SHOWROOM STOCK
RACE CAR PREPARATION

Nigel Macknight

First published in 1992 by Motorbooks International Publishers and Wholesalers, P O Box 2, 729 Prospect Avenue, Osceola, WI 54020, USA

© Nigel Macknight, 1992

All rights reserved. With the exception of quoting brief passages for the purposes of review no part of this publication may be reproduced without prior written permission from the publisher

Motorbooks International is a certified trademark, registered with the United States Patent Office

The information in this book is true and complete to the best of our knowledge. All recommendations are made without any guarantee on the part of the author or Publisher, who also disclaim any liability incurred in connection with the use of this data or specific details

We recognize that some words, model names and designations, for example, mentioned herein are the property of the trademark holder. We use them for identification purposes only. This is not an official publication

Motorbooks International books are also available at discounts in bulk quantity for industrial or sales-promotional use. For details write to the Special Sales Manager at the publisher's address

Library of Congress Cataloging-in-Publication Data
Macknight, Nigel
   Showroom Stock Race Car Preparation/Nigel Macknight
     p. cm.
   Includes index
   ISBN 0-87938-652-5
   1 Automobiles, Racing - Design and construction - Amateurs' manuals I. Title.
   TL236.M32 1992
   629.228 – dc20   92-33696
                               CIP

Printed and bound in the United States of America

All photos by Norman Blake/Classic Photographic, Maidstone, England – except as credited below.

Front cover (top), Geoffrey Hewitt; front cover (bottom), Steve Jones; page 1, Geoffrey Hewitt; page 7, Bridgestone/Firestone Inc. /Dennis Ashlock; page 25, Bridgestone/Firestone Inc.; page 24 (left), SCCA; page 29, BARC/RAC MSA; page 92 (top), HEAT/Keith Morton; page 92 (bottom), HEAT/Keith Morton; page 98, Aero Tec Laboratories; page 99 (top), Aero Tec Laboratories; page 104, Garth Burgess; page 109, Garth Burgess; page 119 (bottom), Garth Burgess; page 126 (bottom right), Garth Burgess; page 129, HEAT/Keith Morton; page 130, HEAT/Keith Morton; page 131, HEAT/Keith Morton; page 132, HEAT/Keith Morton; page 133, Bridgestone/Firestone Inc./Dennis Ashlock; page 135, Brigestone/Firestone Inc./Dennis Ashlock; page 137 (top), Competition Photographers/Ken Brown; page 137, (bottom) Mark Weber; page 138, Mark Weber; page 139 (top), Rupert Berrington; page 139 (bottom), Mark Weber; page 140, Mark Weber; page 141, Mark Weber; page 142, Tim McKinney; page 143, Bridgestone/Firestone Inc. /Dennis Ashlock; page 144, Geoffrey Hewitt; page 145, Bridgestone/Firestone Inc./Dennis Ashlock; page 146, Bridgestone/Firestone Inc.; page 147 (top), Bridgestone/Firestone Inc.; page 147 (bottom), Bridgestone/Firestone Inc.; page 148, Consulier Automotive; page 149, John Colley; page 150, John Colley; page 151, John Colley; page 152, David Dickson; page 153 (top), John Gaisford; page 153 (bottom), John Gaisford; page 154, Fiat Auto (UK) Ltd.; page 155, John Colley; page 156, John Colley.

Diagrams: Terry Godfrey Graphics, Nottingham, England

Page design: Macknight International, Grantham, England

Page makeup: GA Graphics, Stamford, England

On the front cover: (Upper photo) A Paul Rossi-entered Eagle Talon TSi leads a T.C. Kline-entered Honda Civic Si in the opening round of the 1992 Firestone Firehawk Endurance Championship, held at Sebring, Florida. (Lower photo) Dane Motorsport's Ford Sierra Cosworth, driven by David Bartrum, accelerates out of the hairpin at Mallory Park, en route to third place in the opening round of the 1992 BRDC/BRSCC Saloon Car Championship. Much of this book is based on Dane Motorsport's preparation of a replacement for this car.

On the title page: Cars stream through a series of bends at the Sebring circuit in Florida, during a round of the 1992 Firestone Firehawk Endurance Championship.

Contents

Acknowledgements 4
Introduction 5
Chapter 1: Before you start 6
Chapter 2: Preparing the bodyshell 30
Chapter 3: Engine preparation 68
Chapter 4: Rebuilding the car 84
Chapter 5: At the racetrack 130
Chapter 6: The major championships 136
Supplier/services directory 157
Index

Acknowledgements

This book would not have been possible without the wholehearted support of two individuals in particular: David Bartrum of Dane Motorsport and Paul Chopping of Mike Taylor Developments. They generously permitted their race car preparation activities to be the subject of intense scrutiny for a period of several months. Thanks also to Neil, Neville, and Will at Dane Motorsport.

I am also indebted to Norman Blake of Classic Photographic, for so painstakingly documenting every step of the race-preparation process - and must record my appreciation of Roger Smith and Garth Burgess for their assistance when this project was in its infancy.

Finally, my thanks to Tim Parker, Michael Dregni and Mary LaBarre at Motorbooks International, and to the many individuals who reviewed sections of the manuscript prior to publication and made suggestions. Their names appear alongside those of the companies and organizations they represent.

Steve White/Aero Tec Laboratories, Bletchley, Milton Keynes, Buckinghamshire, England.

Tommy Archer/Archer Brothers Inc., Duluth, Minnesota, USA.

Al Thom/Autotechnica, Milwaukee, Wisconsin, USA.

Wayne Peeling/Autocraft Accident Repair Center, Peterborough, Cambridgeshire, England.

Bill Stilwell/Danny Stilwell/Belle Vue Motorsport, Southend-on-Sea, Essex, England.

Ian Benfield/Benfield Motorsport, Wickford, Essex, England.

Brian Cohen/Brian Cohen Racing, Chesterfield, Missouri, USA.

John Taylor/Bridgestone/Firestone Inc., Nashville, Tennessee, USA.

Enid Smith/Dale Wells/British Automobile Racing Club, Andover, Hampshire, England.

Dave Arnold/Brubaker & Associates, Hudson, Ohio, USA.

Roy Chapin/Consulier Automotive, Riviera Beach, Florida, USA.

Colin Folwell/Corbeau GT Seats, Hastings, East Sussex, England.

Wiley Timbrook/Coyote Racing, Golden, Colorado, USA.

Bill Salter/CSC Racing Products Inc., Concord, Ontario, Canada.

Doug Rippie/Doug Rippie Motorsport, Plymouth, Minnesota, USA.

David Bartrum/Dane Motorsport, Maidstone, Kent, England.

Mike Southall/Enterprise Racing, Oldbury, West Midlands, England.

Paul Hacker/Hacker Express, Valatie, New York, USA.

Christine Baldwin/Bob Manry/International Motor Sports Association Inc., Tampa, Florida, USA.

David Stone/Kelly Moss Racing, Madison, Wisconsin, USA.

Graeme Lee/Lifeline Fire & Safety Ltd., Newport, Isle of Wight, England.

Doc Bundy/Robbin Herring/Lotusport Inc., Lawrenceville, Georgia, USA.

Edwina Overend/Mallory Park (Motorsport) Ltd., Kirby Mallory, Leicestershire, England.

Paul Chopping/Mike Taylor Developments Ltd., Northallerton, North Yorkshire, England.

Ivor James/Malcolm Sweatnam/Mountune Race Engines, Morden, Essex, England.

Sam Nelson/Nelson Engine Services, Calne, Wiltshire, England.

Roger Smith/Oselli Engineering, Oxford, Oxfordshire, England.

Paul Dybro, Pfanner Communications, Tustin, California, USA.

Hugh Webb, Radbourne Racing, London, England.

Roger Nevitt/R&D Motorsport, Daventry, Northamptonshire, England.

Simon North, Renault UK Motorsport, London, England.

Robin Bradford/Robin Bradford Associates, Harlington, Bedfordordshire, England.

Chris Belton/Rover Sport, Wallington, Surrey, England.

Roy Fewkes/Mike Garton/Tony Parsfield/John Taylor/Colin Wilson/Royal Automobile Club Motor Sports Association Ltd., Colnbrook, Slough, Surrey, England.

Tony Fall/Fred Young/Safety Devices, Newmarket, Suffolk, England.

Nick Topliss/Spax Ltd., Bicester, Oxfordshire, England.

Bill Mitchell/Special Vehicle Developments, Cheshire, Connecticut, USA.

John Clagett/Rob Elson/Sean Marchant/Dick Martin/Sven Pruett/Sports Car Club of America Inc., Englewood, Colorado, USA.

Dave Clarke/SP Tyres UK Ltd. (Dunlop), Birmingham, West Midlands, England.

T.C. Kline/T.C. Kline Racing, Columbus, Ohio, USA.

Russell Pain/Tim Swadkin/Warrior Automotive Research, Uckfield, East Sussex, England.

Peter Wilkinson/Viewpride Ltd., Wolverhampton, Staffordshire, England.

Introduction

This book is about race-preparing the types of cars which other people drive to work! Before proceeding further, let's be clear in our definition of the cars which interest us.

Our interest lies in large scale, series production cars which, when race-prepared, retain their original bodyshell, engine, gearbox, drivetrain and suspension layout – and, hence, their *roadgoing character*. The regulations, though they vary slightly from one championship to another, universally maintain strict limits on the number and nature of modifications competitors can undertake. They also stipulate that the cars be fitted with an approved roll cage, a fire extinguisher and other items of safety equipment.

This book does not concern itself with the category of cars which, whilst retaining a strong external resemblance to their production line cousins, feature such exotic refinements as full-race engines and competition-specification suspension layouts and drivetrain elements. Operating such cars tends to be highly expensive. Being showroom specification models with limited modifications, the cars which interest us don't require mega-budgets, though it would be wrong to think of this as a 'shoestring' racing category. Being competitive still costs money.

For the manufacturers of roadgoing cars, the attraction of this type of motorsport is obvious: the cars are of direct relevance to the buying public. In the words of Jan Thompson, Vice President of Marketing for Mazda Motor of America, *"We can race the production RX-7 on the track against the cars we compete against in the showroom."*

Although the regulations vary between championships, the techniques applied when preparing these cars for competition are the same: the only variable factor is the *extent* to which cars may be modified within the regulations in force. All of the necessary steps are detailed sequentially in Chapters 2, 3 and 4, while the major championships are summarized in Chapter 6.

Chapter 5 features suggestions for a track test program – an essential prelude to the car's first race outing – while Chapter 1 offers guidelines for selecting a suitable championship and the right car with which to contest it, budgeting for a race program and establishing a properly-equipped workshop. It also examines the relationship between the competitor and those who make the rules. Race-preparing a car is a demanding, but thoroughly stimulating, challenge. I wish you every success!

Nigel Macknight
Lincolnshire, England
October 1992

Guide to nomenclature

We have standardized the terminology within this book to account for language differences between North America and Great Britain: our target markets. The notable variations are listed in alphabetical order below, with the versions employed in this book denoted in italics on the left hand side.

In view of the incompatibility of American Wire Gauge with British Standard Wire Gauge, we have avoided references to either. For universality, material thickness are expressed in American Standard/British Imperial values, with approximate Metric equivalents in parenthesis. The same applies to other forms of measurement.

We wholeheartedly endorse the participation of women in every aspect of motorsport. The masculine pronouns 'he', 'him' and 'his' are used generically, without actual reference to gender.

Alternator = generator (AC)
Antenna = aerial
Bubble level = spirit level
Dashpanel = dashboard
Drill press = pillar drill
Duct tape = tank tape
Dynamo = generator (DC)
Fender = wing
Forward chassis rails = frame horns
Fuel = gas(oline)/petrol(eum)
Ground = Earth
Head liner = roof lining
Hood = bonnet
Hose clamp = Jubilee clip
Muffler = silencer
Quarter window = quarter light
Rocker panel = sill
Sedan = saloon
Stabilizer bar = antiroll bar
Tech inspector = scrutineer
Trunk = boot
Windshield = windscreen
Wrench = spanner

1
Before you start

Selecting a championship
Within this category of motorsport, there are a wide variety of championships. The would-be competitor must decide which one suits him, and his pocket, best.

Some championships permit cars to be modified fairly extensively, within the overriding constraint that their roadgoing nature is preserved. This inevitably pushes costs up, but the more determined privateers can usually raise the necessary funds. Further down the scale, some championships have such stringent regulations that competing cars are virtually identical to their production line counterparts. They must, for example, have standard roadgoing tires, as opposed to racing covers, and the potential for engine modifications is very strictly limited. These cars are obviously far less costly to prepare and operate, though a considerable amount of work goes into squeezing the maximum performance from them within the very tight regulatory restrictions. They are usually totally disassembled and rebuilt, and nothing is left to chance.

Cost considerations aside, your own enthusiasm for a particular make or model may determine which championship you enter. If, for example, you're keen to run a Honda Civic, you are obviously limited to championships for which the Civic is eligible.

In addition to the 'mixed model' championships, there are some championships which cater for devotees of particular models. These are generally administered by the manufacturer or one of its representatives: typically, its national dealer organization or a franchise holder. They publish their own eligibility requirements, but the events are in most cases still sanctioned by one of the major motorsport clubs, whose general regulations – particularly those pertaining to safety – are adhered to.

If your interest lies in exotic modern sports cars, there are several championships for them. If, on the other hand, you must cut costs to the bone, there are events to which competitors must *drive* their race cars, not tow them. The cars must be taxed, registered and insured for the road, and mustn't deviate from their production specification in any way – though they must still have certain safety features, such as a roll cage and a fire extinguisher.

In most championships, the cars have widely varying performance capabilities. To ensure that there is fair competition, they are divided into separate classes. These are sometimes defined simply by engine capacity, but more often, a complex performance-related formula is employed to determine which class a car belongs to. Cars belonging to different classes sometimes race side by side, but it's more usual for a championship meeting to consist of several independent class races.

Almost universally, a Drivers' Championship and a Manufacturers' Championship are contested in parallel, creating class-winning drivers and manufacturers at the end of each meeting, and championship-winning drivers and manufacturers at the end of each season. Where geographical factors might limit the size and quality of the grids, the rulemakers organize events on a regional level. This is particularly true in North America, where the SCCA's Showroom Stock category is a good example. Instead of one all-embracing national series, there are eight divisional Showroom Stock championships. At the end of the season, the top four divisional championship contenders in each class battle for the ultimate honors at an event called the Valvoline Run-Offs.

The championship you ultimately select will depend on your own specific interests, your budget, and mundane logistical considerations. Newcomers to race car preparation should get to know other people who are, or have recently been, involved in that particular championship. Despite their competitive instincts, established participants are usually more than willing to offer encouragement. By joining a national and/or regional motorsport club, newcomers have a forum for making some initial contacts.

There are some useful addresses in the Directory at the back of this book.

Selecting a car

To be competitive, it's vital to start with the right car. We assume that you're going to purchase a roadgoing car and convert it yourself, rather than buying a car which has already been race-prepared. The first step is to establish which cars are eligible for the championship you intend to contest, then you know what the options are. Every set of championship regulations either lists the eligible models, or refers competitors to a list compiled by a higher sanctioning body. A cautionary note: a model may be eligible one year, but not the next.

If the championship you're going to contest has been run over previous seasons, it's easy to find out which models have been doing well in each class. In championships where cars in different classes compete side by side, it's a particularly good sign when one model regularly beats cars belonging to the class above. It does happen, and it's invariably the mark of a super competitive model.

As a general guideline, focus on models that are well proven in competition: cars with a 'sporty' nature. Such a model may well have four valves per cylinder, and may be fuel-injected or even turbocharged. You should concentrate on cars that have been optimized for performance – as opposed to simply fuel economy, or extra leg room – because if you opt for something too pedestrian it won't be competitive, however much work you put into it. Why start with a model which produces 120hp, if a model with an identical engine capacity turns out 150hp?

If it's your first season, don't opt for an untried model. Granted, in some championships, the rulemakers welcome competitors introducing new models, but if the model concerned had real potential, one of the more seasoned campaigners would have got there first.

There are other factors to take into account when selecting a car. Odd as it may at first seem, it's often better to acquire a model from the bottom of the range than a de luxe model – provided it has a comparable performance. Models higher up the range tend to feature 'luxury extras' which, whilst desirable for road use, generally represent unnecessary weight, additional cost, and an increased workload when you come to prepare the car for competition. The items in question are: an antilock braking system (ABS), electric windows, electrically adjustable mirrors, air conditioning, and any type of sunroof.

We've heard purists put the case that, because 'luxury extras' can be removed later, this shouldn't be an influencing factor when selecting a car. As unrepentant pragmatists, we think it most certainly *should* – unless money and time are no object.

Of course, there are exceptions to every rule. Whilst in almost every case, electric window mechanisms are heavier than manual winders, the opposite is the case with a small number of models: late model IROC Camaros, for example. When preparing a car for competition, factors such as this must be taken into account. The subject of weight saving is dealt with in greater depth in Chapter 4.

In the course of writing this book, we maintained close ties with several teams as they prepared a wide variety of cars for championships on both sides of the Atlantic. One team, in England, was the subject of particularly close scrutiny: the Dane Motorsport outfit, based in Maidstone, Kent. Team owner/driver David Bartrum opted to prepare a Ford Sierra Sapphire Cosworth for Class A of the BRDC/BRSCC Saloon Car Championship, for the second consecutive year. He did so because this model had established an excellent record in competition use, and because he already possessed a sound working knowledge of it, both in his professional capacity as the operator of a successful automotive repair shop, and as an everyday motorist: he also owns a roadgoing version.

Even in its standard production form, the Sierra Sapphire Cosworth represents a formidable package, possessing all the ingredients necessary to make it a potent force on the racetrack.

Choosing the right car is of paramount importance. No matter how much work you put into it, a mediocre model won't be competitive. General Motors unveiled the Saturn SC in the Touring Class of IMSA's Firestone Firehawk series in 1991. Peter Farrell (pictured) won five races and captured the driver's championship.

Budgeting/sponsorship

Racing requires resources! Even before converting your car to race specification, calculate how much you can afford to spend during the course of the full season. In common with the majority of competitors, you're likely to have a mortgage to maintain and several mouths to feed, so don't lose sight of your obligations. Driving home from a race feeling guilty because you've neglected your other financial responsibilities, can take a lot of the pleasure out of it.

This section is intended to provide only general guidelines about budgeting, as to do otherwise would unnecessarily duplicate much of the content of the other chapters. Carefully scrutinise the rest of this book as part of your financial planning, refining your projections as you go along. There are many small, but important, items requiring consideration.

A lot of work goes into producing a very accurate budget, but you can make a worthwhile effort on a 'rule of thumb' basis. If you're doing this for the first time, ask someone in the know what they might expect to pay for this and that: someone who has run the same model as yours in the recent past. Above all else, be realistic when you draw up your budget, or you could be left high and dry in the middle of the season, with no money left to go racing. Don't, for example, bank on attracting mega-sponsorship in mid season on the strength of your amazing performances!

Some people fall into the trap of spending all their money on purchasing and preparing their car, leaving insufficient funds to actually run it. Imagine enthusiastically contesting a championship, perhaps even doing well in it, only to find that you don't have enough money to complete the season. It's essential to plan well, and realistically – to know where the money for your racing program is going to come from.

There are three primary areas of expenditure in this category of motorsport: the capital outlay required to acquire the car and establish suitable facilities to support it; the capital outlay required to put the car into raceworthy condition; and the ongoing outlay required to run the car from race to race during the course of the season.

First among the major expenses is establishing a workshop. If you rent premises, chances are the owner will want several months' rent in advance. The cost of equipping a workshop with all the necessary tools and equipment can vary considerably, depending on what you already possess, and whether you purchase new equipment or opt for some quality preowned items. Another factor is the standard to which you equip your workshop. It's possible to save money by doing without the more specialised items of equipment, though you must then add a percentage to your budget for paying specialists to undertake certain tasks for you.

Some competitors convert their current roadgoing car to race specification and find another way to get to work! Putting this radical solution aside, your largest single capital expenditure item will be the car itself. Assuming you're going to buy a roadgoing vehicle and race-prepare it yourself, the logical way to save money is to purchase a preowned car: only the big-buck teams go to the expense of purchasing a brand new vehicle. Look through the advertisements in the automotive/motorsport press, and local newspapers, to see what's available.

After purchasing the car, you have to pay for the hardware and professional help required to upgrade it to race specification: these are detailed in Chapters 2, 3 and 4. The most expensive items are the roll cage, assorted race-specification wheels and tires if these are permitted, and the fee for getting the engine – possibly parts of the transmission, too – professionally race-prepared. The only way to quantify the cost of these and the other necessities is to spend time on the telephone discussing your requirements with motorsport suppliers and service companies. A good place to start is the Directory at the back of this book.

Spare parts represent a 'hidden', but substantial, capital expense. The amount you spend will largely depend on how well you equip yourself. A spare engine can be a very useful asset, as it's feasible to replace an engine in time for the race in the event of a major breakdown during qualifying – even when qualifying takes place on the morning of the race. Many competitors manage without a spare engine, but they run the risk of missing the race if their sole engine lets them down.

It's essential to carry *some* spares to race meetings. The better-financed teams carry a spare gearbox. Again, there's time to change the gearbox between qualifying and the race, even during a one-day meeting. Carry as many spares as you can reasonably afford, and certainly ensure that you have a backup supply of all the smaller breakable items: wheels, hoses, spark plugs, fan belts, cam belts, and so on.

Of course, you'll need some way of moving the race car from place to place. Your budget projection should include the cost of a new or preowned trailer, and the appropriate towing gear for your road car. Better still, if you can afford it, buy a *van and a trailer* and dedicate both of them to your racing activities. Whatever you opt for, make sure that you have a reliable means of transportation. It's heartbreaking to spend hours meticulously preparing a car for an important event, only to have a mechanical breakdown on your way to the racetrack, arrive too late to sign on, and be barred from taking part.

There's a trend towards attendance at an approved racing drivers' school being compulsory for people seeking their first competition license, or those who've let an earlier license lapse. Depending on your circumstances, you may have to budget for the cost of a special introductory course.

In addition to the major items of expenditure, there are a host of smaller startup costs. They include the annual championship registration fee, made payable to the organizing club, the cost of race regulations and other essential documentation, a medical certificate, and a competition license. If you don't already subscribe to one of the motorsport magazines, you'll probably want to do so now, as it's important to be well informed. Also purchase the manufacturer's service manual for your particular model.

Another potential one-off item of expenditure to consider is the fee for a qualified engineer – or a reputable test driver – to help you set the car up prior to the first race of the season. There are several specialists whose services can be engaged to optimise the suspension for a specific racetrack to gain the maximum advantage. You may well be racing at a particular circuit several times during the course of a season, so think of the financial outlay for a setting-up session as a long term investment. To put the outlay in perspective, one setup session costs about the same as a racing tire. If money is tight, select just two racetracks – one high speed track and one slower track – and treat them as representative of the range of circuits you'll be racing on during the course of the season.

After making all that investment in machinery, consider the human factor! A driver's racewear, including the helmet, can represent a goodly sum these days. You may also wish to purchase sets of overalls for you and your helpers.

The 'money-go-round' doesn't stop when you have your workshop established and the car thoroughly race-ready. At that point, you tread the next fiscal tightrope: meeting the day to day, race to race expenses. For detailed information, turn to the accompanying list of running costs.

It's only fair to point out that, at this level of motorsport, you see far more money going out than coming in. However, there are *some* sources of income. After compiling your list of spending requirements, complete your

Of course, you'll need some way of moving the race car from place to place. Your budget projection should include the cost of a new or preowned trailer, and the appropriate towing gear for your road car – or, better still, a van and a trailer. The van need not be as grand as this support vehicle, operated by one of the top professional outfits, but it must be reliable.

budget projection by considering the income element. Discounting prize money (which you are unlikely to receive if it's your first season), you have two potential sources of income: commercial sponsorship, and the income derived from selling your car at the end of the season – unless, of course, you plan to run it again the following year. Bear in mind that, as with a roadgoing car, but to a greater extent, a race car's monetary value decreases with usage.

Raising sponsorship is a tough task, but many competitors manage it year after year. Of course, the top teams have turned sponsorship hunting into an industry in its own right, and secure very substantial incomes with which to mount their race campaigns. Lower down the scale, the priorities are different. Competitors regard motorsport as a hobby and seek only modest sponsorship to defray their running costs.

If it's to be your first season in competition, you won't have a previous record of race successes with which to promote your cause. Nevertheless, you may be able to persuade a local company, perhaps a company with which you have some connections, that it could benefit from the attention your car will attract if it is displayed in a prominent place from time to time. In return, the company might agree to have your car painted professionally in their house colors, at their expense, where they get their own vehicles painted.

One worthwhile step is to establish contact with the local dealership for the make of car you are going to campaign. In return for borrowing your car to display in their showroom occasionally, they might agree to supply parts free of charge, or even inject some finance.

The quality of your race-preparation effort is of paramount importance for several reasons, not least of which is the impression it makes on others. A potential sponsor is far more likely to associate itself with a professional-looking car than a car of indifferent appearance.

If you're fortunate enough to attract sponsorship, always keep your sponsor informed of your progress and take his interests into account. If you simply 'take the money and run', you'll do yourself out of the chance of backing for another season and generally bring motorsport into disrepute. One excellent way of providing a good service to your sponsor, thereby advancing your own cause, is to keep the local press up to date on how you're doing as the season progresses. Better still, write short news updates yourself, or get a friend with literary aspirations to do it for you, and submit them regularly for publication. Local newspapers are often on the lookout for fresh material.

The other source of income – the income from the sale of the car – can only be realized at the end of the season, of course. You'll be able to get a good idea what your car is worth by looking through the advertisements in the motorsport press to see what the asking price is for your particular model in race trim. You may plan to use the proceeds from the sale of your car to pay off a loan taken out at the start of the season. Alternatively, you might allocate the money to your budget for the following season.

Running costs

Use this alphabetical listing for your budget projection.

Accommodation: The degree to which you require overnight accommodation depends very much on the format of the race meetings you'll be contesting, and your geographical circumstances. If the meetings are two-day affairs, with qualifying on one day and racing the next, you will probably need to budget for at least one night's accommodation in the vicinity of the circuit. If some of the races are held at far-flung locations, you will require the occasional night's accommodation, regardless of whether they're one-day or two-day meetings. In fact, in the latter case, you may require *two* nights' accommodation.

If, on the other hand, the race meetings have a one-day format, with qualifying in the morning and racing in the afternoon, and all of the circuits are within a reasonable driving distance of your home, you may never need to stay away overnight.

Brake pads: Almost universally, the rulemakers permit the car's original brake pads to be replaced with race-specification pads, which have much better wear characteristics. They are, of course, considerably more expensive – particularly if they're made from exotic materials. Carbon metallic pads are the most expensive.

On most racetracks, one set of pads will last all day, but you may need to budget for a second set when competing on the twistier circuits.

Clutch discs: It's customary for the rulemakers to permit the standard clutch disc to be replaced with a more robust racing version. Budget for at least one replacement clutch disc per season.

Contingency funds: It's difficult to predict the unpredictable – but try! An important element of a realistic budget is the leeway incorporated into it for mishaps, such as an engine blowup or a rollover accident which destroys the shell. If at all possible, plan for a worst-case situation by ensuring that you can afford to reshell your car, or have the engine completely rebuilt, at short notice at any point in the season (see *Insurance*).

Close racing between evenly-matched cars is part of the attraction of this type of racing, but that can also mean coming into physical contact from time to time. Therefore, budget for the replacement of such items as bumpers, fenders, door skins and light clusters.

Thankfully, mechanical failures are few and far between in this category of motorsport, as the races (with the obvious exception of endurance races) are comparatively short, and only a relatively small number of components are highly stressed. The weakest links are elements of the transmission, where standard components are being subjected to horrendous abuse.

Engine rebuilds: The frequency of engine rebuilds depends on the model you intend to run, your budget, Lady Luck, and the level you're competing at. At the inexpensive end of the scale, characterized by SCCA Club Racing's Showroom Stock category, even the top competitors make one engine rebuild a year (prior to the end of season Run-Offs) suffice.

Turbocharged engines generally require more maintenance than normally aspirated units. Talk to a specialist race engine-tuner to ascertain what the rebuild requirements are likely to be at the level you plan to compete at.

Entry fees: There is an entry fee for each race, made payable to the organizing club.

Filters: You should budget for changing your air filter and oil filter before every race: it doesn't cost much. A blocked air filter hinders performance – the better the airflow into the engine, the higher its power output – while keeping the engine oil free from impurities is only sensible.

Fuel: Allow for the cost of fuel for your race car at each event and test session. Naturally, the cars consume considerably more fuel when they're racing than they do in road use. Typically, fuel consumption might range from 9mpg for a car with a turbocharged engine, to 13-15mpg for a car with a normally aspirated engine.

Remember, also, to budget for the considerable amount of fuel needed to get you, your helpers and the race car to and from each circuit.

Gearbox rebuilds: Many competitors budget for the gearbox to be stripped and rebuilt every two or three race meetings. The philosophy here is that prevention is better than cure: if a gearbox fault can be detected before it induces a breakage, you'll save money in the long run. At the other extreme, we know of one very competitive driver (in SCCA Club Racing's Showroom Stock category) who undertook three consecutive seasons on just one gearbox rebuild!

Insurance: Many competitors don't insure their race cars, but many more do, and insurance cover is actually mandatory in some championships. There are specialist brokers who underwrite race cars, but the high risk factor means that premiums, too, are high. If insurance cover isn't mandatory and you have a choice in the matter, you must weigh the cost of insurance premiums against the risk of your car being wiped out in a major accident.

You will find that the cost of insuring your car against total destruction is prohibitively high, but a well-prepared car is probably worth insuring against a full rebuild around a new shell. Even then, motorsport policies don't tend to cover the labor element of repairs and rebuilds, only the cost of the parts. This is because rebuilding a race car is extremely labor intensive and the labor element represents the largest single cost. Therefore, you won't get anywhere near all your money back, but you can take the sting out of a big accident.

It's only fair to say that some competitors have had good reason to question the benefits of race car insurance. Many have found they had to pay an sizable excess before an insurance company would pay anything towards the cost of repairing even minor accident damage, while some embittered individuals complain that you effectively have to have your car written-off before the insurance company will pay up.

Miscellaneous: A whole host of minor running costs must be taken into account. They include postage, telephone bills, and bank charges (consider having a separate account for your racing activities). When you require spare parts in a hurry, you may occasionally incur freight costs, so make due allowance for this, particularly for overnight delivery services, which can be fairly expensive. If you're running a foreign car, parts may even have to be freighted in from overseas.

Oil: It's advisable to change the engine oil after every two races, at the outside – and certainly before an endurance race, during which the oil consumption can be very high. Synthetic oil is far superior to the regular multigrades, but it's more expensive. Then again, it lasts longer.

The oil in the gearbox (and the differential, if this is an independent unit) should be changed at least as frequently as the engine oil: indeed, some competitors change the gearbox oil between the qualifying session and the race itself, as the gearbox is subjected to fearsome punishment.

Personnel: Even if you're planning a fairly modest campaign, you will need someone to help you fettle the car on race day, and to handle pit signalling and so on. You shouldn't find it too difficult to recruit a volunteer to help you go racing. Alternatively, pay a qualified automobile mechanic to go with you.

Also budget for sustenance for you and your crew. Morale will plummet if helpers aren't kept fed and watered.

Testing: Testing is essential, as there isn't enough time to make a meaningful series of adjustments during qualifying. If your budget allows, try to test at every circuit before you actually race there. Budget for the cost of replacement brake pads and tire wear incurred on test days. There's also a fee for each test day, made payable to the racetrack.

Tires: The cost of replacing tires varies enormously, depending on the level you're competing at. Racing tires are permitted in some championships, while others limit competitors to roadgoing covers. At higher levels, a set of tires can be worn out every two meetings. Further down the scale, you might be able to make a set last half a season and still be reasonably competitive.

Competitors with healthy budgets will always enjoy the advantage of having new tires for every race. If your budget is tight, you'll learn to live with this fact: one of the many tradeoffs between competitiveness and cost.

In some championships, the regulations limit the number of tires that can be used during the course of each race meeting, in order to give less well funded competitors a better chance. Typically, in such cases, each competitor is limited to six tires per meeting, but this does not include wet weather tires, the quantity of which is unrestricted.

If you're planning to compete in a championship which limits competitors to roadgoing tires, allow for the cost of having the treads of the covers you earmark for use in dry conditions buffed down by a specialist to improve their performance.

Wheel bearings: Most competitors budget to replace the wheel bearings every three or four races, and you should certainly replace them once a year: preferably at the mid-season point. A new set should be fitted before an endurance race.

Establishing a workshop

Before acquiring a car, establish a workshop. You want a fairly large work area, not just an average garage-sized building, as you'll need plenty of maneuvering space. Unless you're fortunate enough to have such a facility at home, you must either rent a purpose-built workshop, or establish yourself in a building (or a sizable part of it) being used for some other purpose. It could be anything from a warehouse to a well-swept stable.

Aside for being adequately-sized, the workshop should be well- ventilated, so that fumes generated when welding don't overcome you. Even the fumes from certain cleaning fluids can pose a health hazard, so ensure that there's a positive flow of fresh air. If the building is centrally heated, so much the better. If not, you will need to organize your own source of heat. You'll need a plentiful supply of hot water: not only to wash yourself, but also to degrease components. You also want good lighting conditions: florescent strip lights are best.

Paint the walls white to make the most of reflected light and illuminate shadowed areas. Gloss paint is best, as it can be wiped clean periodically with a damp, soapy cloth.

Create a dedicated storage area away from the work space, where tools, equipment and spare parts can be housed in safety. Lofts are ideal for storing spares, but tools and equipment need to be somewhere within easy reach. Since your first acquisition is likely to be a substantial workbench, consider positioning most of your equipment around that, as it'll give you immediate access to each item as and when you require it.

Also install a comfortable chair, as some tasks can be undertaken better in a seated position. Besides, you'll want to take a break once in a while.

If you're starting with a bare workshop, set aside some time to shop around for a wide range of tools, both hand- and power-operated. Some tools are essential, others merely desirable. You almost certainly already possess a selection of wrenches and screwdrivers. There's likely to be a preowned equipment center near you, so check it out. Also check your local newspapers, or the automotive/motorsport press, for advertisements for both new and preowned equipment.

Invest in quality if you possibly can. It's false economy to buy inferior tools and equipment. Bear in mind, if you're establishing a workshop for the first time, that you're likely to enjoy motorsport so much that you'll want to continue indefinitely. If you've invested in good equipment, it'll be there for many years to come.

If money is tight, you can start with a set of essential tools, then add the 'desirable' items over time, spreading the cost. There's no need to buy every conceivable size, either. With wrenches, for example, you'll find that if you acquire what you need on an *ad hoc* basis as your

Although a modernized version is widely available, there's still a lot to be said for the 'old-style' Allen key! A selection of both versions is pictured here. Acquire a full set of either type, sized to fit your particular model.

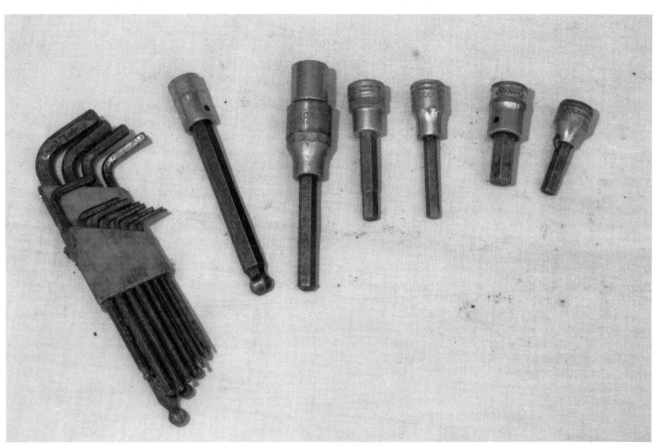

race-preparation project progresses, you won't actually require a full set, and will therefore have saved a certain amount of money.

Over a period of time, you'll accumulate various inexpensive bits and pieces which make life easier. For example, four short planks of wood with chamfered front edges will allow you to drive the car to an elevated position, making it easier to get a floor jack under it.

Before you acquire any tools, check which standard the manufacturer works to, as this varies according to the car's country of origin. Cars originating in North America are built to American Standard measurements, which – in the majority of cases – equates to the 'old' British Imperial standard, while cars emanating from Europe and Japan are built to Metric measurements. Aside from that major differentiation, there are more subtle variations. If you're working on a French car, you're likely to require wrenches with even-numbered Metric sizes, such as 12mm, 14mm, 16mm and 18mm, whereas British and German manufacturers tend to employ the more traditional odd-numbered Metric sizes, such as 13mm, 15mm, 17mm and 19mm.

Even then, uniform standards don't apply. For example, Japanese manufacturers tend to employ fine-pitch threads, while manufacturers from other countries tend to favor conventional, coarse-pitch threads.

One important decision you must make at this stage is whether to augment the traditional range of tools with air- or electric-powered tools. To a large degree, the decision will depend on your financial circumstances. Ideally, opt for air tools: they're highly versatile and will reduce your workload considerably. The downside is that air tools can only be operated in conjunction with a compressor, which is an added expense. However, you may find ownership of a compressor an advantage in its own right, as you can use it for blast-cleaning engine components, spark plugs, and so forth.

The range of air tools duplicates the range of electrical tools: there's air chisels, air hacksaws, and so on. The disadvantage of electric-powered tools – and the reason why very few teams use them – is that most people have reservations about operating them in rain, or in the vicinity of fuel vapor. In fact, electric tools are actually banned from the pits when an endurance race is in progress, as fuel vapor is likely to be present during refueling stops.

When equipping your workshop, use this alphabetical checklist, which combines essential and desirable tools with some of the 'odds and ends' employed in race car preparation.

Air-pressure gauge: This is essential, for taking tire pressure readings.

Allen keys: Although a modernized version is widely available, we reckon there's still a lot to be said for the 'old-style' Allen key! Acquire a full set, sized to fit your particular model.

Axle stands: Invest in a set of four adjustable, triangular axle stands, and get into the habit of positioning them under the car every time you use the floor jack. Be safe, not sorry.

Invest in a set of four adjustable, triangular axle stands like these, and get into the habit of positioning them under the car every time you use the floor jack. Safety is key to good workshop practice. It's perfectly safe to clamber around inside the car while it's mounted on axle stands.

Bending equipment: You'll definitely need some way of bending steel and aluminium of different thicknesses, up to a maximum of about 0.1in (2mm). A purpose-built bending machine is a very expensive commodity, so acquire two pieces of 0.2in (5mm) angle iron, each about 3ft (1m) long, and improvise a bending apparatus by putting them in the vice and using your hands to bend material between the two straight edges.

Cover the inner faces of the angle iron with masking tape beforehand to 'soften' them, or they'll disfigure the surface of the material. To bend a piece of steel or aluminium, simply mark a line with a pencil where you want the bend to go, and align this with the inner edges of the angle-iron. A pencil is better than a scribe, as it doesn't permanently mark the surface. When bending thicker material, use a couple of G-clamps to stop the ends of the angle irons from opening up.

Body jigs: We recommend that you fabricate a pair of spit-type body jigs, as the ability to rotate the bodyshell by hand through 360 degrees and lock it in any position will greatly reduce your workload when welding and painting. The procedure is described under a separate heading. Don't install the engine while the shell is on spits, as they won't take the weight.

Bubble level: You may need a bubble level for use in conjunction with a camber/caster gauge. A bubble level is

Fabricating spit-type body jigs

We strongly recommend that you fabricate a pair of spit-type body jigs. With this arrangement – once the bodyshell has been raised to the correct height – tubular prongs at the top of the jigs are pushed into the apertures at both ends of the chassis rails, supporting the full weight. The shell can then be rotated by hand through 360 degrees and locked at any angle, providing all round access.

Spits are inexpensive and very straightforward to make and you'll find them invaluable when seam welding and repainting the car. These guidelines link with the diagram opposite.

You'll be fabricating two virtually identical jigs, one for each end of the car. Each jig comprises an inner and outer vertical post rising from a horizontal base. The inner post carries a pivoting frame bearing the two prongs. To ensure that the spits provide sufficient ground clearance for the shell when it's rotated, measure the distance between the edge of the roof above the door pillar on one side and the edge of the rocker panel at the diagonally opposite side. That distance represents the maximum outer diameter the shell will prescribe in the course of one complete revolution. Therefore, the jig's vertical posts must be a minimum of half that distance in height if adequate ground clearance is to be maintained.

Now make the same measurement from the opposite side. The point where the two imaginary lines cross denotes the correct location for the pivots at the top of each post: a point directly in line with the center of the shell. This second measurement is just as important as the first, because unless the pivots are located precisely at the center of rotation, the shell will not be properly balanced and will be difficult to turn.

Finally, measure the dimensions of the two apertures at the front of the main chassis rails and the two at the rear, then the horizontal distance between them. This is to ensure that the prongs will fit snugly and are correctly sited.

Armed with all this information, purchase from your local steel stockist a suitable length of rectangular-section mild steel tubing for the vertical and horizontal jig elements. This tubing should have a minimum wall thickness of at least 0.2in (5mm). You'll also need about 4ft

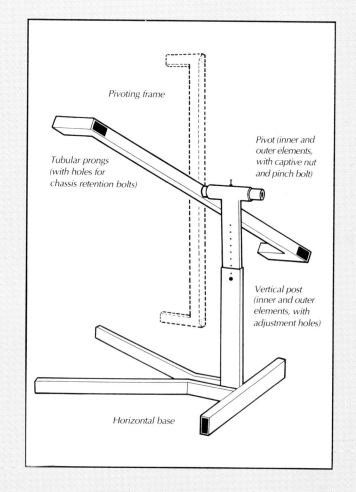

also useful for ensuring that items such as airjack tubes are properly oriented before welding them in.

Cellular phone: It makes a lot of sense to equip yourself with a cellular phone, as it offers flexibility in a field where communications are important. It may be that your workshop doesn't have a telephone line installed: a cellular phone will save you the trouble and expense of having one put in. A cellular phone can be useful on race days, too – although most racetracks offer telephone facilities. If you're unfortunate enough to sustain a broken windshield during qualifying, for example, you can contact one of the emergency replacement services there and then and get another one fitted in time for the race.

There are a couple of important points to bear in mind if you haven't owned a cellular phone before. Don't develop a habit of using it all the time, or you'll get a nasty shock when the first bill arrives. Think of it primarily as a means by which *other people can contact you*, wherever you may be. Secondly, resist the temptation to distribute your number to all your buddies. They're likely to call at inconvenient times – like in the middle of an event, eager to hear how well you're doing – and you'll be footing a sizeable proportion of the bill!

Chisels: A chisel may come in handy once in a while, but it's rather crude for this type of work. An air chisel is a different matter, as it's useful for such tasks as dislodg-

(1.2m) of circular-section tubing for the pivot assemblies – each comprising a short length of tube rotating freely within a fractionally larger tube – and around 12ft (3.7m) of rectangular-section tubing to fabricate the four prong assemblies. When specifying dimensions for the latter, ensure that the tubing from which the prongs will be made will slide comfortably into the apertures at the ends of the chassis rails.

When all the structural elements have been welded together in the manner indicated in the diagram, drill a series of holes in the posts to facilitate vertical adjustments. Also drill holes in all four prongs, so that bolts can be passed through into the chassis bumper holders to hold the shell firmly on the jigs.

There only remains the task of mounting locking devices on both spits, so that the shell can be locked firmly in one position. Drill a large hole through the top of the outer pivot tube and weld a captive nut over it, then screw a bolt of corresponding dimensions down through it to pinch the inner pivot tube.

stubborn pieces of sound proofing material during bodyshell preparation. Always wear eye protection.

Compressor: A fairly substantial compressor is required if you elect to equip your workshop with air tools. It would be logical to look at the preowned market first, as new ones can be expensive. A single-phase compressor simply plugs into a wall socket, and is ideal if your budget is limited. If you want to operate a compressor at race meetings, though, you may well need one of the more sophisticated models which run independently on gasoline, as not all racetracks provide an electricity supply to the pit garages.

Consumables: These are the items you use almost without thinking, but miss terribly if they're not there! Used in the workshop and at the racetrack, they include: an assortment of lubricants; WD-40 (excellent for loosening tight-fitting nuts and bolts); an anti-seize agent, such as Copperslip (which should be applied as early as possible to prevent excessive wear on wheel nuts and suchlike); grease for repacking wheel bearings; an assortment of cleaning materials, such as shop towels, rags, paper towels, biodegradable cleaning fluid, and aluminium cleaner (the latter is particularly good for removing brake lining dust and rubber deposits from wheels after a race); antimisting spray for the interior surfaces of windows; T-Cut, to remove blemishes on paintwork; polish; top quality duct tape; and adhesive racing numbers.

Cornerweight scales: These can be very beneficial when building a race car, helping you position items of hardware so as to achieve the optimum balance. Get a set of mechanical scales, as electronic ones are very expensive.

A fairly substantial compressor is required if you elect to equip your workshop with air tools. A single-phase compressor, like this one, simply plugs into the wall and is ideal if your budget is limited. If you want to operate a compressor at race meetings, you'll need a more sophisticated version.

Cutting tools: You'll be cutting steel and aluminium often, so require a range of cutting implements. A normal household jigsaw is perfectly adequate for most tasks, provided you get blades suitable for cutting metal, as opposed to wood.

You'll find an air hacksaw very useful indeed, because it can get into places an ordinary hacksaw can't. It's handy to have an ordinary hacksaw, too, for smaller jobs.

Also acquire some circular cutters, which fit into drills. Get various sizes, ranging from small diameters for making holes in bulkheads for lines and cables, to large diameters for making holes to accommodate roll cage elements.

Deburring tools: Deburring tools get rid of the jagged edges on the reverse side of holes you drill. You'll need two or three different sizes, including one which fits into an electric drill, banishing burrs instantly. Larger holes can be deburred with a hand-held version.

Domestic scales: These are essential, as you must make a series of weight calculations as the car is rebuilt to ensure that it neither exceeds the mandatory minimum weight by an unacceptable margin, nor falls below it.

Drilling equipment: You want a really sturdy electric drill, as a standard household drill won't stand up to the punishment of this type of work for very long. Get a drill with a 1/2in chuck, as circular cutters (see above) will only fit into the larger chucks. Acquire a full range of drill bits. The bits you'll be using most frequently are in the 1/8in to 5/16in range.

It's handy to have a cordless drill for quick jobs, when you don't want to go to the trouble of attaching an extension lead. When it's not being used, you leave it plugged into a wall socket to keep its nickel-cadmium battery charged.

If your budget allows you to acquire more than just the essential items, install a drill press. This is a superior way to drill holes when great precision is required. There's the added benefit that you don't tend to break as many

This is but a small part of the range of accessories loosely termed 'consumables', employed to clean and lubricate parts. They're items you use almost without thinking – both in the workshop and at the racetrack – but miss terribly if they're not there.

drill bits! If a drill press proves too expensive for you to buy outright, perhaps you can arrange occasional access to one locally.

Engine hoist: This is another item worth buying on the preowned market, as new ones can be expensive. Get a quality one with wheels and a folding boom which extends over the engine compartment.

Eye protectors: These are but one of several safety- related items which every workshop must have. Eye protection is of paramount importance when you are welding, drilling (particularly drilling upside-down) or grinding: in fact, whenever you might be exposed to flying swarf.

Purchase a pair of industrial 'spectacles' with transparent side panels, and/or a pair of goggles. Some people wear a full-face mask. These are fine most of the time, but can be rather cumbersome when you're working inside the bodyshell.

Files: Get a selection of files of different sizes and profiles: flat, round and half-round.

Fire extinguisher: Every workshop should be equipped with an approved fire extinguisher, wall-mounted and instantly accessible. Quite apart from your own safety and that of people occupying adjacent premises, consider the monetary value of your car and all the workshop equipment.

Floor creeper: By making spit-type body jigs, you won't have to crawl under the bodyshell in the initial stages of the build project, but the car won't be on spits once the engine's been put back in. To keep yourself clean, and keep the cold off your back, buy a floor creeper. Always store it vertically against a wall when it's not needed, as it makes a very poor skateboard.

Obtain a quality hoist – a reconditioned one if money is tight – with wheels and a folding boom which extends over the engine compartment. Remove any components which might get damaged when the hoist chains are put under tension: valve covers, for example.

If your budget allows you to acquire more than just the essential items, install a drill press. This is a superior way to drill holes when great precision is required, with the added benefit that you don't tend to break as many drill bits!

Floor jack: Invest in a trolley-type jack capable of lifting no less than 1.5 tons. Unless you know it's been well maintained, don't risk your ribcage and pelvis to just any preowned jack. If you want to save money, buy an approved reconditioned jack, which will be as good as new.

G-clamps: These are handy for several tasks, not least of which is fitting the roll cage. Get several sizes.

Generator: A generator can certainly be useful at times, bestowing the luxury of a 240-volt electricity supply wherever you may be. However, you won't need one unless you're planning to work on the car away from the workshop at night – during a 24-hour endurance race, for example – when you'd need it to operate an elaborate lighting system. Newcomers to race car preparation are unlikely to attempt a 24-hour race in their first season, as this requires considerable resources.

Geometry equipment: In order to make meaningful adjustments to the car's setup at test sessions, you'll need specialist equipment – a camber/caster gauge and a track alignment gauge – to ensure that the wheels are properly aligned and the suspension geometry is correct. Approach the appropriate department of the race tire manufacturer and ask for advice as to the best settings for their particular products and the types of equipment you should acquire, as there are dozens to choose from and a wide price range.

Grinding equipment: Acquire an angle grinder, together with some soft- and hard-faced discs. Being portable, it can be used for sharpening tools in the workshop and at the racetrack. You can also use it to fashion things. For example, if you're going to use carbon metallic brake pads, it's not always possible to get ones which fit your

You'll need several tools for grinding. Acquire an angle grinder, together with some soft- and hard-faced discs. Being portable, it's particularly versatile: tasks range from sharpening tools to fashioning oversized brake pads to the required shape.

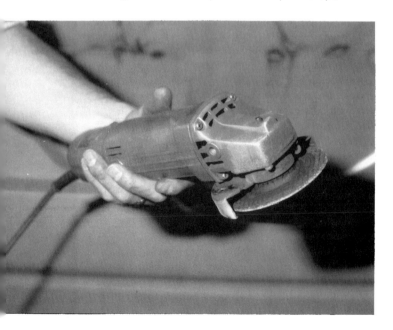

Good workshop practice

No matter how well equipped a workshop may be, it is only as effective as the person using it. There are several facets to good workshop practice, but the most important one is safety consciousness.

One vital safety precaution is to put the axle stands under the car whenever the floor jack is in use. To ensure that the car doesn't slip off the jack whilst being raised, check that the gearbox is in neutral and release the handbrake first, then raise the front of the car and put two axle stands into position. Engage a gear and/or apply the handbrake, then lower the jack.

Never climb into a bodyshell while it's mounted on spit-type body jigs, as they are highly likely to collapse under the excess weight. Only when the shell is mounted on axle stands is it safe to clamber around inside it.

A person's attitude toward safety in the workshop is reflected in his attire. Wear sensible footwear at all times and ensure that your eyes are properly protected when you're welding, drilling, grinding or using a wire brush. Keep loose clothing, such as ties and cuffs, well clear of moving mechanical parts, and remove your wrist watch and rings before getting down to work. If you're handling sheet metal, wear gloves if at all possible. This is especially important if you only perform manual work on a part-time basis, because the skin on your hands may not be as tough as someone who does this type of work every day. Lots of little nicks can become very painful after a while.

Don't feel self-conscious about wearing gloves in the workshop. All that 'macho' stuff went out with the Ark.

Another tip about personal wellbeing: use barrier cream on your hands before undertaking dirty jobs. As well as providing protection against the risk of infection, this makes it easier to wash the dirt off afterwards.

Bear in mind the toxic nature of some of the substances you come into contact with – carb cleaner, for example – and dispose of toxic materials in a responsible manner. In many cases, State laws require retail outlets to reclaim and recycle the cores of batteries, while automotive oils should be sent for reprocessing into fuel oil.

Orderliness is important in the workshop. Put tools away after you've used them, or it'll be difficult to find things when you need them. It's good to get into the discipline of tidying rubbish off the floor at the end of each day. Trash is a hazard, and accumulates rapidly. Don't leave spilt oil on the floor, as you could slip on it. A well ordered workshop is conducive to productivity and engenders a positive attitude. If you've tidied the workshop at the end of the day, you can start work the following day straight away, without having to fight your way through a mountain of garbage.

Keep children and pets out of the workshop if at all possible, and don't under any circumstances leave them unattended.

Finally, take precautions to reduce the risk of fire. Don't smoke in the workshop, and don't allow fuel vapor to accumulate. If possible, store gasoline outdoors. Make sure that you have a fire extinguisher suitable for fuel and electrical fires close to hand at all times, and never attempt to tackle a fuel or electrical fire with water.

Every workshop should be equipped with an approved fire extinguisher, wall-mounted and instantly accessible. Quite apart from your own safety and that of people occupying adjacent premises, consider the monetary value of your car and all the workshop equipment.

A person's attitude toward safety in the workshop is reflected in his attire. Ensure that your eyes are properly protected when you're welding, drilling, grinding or using a wire brush.

19

A parts washer is nice to have, if your budget can stretch to it. It saves time when you're cleaning components prior to reconditioning them. If money's in short supply, you may be able to hire a parts washer for the short time it's required: the early stages of the build project.

particular model. With an angle grinder, you can fashion them to the required shape.

It's also very useful to have a rotary file, together with a set of interchangeable heads: different head profiles suit particular tasks, and the materials from which they are made (including stone) provide varying levels of abrasion.

If your budget permits it, it's also handy to have a bench grinder installed the workshop. Buy a wire wheel attachment for it, as these are useful for removing paint from small components. Get into the safety habit: use the bench grinder's transparent eye guards every time.

Hammers: Acquire a broad selection of hammers, for applications ranging from tapping tight-fitting bolts out of axles to straightening dents in the bodywork. Get various sizes of soft faced hammers, with detachable, replaceable, faces. Also acquire small, medium and large ballpeen hammers.

Heating equipment: To ensure that the workshop area is adequately heated in the absence of central heating, we recommend that you acquire a portable propane-fired space heater. These are especially good if you're working in one specific part of a larger area, because you can direct the flow of heat precisely where you want it instead of wasting money heating a large unoccupied expanse.

Medical kit: Some excellent medical kits are available from drugstores and elsewhere. Ensure that your kit includes something to null the pain of minor burns. You're bound to burn yourself at some point, so you might as well be prepared. Other essential items include: medical tissues to swab a wound; antiseptic cream to prevent infection; dressings to protect the wound, and a supply of non-prescription pain killers. An eye bath is also recommended. *Mount your medical kit somewhere readily accessible.*

Oddments: Lots of smaller items are needed to make a workshop fully operational. These include rivets, wire clamps, an assortment of cable ties, and a box of rubber grommets (various sizes) to replace those you damage.

Parts washer: A parts washer is nice to have, if your budget allows. It saves time when you're cleaning components prior to reconditioning them. Buy a preowned unit. Alternatively, you may be able to hire one for the short time it's required – the early stages of the build project.

Pliers: You'll need a wide selection of pliers, including needle nosed versions and mole grips. Also acquire a set of crimping pliers. These are essential if you plan to make any alterations to the car's electrical system, and for running repairs. Lockwire pliers have been largely superseded by Loctite in the tool boxes of competitors who contest sprint races. Members of the endurance racing fraternity have a different outlook, and wouldn't be at all happy to loose theirs! Lockwire pliers prevent bolts from working loose by tying them back to the head of an adjacent bolt with a length of braided wire. In endurance racing, components are more likely to work loose as a result of prolonged exposure to vibration.

Lockwire can also be used to secure larger items, such as the oil filter canister. Tighten a hose clamp around the canister, then place the clamp under tension by lockwiring it back to an adjacent bolt.

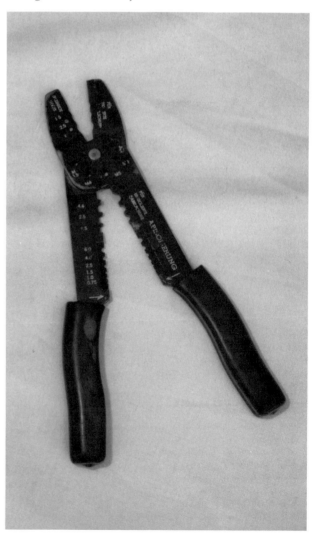

Portable lighting: Get a lead light to provide localized high-intensity lighting. It can be hung under the hood, powered by a 12-volt battery. Keep portable lights well away from any source of dripping gasoline: when you're removing a fuel pump, for example.

Rivet gun: You must certainly have the ability to undertake rivetting. Get an *adaptable* rivet gun, as you'll want to use various sizes of rivets.

Sanding equipment: Acquire a random orbital sander. These vibrate and rotate simultaneously, providing a truer finish. You'll also need a selection of wet-or-dry paper discs. The latter, when wet, are much less abrasive, leaving a smoother finish.

Always wear goggles and use a face mask when you're sanding, as inhaling dust is a major health hazard.

Screwdrivers: You need various sizes of Phillips- head and flat-bladed screwdrivers, to suit your particular model. Also invest in an electric screwdriver, which saves an awful lot of effort.

Sockets: You don't require a full set: only buy the sockets you actually need for your particular car. Typically, you'll require 1/2in and 3/8in drive sockets (or the Metric equivalent), unless your car has exceptionally-sized hub bolts, in which case you'll require a 3/4in drive socket.

Storage boxes: Keep your little bits and pieces in those neat plastic storage bins, which are modular and can therefore be attached to one another, building your storage capability as required.

Tire temperature gauge: This is a fairly expensive acquisition, but very useful when setting-up the car.

Trash can: You'll need somewhere to put trash, even if it's just the sawn-off bottom half of a 30-gallon oil drum.

Vice: Bear in mind that you'll want to grip large as well as small items in your vice, so get one that's fairly substantial and secure it firmly to the workbench. We recommend a vice with 5in (13cm) jaws: cut two short lengths of angle aluminium to serve as jaw covers.

Welding equipment: There are several welding methods, each of them suited to a particular application. For the tasks we'll be undertaking, you should have facilities for both gas welding and MIG welding.

Gas welding employs a mixture of oxygen and acetylene (oxyacetylene), bottles of which are available locally: check *Yellow Pages*. The only places where gas welding should be applied is where two or three sheets of steel come together at an angle, because the rigidity inherent in this type of joint is an effective counter to heat distortion.

MIG welding (the initials stand for Metal, Inert Gas) creates a very localised heat pattern, and is recommend

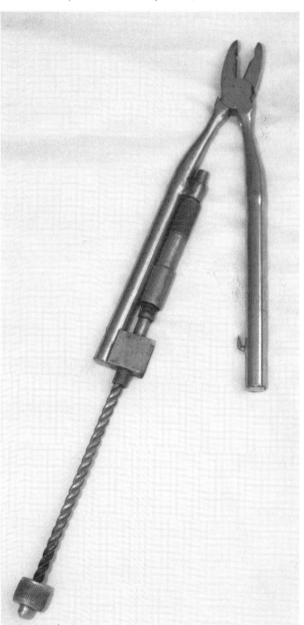

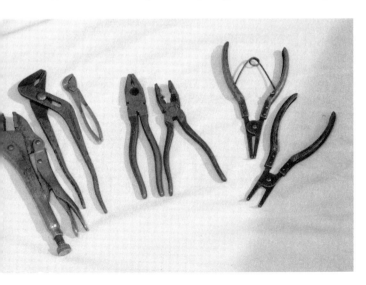

A wide variety of pliers are needed, including needle nosed versions and mole grips (top). Also invest in a pair of crimping pliers (left) for electrical work. You'll also need a pair of lock-wire pliers (right) if you plan to contest endurance races, as they prevent components working loose under prolonged exposure to vibration.

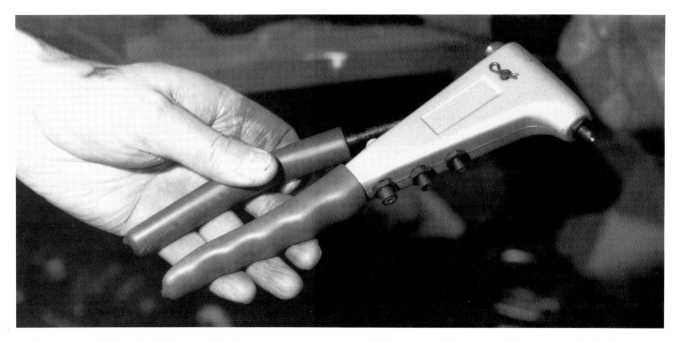

You must certainly have the ability to undertake some rivetting. It's far better to invest in a rivet gun which features several adaptors, like this one, as you'll need to fit various sizes of rivets as the race-preparation project progresses.

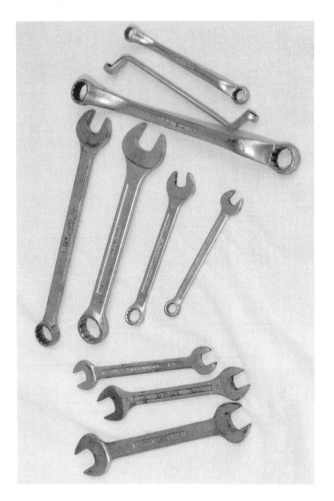

ed for seam welding around box sections and chassis rails, and welding steel components to the bodyshell. A new MIG welder is fairly expensive, but you can acquire a preowned unit at a reasonable price.

Workbench: Although it appears near the end of this alphabetical listing, a workbench should be your first acquisition. Invest in something fairly substantial, but avoid built-in shelves and drawers, as it's handy to be able to store items such as axle stands under the bench, out of the way, when they aren't in use.

Consider acquiring a mobile workbench, as opposed to a conventional one, as this will offer greater flexibility. There will be wheels at only one end, so make this the 'heavy' end and put the vice there. Pit garages are often rather austere places, virtually devoid of facilities. By moving your own workbench in, you can transform your surroundings and get the job done properly (the last thing you want to do is strip a gearbox on the floor). People often tend to think of mobile workbenches as being on the small side, but there are some very substantial ones available.

Wrenches: You'll require a variety of wrenches matching the standard of measurement employed on your particular model. We prefer to use combination wrenches – combined open-ended/ring-ended – as they're more versatile. Also acquire a monkey wrench and a torque wrench.

If you opt for air-driven tools, an air wrench is a must, as it greatly reduces the time needed to remove and replace wheels and so on. Get a set of drives to match your model, including a right angle drive for access to awkward places.

You'll require a variety of wrenches matching the standard of measurement employed on your particular model. We prefer to use combination wrenches – combined open-ended/ring-ended – as they're more versatile (left). Also acquire a monkey wrench and a torque wrench (right).

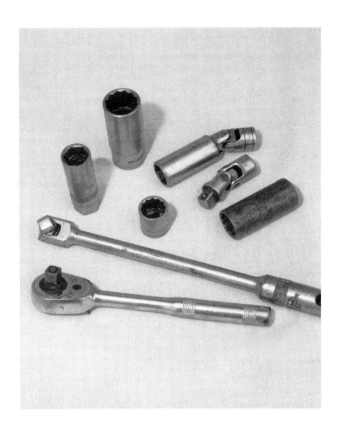

Only buy the sockets you actually need for your particular car, not a full set. Typically, you'll require 1/2in and 3/8in drive sockets (or the Metric equivalent), unless your car has exceptionally-sized hub bolts, in which case you'll require a 3/4in drive socket.

This impressive array of storage boxes was pictured in a professional workshop. Even if you have comparatively modest storage requirements, keep rivets, hose clips, wire clamps, cable ties, rubber grommets and suchlike in modular plastic storage boxes.

A new MIG welder is fairly expensive, but you can acquire a preowned unit at a reasonable price. MIG welding creates a very localized heat pattern, and is recommended for seam welding around box sections and chassis rails, and welding steel components to the bodyshell.

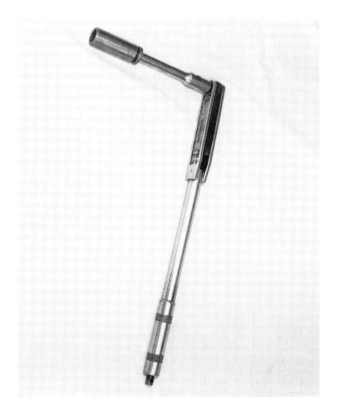

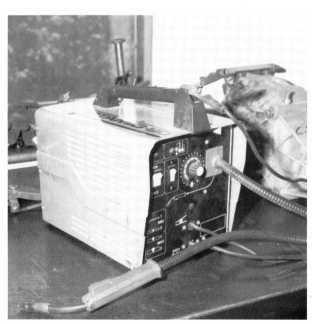

The rulemakers and you

The following three chapters describe in detail the full range of modifications allowable in this category of motorsport. However, a car incorporating *all* of them would not be eligible for any championship we are aware of. The modifications you undertake when preparing your car for competition must comply with the regulations in force in the chosen championship – and competitors are only allowed to do so much.

A love-hate relationship exists between the competitor and the regulatory authority which sanctions the championship he contests. The rulemakers decide which models are eligible to compete, and dictate what you can and cannot do to your car. You have no choice in the matter. In the category of motorsport we're concerned with, the regulations are aimed at preserving the roadgoing nature of the cars, but limited deviations are permitted in the interests of increasing performance and enhancing safety.

The specification of each model in its original roadgoing form, as published by the manufacturer, is the rulemakers' benchmark. The manufacturer records, in minute detail, the dimensions and weights of virtually every component, and the materials from which they are fabricated. The rulemakers try to ensure that the only deviations are those which they themselves have allowed, but it's a cat and mouse game. Ingenious interpretation of the regulations is the essence of showroom stock race preparation.

In the United States, the regulators interpret vehicle specifications in accordance with 'Specification Sheets' they issue for each eligible model, and on the contents of the manufacturer's service manuals. Furthermore, a model will not even be considered for eligibility unless its manufacturer achieves a specified minimum annual production output. This ruling ensures that competing cars really are series production models and not one-off racing 'specials'. One of the premier American sanctioning bodies, SCCA Club Racing, will not admit models with production outputs lower than 3,000 units per year. At the opposite extreme, IMSA admits models with production outputs as low as 200 per year.

The system is somewhat more stringent in Great Britain and Continental Europe, where national championship regulations tend to parallel the guidelines of the global regulatory authority, the Federation Internationale du Sport Automobile (FISA), based in Paris. National regulatory authorities generally demand that each model conforms to amended versions of production specifications submitted to FISA by its manufacturer. If these specifications receive FISA approval, they are released in the form of 'Homologation Papers', and the model in question is said to have been 'homologated for competition'. In this category of motorsport, a manufacturer can only apply to

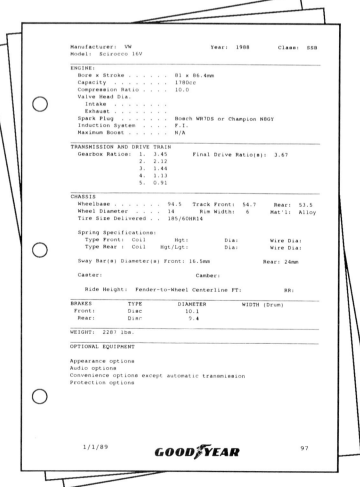

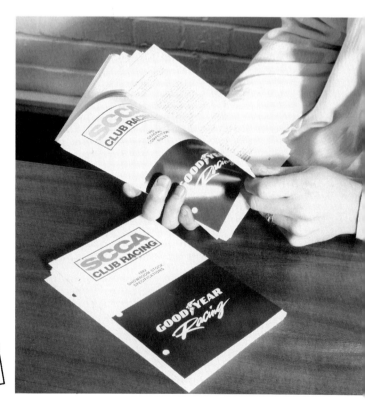

In the United States, the regulators interpret vehicle specifications in accordance with 'Specification Sheets' they issue for each eligible model, and on the contents of the relevant manufacturer's service manuals.

FISA for a model to be homologated when a minimum production output of 5,000 units has been achieved over a twelve-month period.

It is usual for homologation to lapse five years after the date on which production of the model in question ceased, or if annual production falls below ten percent of the minimum level required for homologation: in this case, 500 units per year.

If you don't encounter references to homologation, there's no need to concern yourself, as the principle is by no means universally applied. In America in particular, the regulatory authorities are not overly influenced by FISA's way of doing things.

Besides stipulating minimum production outputs, there are other ways the rulemakers can determine which models make up a grid. The regulations for some championships state that cars must have at least four seats, and correspondingly generous interior dimensions, effectively barring sports cars – even large scale production models, such as the Porsche 911 and the Lotus Esprit. Another ruling can be employed to exclude models thought to have deviated too far from their standard production counterparts. It prohibits what are sometimes termed 'evolutions' of the basic model – in other words, high-performance special editions – and it is enforced particularly vigorously in Europe. Again, a more liberal policy is adopted in some of the American championships.

Rulemakers can even influence how competitive one model will be against another! They reserve the right to 'even the score' by amending the regulations during the course of the season. That right is exercised to varying degrees by different groups of rulemakers, but it's usually brought into play just enough to ensure that no particular model enjoys runaway success throughout a season. As one might expect, this method of achieving parity is a frequent source of controversy – and, it must be said, not a little gamesmanship...

When you've selected a championship and acquired a car with which to contest it, the time has come for some serious work. Before we delve too deeply into *what* needs to be done, let's dwell for a moment on precisely *why* it will be done. In this category of motorsport, the two areas where the greatest scope exists for gaining a performance advantage are in reducing the overall weight of the car, and in increasing the power output of the engine. Acceleration is a mathematical equation based on the

Besides stipulating minimum production outputs, there are other ways the rulemakers can determine which models make up a grid. The regulations for some championships state that cars must have at least four seats, and correspondingly generous internal dimensions, effectively barring sports cars – even large scale production models, such as the Porsche 911 (pictured here) and the Lotus Esprit.

power to weight ratio: if you decrease the vehicle weight and increase the engine power, the car will go faster.

The regulations state a minimum weight for each model. This figure is based on the weight of that model in production form, but makes allowance for the additional weight of the roll cage and the fire extinguisher (and an airjack system, if this is permitted). Obviously, when you rebuild the car to race specification, the closer you can get to the minimum weight limit, the better your chances of being competitive. In the chapters which follow, we'll indicate how – even within the limited scope allowed by the regulations – there are plenty ways of saving weight

Acquire a full set of regulations, together with any other essential documentation, at the earliest possible opportunity. Materials distributed by regulatory authorities range from the comprehensive 'starter pack' despatched to newcomers by Britain's RAC MSA, to the frugal IMSA Code. Also try to augment the essential documentation with some of the manufacturer's technical material on your particular model, as this may support your case in the event of a dispute.

when rebuilding the car.

Increasing the engine's power output is the other critical area for improvement. Here, the subtle art of 'blueprinting' is applied: the term is derived from 'blueprints' – the manufacturers' published specifications. Blueprinting is achieved by a combination of balancing and machining, ensuring that a car conforms to the manufacturer's specifications, as amended by the regulations, *but does so in a manner which is to the competitor's maximum advantage*. Manufacturers produce every component to specified tolerances, with each of the quoted dimensions and weights having corresponding maximum and minimum tolerable values: tolerances are normally expressed as percentages. If those fractional tolerable variations are brought into harmony, a car's performance will be enhanced – *without deviating from the manufacturer's original specifications*.

Take one example. A manufacturer might specify that the pistons in a particular model weigh 20.5oz (585g) apiece, but will qualify this by stating that the figure is accurate to one percent: in other words, there is an acceptable tolerance range of 0.25oz (5.85g). While such variations are perfectly acceptable for roadgoing use, for competition applications – where performance is paramount – they are wholly unacceptable. A specialist tuner preparing that engine for competition will undertake a painstaking matching process, selecting systematically from a large batch of pistons to ensure that he obtains a set with virtually identical weights. The engine, whilst conforming to the original specifications, will then be better balanced than before, and will therefore run more smoothly and deliver slightly more power.

This is but one example of blueprinting: there are dozens of them. In each case, the improvement to performance is only slight, but the cumulative effect of dozens of fractional improvements becomes significant in a category of motorsport which offers little scope for enhancing performance.

Blueprinting should be entrusted to an expert, as it is a highly-specialised skill requiring equipment not found in ordinary workshops. Although it is an art applied almost exclusively to the engine – the subject of Chapter 3 – there is scope for blueprinting certain elements of the transmission, particularly within the gearbox.

In some championships, the regulations state that blueprinting is contrary to the 'spirit of the regulations' and declare it illegal. However, the rulemakers are powerless to prevent certain types of blueprinting – such as balancing of the pistons (and the other reciprocating components) in the manner outlined above – because there's no way they can prove that this has taken place. You may therefore have your engine blueprinted to that extent with impunity, but must instruct your engine-tuner to exercise great care if he *machines* any components to achieve balance, as in many cases this *is* detectable (to avoid detection, engine-tuners emulate the manufacturer's machining methods).

The regulations are seldom so easily circumvented. If you stray into the vast areas where detection *is* possible,

SCCA Pro Racing's regulations book, which deals with its showroom stock series, the World Challenge.

FISA's famous "Yellow Book" of regulations, upon which most national championships in Europe are based.

you are likely to get caught – and the penalties can be severe. The rulemakers have the power to deduct all points gained in previous races if they have good reason to suspect that a competitor's indiscretions have gone undetected for some time. In extreme cases, they can even disqualify a competitor from future events for an extended period.

It isn't just the hard and fast rulings that can be the competitor's downfall, either. Some regulatory authorities reserve the right to invoke the 'spirit of the regulations' principle if they suspect that a competitor is taking advantage of ambiguities in the wording of the regulations to exploit a loophole (i.e. resorting to semantics). It is typical, in such cases, for the regulations to state that *"All modifications which are not allowed are expressly forbidden"*. In other words, unless the regulations specifically state that you can do it, *don't* do it – period!

Acquire a full set of regulations, together with any other essential documentation, at the earliest possible opportunity. Also try to augment the essential documentation with some of the manufacturer's technical material on

In Great Britain and Continental Europe, national regulatory authorities generally demand that each model conforms to amended versions of production specifications submitted to FISA by its manufacturer. If these specifications receive FISA approval, they are released in the form of 'Homologation Papers', a set of which are being perused here.

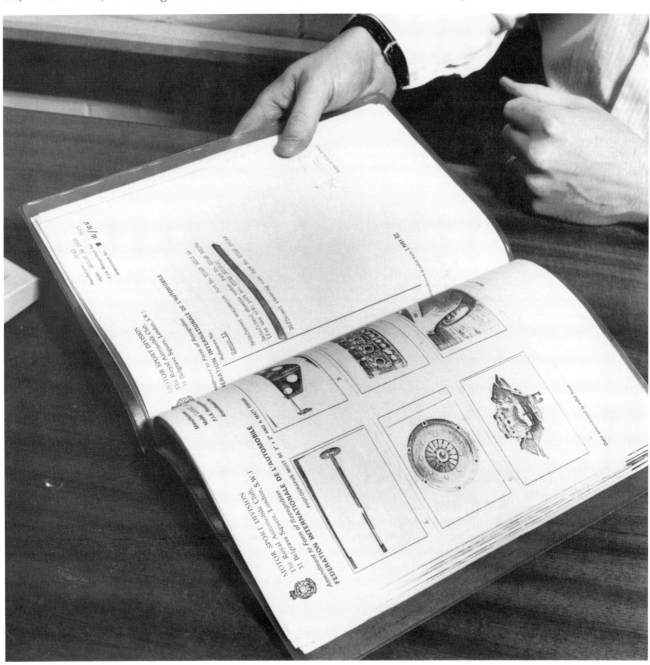

your particular model, as this may support your case in the event of a dispute. It has even been known for technical information contained in manufacturers' sales promotional brochures to settle disputes as to what is, and what is not, a legitimate production specification. There have also been cases of disputes being settled by tech inspectors and competitors visiting nearby showrooms to compare standard components with those installed in race cars! Before you start work on your car, establish telephone contact with a technical representative of the club which sanctions the championship you intend to contest. He will be qualified to offer guidance as your race-preparation project progresses, especially if you suspect that a particular modification might infringe the regulations.

These pages from the British Automobile Racing Club's eligibility papers for the Ford Sierra RS Cosworth provide an insight into the rulemakers' approach.

22: (A) Engine reciprocating

- Bore .... 90.82 .... mm
- Stroke .... 76.95 .... mm
- Swept volume per cylinder (Vs) .... 498.49 .... ml
- Nominal compression ratio .... 8.2 : 1
- No of cylinders .... Four
- Block Part No & Material V.86HF6010AA Cast Iron
- Head   Part No & Material V.86HF6085AA Al. Alloy
- Combustion chamber in head .... Yes
- Volume (Vh) .... 51 Noml .... ml
- Finish (ie as cast, fettled/position, finished or machined) .... As Cast
- Head Gasket
- Compressed thickness .... 0.12 Noml .... cm
- Aperture area (⌀ 92.7 mm) .... 67.5 Noml .... cm²
- Volume allowance (Vg) .... 8.1 Noml .... ml
- Combustion volume in piston & block (Vb) .... 10.1 Noml .... ml

The actual compression will be calculated according to the formula

$$\text{Compression ratio} = \frac{V_s}{V_h + V_g + V_b} + 1$$

The valve so calculated must not exceed the nominal figure by more than 0.2

- Inlet valve head diameter .... 35.2 .... mm
- Exhaust valve head diamter .... 31.2 .... mm
- Inlet valve max lift .... 8.6 .... mm with .... 0 .... mm clearance at Hydraulic
- Exhaust valve max lift .... 8.6 .... mm with .... 0 .... mm clearance at Hydraulic
- Valve springs Part No, No of coils, outside diameter (mm) V86HF6513AA
- 5.75 coils. O/D 30 mm
- Wire diameter (mm) .... 3.9 .... Uncompressed length (mm) 40.1

Registration No 70

RAC PRODUCTION CAR SPECIFICATION SHEET

Registration No .... 70 .... Valid From 1.1.87

This document specifies items which have a major effect on performance and any car which relies upon this document for its eligibility must be in entire conformity with all the data listed herein. Failure to conform in any single respect will be deemed to render the car ineligible. No options are allowed except where specified or authorised and changes in specification are only recognised as the subject of a seperate specification sheet covering a previous or later model variant.

Only original copies having each sheet embossed with the RAC stamp will be valid.

Except where specified otherwise hereafter, tolerances will be allowed according to Appendix J, ie:

1. Tolerances for all machining, excepting bore and stroke: ± 0.2%
2. Unfinished castings: +4% -2%
3. Weight +7% -3%
4. Width of the car at front and rear axles: +1% -0.3%
5. Wheelbase ± 0.5%
6. Track ± 25mm

Maximum and minimum figures have no tolerance allowed.

- Make of car .... Ford .... Model .... Sierra R S Cosworth
- Importer of car (if manufactured abroad) .... N/A
- Production/Import commenced .... June 1986
- Production/Import ceased .... N/A
- Weight, with oil, water, empty fuel tank, spare wheel, if fitted and tools, if supplied .... 1140 Sapdice: 1220 .... kgs
- 610   660 .... kgs
- Weight on front wheels 530   560 .... kgs
- Weight on rear wheels

- ...aner Make/Type .... Ford Plastic Box 81BB2L531AA
- Filter Medium .... Paper element

Registration No 70

2.

- gth overall .... 446.0 .... cm Width overall .... 154.7 .... cm
- le Height .... 40.5 .... cm Measured to Lowest edge of door crease at front of door
- nt .... 42.5 .... cm Measured to Lowest edge of door crease at rear of door
- r ....
- ack (at stated ride height) Front .... 1500 .... cm
-                              Rear .... 1515 .... cm
- mber (at Stated ride height) Front .... 1° 15' Negative ± 30'
-                              Rear .... -1° ± 30'
- eel base at stated ground clearance .... 262.0 .... cm
- adwheel
- m diameter .... 15 .... in
- m width and type .... 7 J .... in Aluminium Alloy
- terial .... 140 .... mm
- fset from mounting face to inner extremity of rim 205/50
- yre size fitted to basic model .... 2½ .... N/A .... kg/cm
- Steering box, turns from lock to lock .... Rate
- 12. Front Springs Part No V86BB5310AA
- Coil Springs:
- No of XXXX coils 5.6
- Diameter of wire .... 11.0 .... mm
- External diameter of spring .... 134 .... mm

Registration No 70

Preparing the bodyshell

Checking the bodyshell alignment

If your car is preowned, and you have any doubts at all as to its history, take it to a well-equipped bodyshop at the earliest possible opportunity and have the alignment of the bodyshell checked for 'true'. The car could have been in an accident at some time before you acquired it, and there's nothing worse than trying to set up a car at the racetrack, only to discover that the shell is twisted.

For evidence that there's been widespread use of filler, a pointer to accident damage, go over the car's structure with a magnet. If your suspicions are confirmed, contact a suitably- equipped bodyshop and discuss your concerns. If possible, go to a shop that's been personally recommended to you. Failing that, consult *Yellow Pages*.

There are a variety of commercial alignment-checking methods in use, but they are all intended for roadgoing cars, and a car destined for competition use might require a more thorough series of measurements. That said, a basic series of checks will provide a good indication as to the alignment of the shell: typically, the bodyshop personnel clamp the car to a special jig, and by offering adaptable brackets up to either the bumper mountings or the suspension pickup points, they can ascertain the shell alignment to a fair degree of accuracy.

To go the extra yard for accuracy, you may need to have the vertical distances between each of the four turret tops and the base of the chassis rails measured. By this method, for relatively little expense, you can put your mind at rest. If some twisting *is* detected, the bodyshop people can usually remedy the problem with some strategic pushing or pulling with powerful hydraulic devices.

The actual point at which you should take your car for the alignment check, assuming you have doubts about it, depends very much on individual circumstances – as does the degree to which the car should be disassembled prior to the measurements being made. You may wish to have the alignment checked before handing over any money for it, but the owner may be unwilling to have his car disassembled for a comprehensive examination without a guarantee that you'll eventually purchase it.

If you plan to have the alignment checked *after* acquiring the car, do it sooner rather than later – and certainly before you install a roll cage. In the unlikely event that the car proves to be misaligned beyond economical repair, you'll be glad you discovered the grim truth before investing precious time and money on it.

Disassembling the car

Confident that the car's structure is properly aligned, you can begin the first phase of the race-preparation process: modification of the bodyshell. The shell must be stripped right down to bare metal, step by careful step. At a later date, you'll be dispensing with some of the car's standard roadgoing equipment. Don't throw anything away at this stage, though. The regulations in this type of racing are aimed at preserving the car's roadgoing nature, so most of what you take out will be going back in.

When you remove seemingly-redundant items from your car, store them together in a safe place, just in case.

Before you get under way, ensure you have enough room to pull bulky items, such as the dashpanel and the seats, out of the car. Also ensure that you have a place to store the items as you remove them: loft space is ideal. Get an adequate number of cardboard boxes or other sturdy containers close to hand, so that as you take pieces off the car, you can store them together in appropriate groupings.

Think safety! Before doing anything else, drain every last drop from the fuel tank and the feed line (and the return line, if the car is fuel-injected). You don't want any flammable liquid around when you start welding, and now is the best time to get rid of it. If the fuel system in your particular model facilitates it, let gravity do the work. If there's a drain plug at the bottom of the tank, use that. If your car doesn't have a drain plug, you may only have to remove the fuel pump and let the fuel run out through both ends of the feed line.

Failing that, you must use the car's own fuel pump to discharge the contents of the tank. However, in most cases, it will only operate for a few seconds when the ignition key is turned, so the tank cannot be adequately drained. If this proves to be the case, remove the battery and the fuel pump and rig up a slave system, by-passing the standard ignition sequence. The battery should be positioned well away from the car, to guard against igniting errant fuel vapor.

Whichever method you employ to drain the fuel, the battery should be removed from the car at the earliest possible opportunity. If you fail to do this, and begin disassembling the car, you risk shorting-out the electrics and starting a fire.

The next step is to locate the jacking points and raise the car onto axle stands. Ensure that all four contact points on the chassis rails are substantial enough to bear the weight of the shell.

In some championships, the rulemakers allow the car's standard fuel tank to be replaced with a bladder-type flexible fuel cell. Whether you intend to do this or not, the fuel tank should now be removed from the underside of the car. It will probably be held in place by two steel straps, and will drop away easily when they're undone. Lower the car back onto its wheels at this point.

With the car in a safe condition, you can begin disassembling it in earnest. A useful tip is to remove all the doors first – and the hatch, if your car has one – complete with their internal and external fittings, because you'll enjoy much better access to the interior with them out of the way. This also avoids the risk of straining the hinges or causing other damage as you try to heave cumbersome items out through the door apertures.

As you remove each door, put it out of harm's way. If you're removing a hatch as well, take particular care not to damage the electric demister in the screen. Some sets of regulations dictate that it must be in working order – and in any case, it could be needed for wet races.

The next step is to remove all the internal fittings, because it's easier to get at them while the car is on its wheels. At this stage, also, you and your car are nice and clean, so it's the best time to be removing items that are easily soiled.

With these, as with all the other items you remove from the car, adopt a firm policy of keeping pieces together in groups, clearly labelled in your assortment of boxes. For example, having removed the dashpanel, you can put the contents in one box, then put the windshield wiper mechanisms in another, and so on. If you don't impose this discipline on yourself, and simply pile the pieces in a big heap on the floor, you'll find putting the car back together a major headache.

Novices and veterans alike benefit from a systematic approach. Make written notes every time there's something particularly tricky that you think you might forget when the time comes to put the car back together. Augment these, if possible, with plenty of still photos – or even some camcorder footage – to provide a really comprehensive record. A regular color print camera with auto focus and flash is cheaper than using a Polaroid camera, and – with one-hour development services widely available – is almost as quick.

Another useful tip is to keep a roll of masking tape close to hand. It's very handy for maintaining the relative positions of certain smaller components as you take things apart. Put screws back into their holes after disassembly, then stick a piece of masking tape over them to hold them in place. Masking tape is also useful for wiring connections. When you undo a connection, stick a small piece of tape to it and write on that where the wire in question is supposed to go: to a headlight, or whatever.

Take large items out of the car first, to make room for yourself. Getting the front and rear seats out is a worthwhile priority, as you'll find the sudden air of spaciousness within the car an instant boost to morale! With the seats lifted clear and the seat frames unbolted from the floor, much of the carpeting will come free.

You'll need to remove the windows and various internal fittings before you can ease the head liner out. If the car has a bonded-in windshield, you may need to employ the services of a specialist to remove it: any reputable windshield replacement company will undertake this task for a moderate fee, should it prove necessary. As with a hatchback, if your car has a rear screen, be careful not to damage the electric demister as you remove it. Keep your hands scrupulously clean when easing the head liner free, as the regulations for most championships dictate that it must go back in, and you want it to look its best.

Next, remove the steering column. Leaving the steering wheel on, locate the knuckle joint at the bottom of the steering column where it goes through the floor, undo it, and ease the column upwards and out. The dashpanel can now come out, together with the associated heating system and/or air conditioning system elements.

If your car has bolted-on fenders, this is the time to remove them. Welded-on fenders should remain in place throughout the build project. If your car has a trunk, remove the lid at this point, lift out the spare wheel and jacking equipment, and remove all the carpeting and trim from the trunk. Also remove any brackets in or around the spare wheel recess.

While the car is still on its wheels, remove the hood and put it safely to one side, then raise the car back onto the axle stands and drain the oil from the engine and gearbox, and the water from the radiator. Next, set about removing the wheels and disassembling the drivetrain, the axle assemblies and the suspension units. It's best to take things out in big chunks – the bigger the better, provided they're of manageable proportions – and strip them down on the bench at a later date. For example, if you have a front-wheel-drive car, you should be able to remove the front suspension units with the driveshaft assemblies and brake units intact.

One word of caution about the driveshafts. Be careful not to damage the constant velocity joints, or split the rubber CV covers, by allowing them to exceed their normal range of working angles as you lift them clear. Hold them as near as possible to their original relative positions as you take them off the car and place them in temporary storage.

It's advisable to remove the radiator next, to ensure that no damage is inflicted when you hoist the engine and gearbox out. With the radiator out of harm's way, disconnect all the cables and hoses that link the engine with the car, and remove the induction system and heating and/or air conditioning system elements from the engine compartment, together with any components which might get damaged when the hoist chains are put under tension: valve covers, for example.

As you proceed with the removal of major components in the sequence outlined above, you'll encounter fuel lines, brake lines and wiring looms, all of which must come out. You may not have adequate access to some components until the shell is virtually denuded. Because disassembling a car is essentially a reversal of the manufacturer's production process, it's often a case of, 'First in, last out.'

Once everything has been removed from the bodyshell, consider having it chemically treated to remove all the paint, and any other deposits. This can save a great deal of weight, and will also make welding easier later. The task must be undertaken by a specialist, who'll immerse it for several hours in a huge vat of alkaline solution. If your car is preowned, it may have had some filler applied to remedy bodywork damage. The acid-dipping process will remove any filler of the isoponic or metalux types (but not polyester-type filler), along with the paint. It will also remove the rubberized anti-chip coating on the undersurfaces, and the gungy sound proofing material which manufacturers apply to the inside of some panels: score these areas with a knife before sending your shell for dipping, to allow the chemicals to penetrate properly.

Put bolted-on fenders, the doors, the hood and the trunk lid in for the same treatment, but not the hatch. The weight saving is negligible with modern hatches, as they're composed almost entirely of glass.

We know of a case where 30kg (66lb) of excess weight was removed from a bodyshell by the acid-dipping process, of which 15kg (33lb) was wax the manufacturer had pumped into the chassis rails and other cavities to limit corrosion. Have a look in *Yellow Pages* to ascertain if chemical treatment services are available locally, and at what cost. We don't recommend bead-blasting or grit-blasting, as these methods – particularly the latter – are likely to pit the shell surfaces.

When you get the shell back to your workshop, rub it down thoroughly with a solvent-soaked cloth to deactivate any acid which may have been retained. You may then have to use a wire brush or a scraper to dislodge remnants of glue from seams, and excessive amounts of undersealant from joints. It may also be necessary to remove pieces of joint sealer mastic still adhering between panels. The joint sealer is soft and gungy in its normal state, but it shrinks and turns fairly hard after prolonged immersion in alkaline solution. Apply a healthy flame from a welding bottle to heat any obstinate remnants of joint sealer through, then scrub them out with a wire brush, taking care not to provoke distortion.

Of course, if the cost of chemical treatment proves prohibitive, paint and other deposits can be removed by hand using a propriety paint stripper and other materials. However, it's an extremely laborious process – particularly getting rubberized undersealant and sound proofing material off. These generally require the vigorous application of a scraper, or an air chisel fitted with a blunt blade.

If you've had the bodyshell chemically treated to remove the paint and any other deposits, rub it down thoroughly with a solvent-soaked cloth to deactivate any acid which may have been retained. You may then have to use a wire brush or a scraper to dislodge remnants of glue from seams, and excessive amounts of undersealant from joints. It may also be necessary to remove pieces of joint sealer mastic still adhering between panels.

Dealing with a sunroof

As stated in Chapter 1, it's better to avoid cars with sunroofs, provided you can get an alternative model of comparable performance. There's usually a weight disadvantage, an additional workload – and, sometimes, financial outlay – associated with rendering a sunroof suitable for competition.

Glass and acrylic sunroofs aren't permitted on the racetrack for safety reasons, so if your car has one you must replace it with a steel sunroof – provided there's one available for your particular model – and bolt it in permanently: this task is detailed in Chapter 4. If there isn't a steel sunroof available for your model, the next alternative is to fit a replacement roof panel: it's almost always possible to get one without a sunroof aperture. Although this task can be undertaken before or after the roll cage has been installed, it's generally preferable to do it beforehand, as you'll have better access. Drill out all of the spot welds around the outer edges of the roof and lift the entire panel off, then slide the replacement roof panel into position and weld it on.

If you're very unlucky, and simply can't get a replacement roof panel without a sunroof aperture, the only course of action open to you is to weld a sheet of steel in to fill the aperture. This task should certainly be undertaken before the roll cage goes in. The regulations usually state that a steel sheet introduced to fill a sunroof aperture must be at least as thick as the rest of the roof, and that it must conform to the contours of the roof line. It's difficult to weld a sheet of steel into the roof panel without causing heat distortion, so exercise extreme care.

All brackets, mounts and mouldings associated with the sunroof can be discarded if a sheet of steel has been welded in its place.

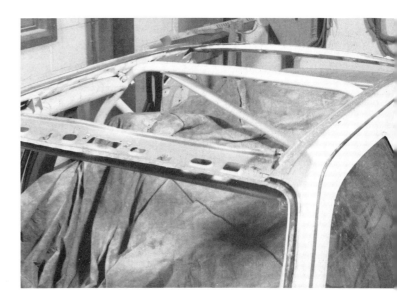

If there isn't a steel sunroof available for your model, the next alternative is to fit a replacement roof panel: it's almost always possible to get one without a sunroof aperture. Drill out all of the spot welds around the outer edges of the roof and lift the entire panel off, then slide the replacement roof panel into position and weld it on.

Fitting a roll cage

When the bodyshell has been disassembled right down to bare metal, the roll cage can be installed. A roll cage is a tubular framework installed inside the car to provide maximum protection to the occupant in the event of a rollover. It can also afford protection in the event of an impact with another car, or with obstacles at the trackside, such as guardrails. Furthermore, roll cages have evolved to the point where they can actually enhance the performance of a car. Rather than being anchored to the bodyshell at floor level only, many cages feature multiple anchor points *above* floor level – on the door pillars and around the roof – bestowing much greater rigidity. These are known as multipoint cages.

Triangulation is the key to a roll cage's structural integrity, preventing lozenging of the structure under cornering forces and impact loadings. As further cage elements are added to the basic design, rigidity and strength are enhanced. Roll cage designs are essentially modular, and there are many permutations. The design you select will depend partly on your personal preferences and partly on the mandatory requirements. In championships which permit only minimal modifications, the roll cage must be of the removable type, and extensive triangulation is considered inconsistent with what might be termed the 'showroom stock philosophy'.

A roll cage's primary elements are: the main hoop, a continuous length of tubing which runs from floor level, up the door pillars and across the full width of the roof; and the back stays, which are supporting members, one each side, bracing the top of the main hoop to the rear turret tops. The regulations sometimes state that the main hoop must be braced by a diagonal strut running from one of the top corners to the bottom corner on the opposite side, and that this must be intersected by a horizontal brace linking the main hoop legs below the window

Installing a bolt-in roll cage is fairly straightforward, provided it's not rushed. Instructions supplied with each kit often include a suggested assembly sequence.

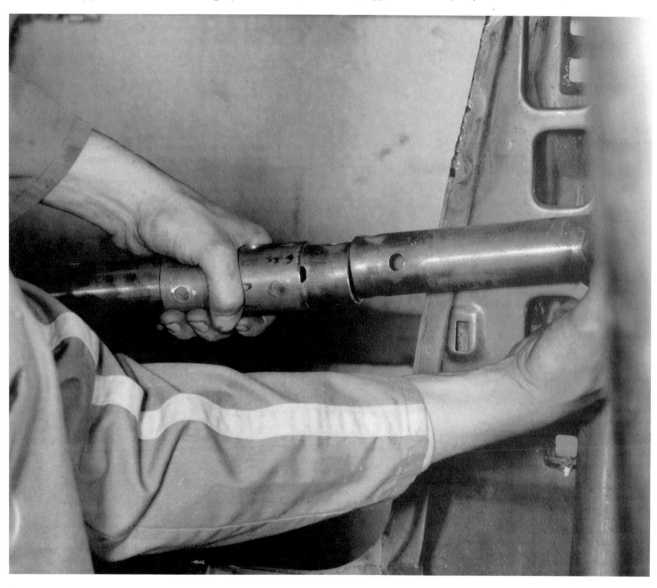

line. Alternatively, some cages feature two near-vertical supports running down from the center of the main hoop to a transverse strut (tunnel bar) linking the main hoop legs.

The regulations often dictate that these cage elements be braced by a strut running diagonally backwards from one corner of the main hoop, just behind the driver's head, down to the base of the back stay on the opposite side. This is known as a crossbar, and some cage designs feature two of them, one from each side, crossing in the middle. Often, the rear turret tops are linked by a transverse bar called a rear strut brace, greatly increasing the rigidity of the back of the car.

With the introduction of these additional elements, the braced main hoop becomes a 'back cage'.

Increasingly, over recent years, regulatory authorities have specified that production-based race cars must feature a 'front cage': a system of roll cage elements extending forward to cocoon the front seats. This greatly improves driver safety, and offers further possibilities for increasing the rigidity of the shell to enhance the car's performance. As with back cages, there are many permutations, so the configuration you specify will reflect personal preferences and regulatory obligations.

The primary elements of a front cage are two continuous lengths of tubing extending forward from the top corners of the main hoop, curving down to conform to the line of the windshield pillars, and attaching to the floor

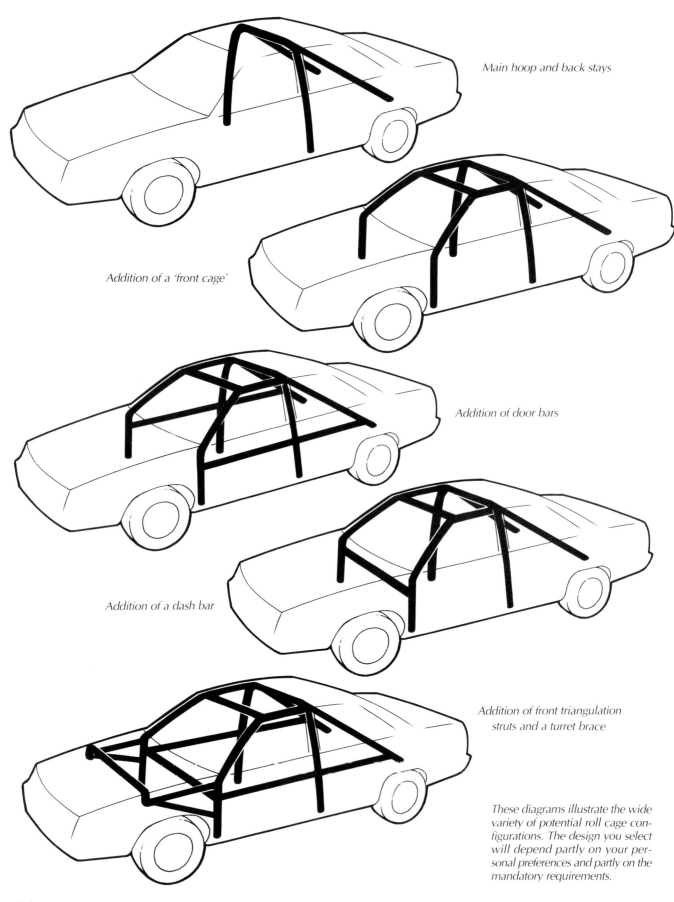

Main hoop and back stays

Addition of a 'front cage'

Addition of door bars

Addition of a dash bar

Addition of front triangulation struts and a turret brace

These diagrams illustrate the wide variety of potential roll cage configurations. The design you select will depend partly on your personal preferences and partly on the mandatory requirements.

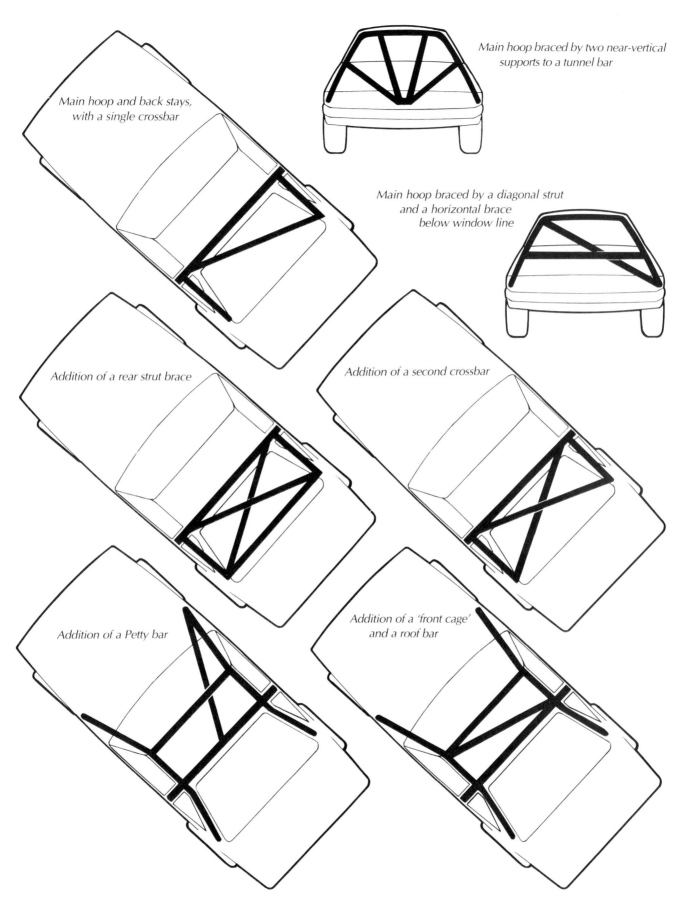

pan just forward of the door apertures. These are known as front legs, and they are linked by a transverse brace running across the roof just above the windshield, forming what is termed a 'front hoop'. In some championships, the regulations specify that the front legs must also be linked further down – though above knee level – by a transverse strut known as a dash bar.

The combination of a main hoop and a front hoop provides opportunities for yet more elaborate triangulation. It is not uncommon for a diagonal brace to be fitted between one corner of the main hoop and the top corner of the front bar on the opposite side. This is known as a roof bar. Another refinement is a diagonal strut running from the center of the horizontal section of the main hoop to the base of the front bar on the passenger's side. This is known as a Petty bar, in honor of the legendary NASCAR driver Richard *"The King"* Petty.

As protection against sideways intrusion by another car in the event of a T-bone impact, it is usual for longitudinal bars to be sited across the door apertures. There may be one or more of these bars on each side, linking the main hoop to the front bars, but they must always be sited below the window line. Known as door bars, they are mandatory in most championships. For safety reasons, the rulemakers limit their maximum height above floor level and their maximum angle relative to the floor pan. Typically, the regulations will state that this angle must not exceed 15 degrees, and that the door bars can only be angled downwards towards the front of the car.

If triangulation is the key to a roll cage's rigidity and strength, it is also the driving factor in its cost. In short, the more complex the triangulation, the greater the labor and material costs and the higher the price. In the category of motorsport we're concerned with, the sophistication of the roll cage is sometimes limited by the

Before you actually bolt the various roll cage elements in, you'll have to weld flange plates (complete with captive bolts) onto the bodyshell floor to reinforce the points where the integral flanges at the foot of each roll cage leg attach to the floor pan.

rulemakers. In most cases, however, competitors are free to fit the best cage they can afford, as driver safety is considered paramount.

The regulatory minimum weight limit for each model makes allowance for the weight of the roll cage, so that cars fitted with comprehensive cages don't suffer an undue weight penalty. Typically, there might be three weight allowances, graduated according to the complexity of the cage: 15kg (33lb) for a basic cage, 25kg (55lb) for a more sophisticated configuration, and 35kg (77lb) for the most comprehensive arrangement.

Regulatory factors, and the simple matter of practicality, make building your own roll cage inadvisable. Even if you were capable of fabricating an adequate homemade cage, you'd be unlikely to get it certified as safe by the rulemakers. When considering your options, it's wise to seek the advice of one of the leading suppliers, some of whom have up to 250 different roll cage designs available 'off the shelf', all fully certified.

At this point, most competitors decide whether to buy a bolt-in roll cage kit and fit it themselves, or have a welded-in cage, which can only be installed at the cage manufacturer's premises by their highly skilled personnel. Not all competitors have a choice in the matter, as welded-in cages are prohibited in some championships in the interests of containing costs. At the other extreme, welded-in cages are mandatory. In cases where competitors have a choice, some regulatory authorities go as far as *recommending* welded-in cages.

Although the range of welded-in cage designs essentially mirrors the range of bolt-in cage designs, welded-in cages are indisputably better. The downside is that they're more expensive. When welded-in, the roll cage becomes an integral, form-fitting, strengthening and stiffening feature of the shell, introducing structural rigidity that simply wasn't there when the car was in its original

Welded-in cages

In the early-1980s, independent of evolutionary advances in safety, came the realization that cars could benefit in pure performance terms from an advanced, well designed roll cage. That realization brought forth the welded-in cage: an integral strengthening and stiffening medium.

Welded-in cages are not permitted in many championships, due to their relatively high cost – but they are the ultimate. A welded-in cage influences the handling and performance of a car in a way that bolt-in cages can't, by virtually eliminating the bodyshell's tendency to flex under cornering loads. There is the added benefit that a competent driver can accurately interpret subtle alterations to the suspension setup, rather than being misled by an unbraced shell's complex flexing characteristics.

A welded-in cage is also better from the safety standpoint, as there are more contact points between the shell and the cage, dissipating impact energies.

As with most things, there's a downside. Some competitors argue that bolt-in cages are better, because in the event of an accident, the cage can be removed and the shell straightened. You can't do that with a welded-in cage, because the shell won't budge!

There was something of an outcry when it became permissible to weld cages into production-based cars, but they are now an accepted part of the scene in several championships: albeit the preserve of the better funded competitors.

Aside from the obvious financial considerations, bear in mind that if you opt for a welded-in cage, you'll need to arrange for the bare shell to be transported to the cage maker's premises, and back, and should plan to be productive with your time while the shell is elsewhere.

If your car has bolted-on fenders, take them off before sending your shell to the cage maker's premises. They are of no use to him, so keep them at the workshop – in a place where no-one can accidentally put a dent in them!

Rather than being anchored to the bodyshell at floor level only, modern roll cages often feature multiple anchor points above floor level – on the door pillars and around the roof – bestowing much greater strength and rigidity. These are known as multipoint cages.

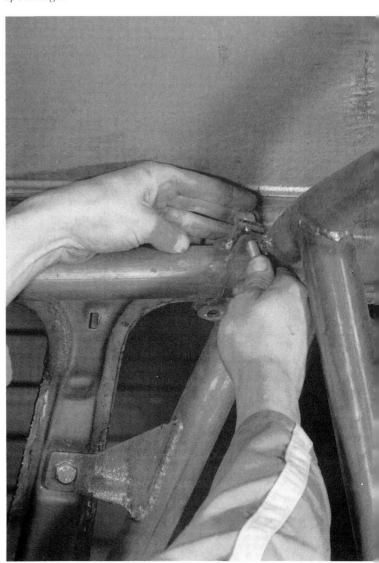

roadgoing form. That rigidity translates into better handling and improved performance on the racetrack.

Since a welded-in cage is beyond the financial resources of most, and building a homemade cage is ill-advised at best – and possibly illegal – the vast majority of privateers opt to purchase a propriety bolt-in cage and fit it themselves. A bolt-in cage doesn't make the bodyshell quite as rigid as a welded-in cage would, but it reduces flexing considerably.

Installing a bolt-in cage is fairly straightforward, provided it's not rushed. Instructions supplied with each kit often include a suggested assembly sequence. Before you actually bolt the various cage elements in, you'll have to weld flange plates (complete with captive bolts) onto the bodyshell floor to reinforce the points where the integral flanges at the foot of each roll cage leg attach to the floor pan. If you've specified a multipoint cage, you'll also have to weld other reinforcement plates in to strengthen the points where the cage attaches to the shell above floor level. All of these plates are supplied with the cage.

Applying heat to localized areas of the shell while it's in a flimsy, stripped-out state can cause warping, so exercise great care.

Start by bolting the primary roll cage elements together inside the car, but don't tighten the nuts until all of the pieces are in position, as this makes fitting the cage difficult. When the cage is in, slide the flange plates into position under each of the integral flanges at the ends of the cage legs. Tackweld each flange plate to the floor, then repeat the exercise with the other reinforcing plates above floor level. At this point, remove the cage and complete the welding, taking care not to overheat the surrounding area. When all the flange plates are firmly welded in, you can bolt the cage in permanently: again, don't tighten the nuts until all of the cage elements are in position.

Typically, the regulations state that there must be three bolts of a specified diameter running through each cage-to-floor mounting point. Although opinion is somewhat divided, we recommend that you apply an anti-seize agent (Copperslip is good) to the bolts before putting the nuts on, so that cage elements can be easily removed during running repairs.

Some sets of regulations specify that roll cages must feature backing plates. These combine with the integral flanges and flange plates to sandwich the floor, anchoring the cage legs even more firmly to the shell. If your cage is to have backing plates, start by following the procedure outlined above, then drill down through the preformed holes in the integral flanges and flange plates, penetrating the shell floor. Taking one attachment point at a time, position the backing plate under the floor with a G-clamp and push the bolts supplied with the kit up through the holes you've just drilled.

It's best to put the bolts in from the outside, as the nuts will then be on the inside of the car, where they're less likely to sustain damage or get corroded in over time. Again, we recommend that you apply Copperslip to the bolts before pushing them through.

Roll cages: more than meets the eye

A roll cage can save your life, so it's worth knowing a little more about them. Roll cages may look straightforward, but their design reflects a revolution which began about a decade ago. The advent of multipoint cages, welded-in cages, and ever more complex levels of triangulation, has refined the basic roll cage to the point where it can contribute directly to the performance of the chassis on the racetrack.

With refinements being made increasingly in the interests of performance, as opposed to purely safety, the rulemakers are rather vague when it comes to the question: when is a roll cage not a roll cage? In recognizing this as a gray area, they seem to have settled on a tacit understanding that, as long as safety criteria are fulfilled, and all of the cage elements are fabricated from similar materials, physically joined together as a single coherent structure, cage manufacturers may do as they wish. This is known as the 'free concept' approach, and it acknowledges the fact that, because they know more about roll cages than anybody, the leading manufacturers should be permitted to experiment, bettering the breed.

Despite that license to experiment, the rulemakers impose limitations on roll cage designers. Under most sets of regulations, cage elements cannot be fitted either forward of the centerline of the front wheels or aft of the centerline of the rear wheels. In their perfect world, cage designers would stiffen the extreme front end of the car by fitting a diagonal brace across the radiator aperture, but this regulation prohibits it.

In addition, roll cage elements must not pass across the windows, where they would limit the driver's visibility, nor must they be in a position where they might interfere with the operation of the footpedals.

As car designers have progressively increased the rake of windshields, there's a tendency for roll cages to become 'flatter', and therefore inherently weaker. The increase in windshield rake has also progressively widened the door apertures, creating a potential Achilles Heel which the cage manufacturers must attempt to protect.

Typically, a set of regulations will state that a cage must be capable of maintaining its structural integrity when a force equivalent to at least seven and a half times the car's weight is applied vertically to the roof: simulating the effect of an unimpeded rollover impact. It would obviously be impractical to subject large numbers of cages to such a comprehensive test, so the rulemakers engage the services of qualified organizations to devise computer programs capable of assessing each design's crashworthiness.

Every time a roll cage manufacturer comes up with a new design, it must submit a schematic drawing of the revised cage for computer analysis. Details of the new angles and/or components are keyed into the computer and the software program is run. Only when the changes are found to meet or exceed the regulations is the new cage granted a certificate of approval.

All of the tubes and braces in a roll cage must be of a minimum specified diameter and wall thickness. Indeed, the regulations sometimes specify that cages must incor porate a small inspection hole in a non-critical area to aid verification of the wall thickness. Minimum sizes are specified for the mounting plates, as plates which were too small would punch through the floor in a rollover impact. The edges of the plates must be bevelled, so they don't present a cutting edge to the floor material: a sharp edge would work its way through the floor in time.

In addition, minimum thicknesses are specified for the mounting plates and backing plates, and for the bolts which pass through them. The fixing method (welding or bolting) is also prescribed, and there are regulations governing the way in which gussets are introduced into joints and lugs are incorporated into multipoint designs.

The materials from which roll cages are built are the subject of innumerable regulations. Most are fabricated from circular-section steel tubing: either CDS (Cold Drawn Seamless), which is drawn from a solid billet, or DOM (Drawn Over Mandrel), which starts out as a tube of smaller diameter and is cold drawn over a mandrel to increase its diameter and reduce its wall thickness, the effect of cold working being a doubling of the tensile strength. Another type of tubing used in roll cage manufacture is ERW (Electro Resistance Welded), which is formed from strips of flat steel rolled and welded down one side. However, ERW is outlawed in some championships, while in others it is only permitted in a heavier wall thickness: for example, in one championship, with cages constructed from 1 3/4in diameter tubing, 0.095in DOM may substitute for 0.120in ERW.

Super rich teams sometimes specify aircraft-grade T45 high tensile steel for their roll cages, particularly if they are of the welded-in variety. T45 is accepted by the rulemakers, because it exceeds their minimum standards. With a breaking strain almost twice as high as that quoted for CDS, T45 permits cage designers to reduce the tube wall thickness, saving weight while achieving the same strength. However, for ductability – the ability to resist damage after the initial impact – many experts argue that there's no substitute for wall thickness to provide resistance after a kink has been sustained. A car can go over five or six times, sustaining multiple impacts on the same points, and the roll cage can disintegrate if the tubing doesn't have adequate ductability.

All of the steel stock supplied to the cage maker is accompanied by a certificate guaranteeing that it has been processed to the regulatory standard. The cage maker then runs a series of tests, in-house, to check the tubing's hardness and graphite content. Welding of all roll cages is to aviation industry standards, and every six months or so the manufacturer sends its welding equipment to be thoroughly tested (the rulemakers also lay down stringent welding standards).

When a cage is structurally complete, some manufacturers put the various elements through a rustproofing cycle. This begins with total immersion in a degreasing tank. When thoroughly clean, the elements are suspended from a gantry and passed at a predetermined speed through a mist cabinet, which crystalizes the surface in a process called phosphating. As well as rustproofing the

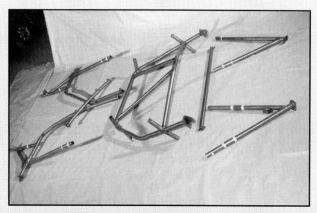

cage elements, phosphating provides an excellent key for the final finish: powder coating with a very hard, polyurethylene-based paint, baked on.

Every certified roll cage has an ID number etched into it. Each cage also bears a material batch number, a safety measure which would enable all cages made from a particular batch of steel to be traced and recalled in the event of quality control problems. Happily, there is no history of recalls in the roll cage business. A top cage manufacturer's reputation is a hard won asset, and great care is taken to preserve it.

This is worth bearing in mind when a refinement is introduced, and you are considering having your car upgraded to the latest specification. That modification will have been thoroughly evaluated by the manufacturer, then tested and certified by the regulatory authority. When a car rolls over, in most cases the damage is limited to a few dented corners. Deformation of the cage structure will absorb energy and save the driver from serious injury. However, on occasion, a car can become airborne. It may be launched off another car, and drop from a considerable height.

When the car is dragged back to the paddock, everyone will gather around to survey the wreckage. The cage manufacturer's logo will probably be in full view, and there will be one of two reactions from the assembled throng: *"Wow! Hasn't it stood up well!"* or, *"I'm not going to buy one of those!"*

At that point, the cage maker's reputation is either enhanced – or dies on the spot.

Bracing the front turret tops

Provided the regulations permit it, you can improve the performance of the chassis still further, and increase safety margins, by fitting front triangulation struts. These extend forward from the front legs, pass through the engine compartment bulkhead, and are attached to the turret tops. To complete the process of triangulating the front of your car, acquire a turret brace. This is a detachable strut which runs transversely across the engine compartment, linking the turret tops (even in a welded-in cage this has to be a bolt-on element, to facilitate engine removal).

Triangulating the front of the car in this way will contribute greatly to its strength and rigidity, reducing the tendency of the forward part of the shell to distort under heavy cornering loads, which adversely effects handling and can be a cause of creeping metal fatigue in the engine compartment bulkhead. Honda broke new ground with the 1992-specification Civic, by introducing a turret brace as original equipment: it is perfectly adequate for competition use.

If you triangulate the front turret tops with the roll cage, the struts must obviously pass through the bulkhead at points where they won't come into contact with the engine block. Physical limitations aside, regulations governing the extent to which components may be relocated to accommodate roll cage elements are usually very liberal, as safety considerations take precedence. It's permissable to make holes in the dashpanel to accommodate the front triangulation struts, provided the holes are no larger than necessary.

With a welded-in cage, the struts are welded directly to the turret tops. Likewise, with a bolt-in cage, it's usually possible to bolt the front triangulation struts directly onto the turret tops. However, on a few models – the Lancia Delta Integrale is one – this isn't possible: a lug has to be welded to each turret top first, then the front triangulation struts are bolted to the lugs. Just cut lugs from a small sheet of steel. If they're to be under 3in (75mm) long, cut them from a sheet 0.1in (2mm) thick. If they have to be slightly longer, it's advisable to cut them from a sheet 0.15in (3mm) thick.

Irrespective of the configuration at the turret tops, the front triangulation struts ideally should lie snugly against the sides of the engine compartment, so that several additional bolts can be passed sideways through them, anchoring them to the sides of the shell to bestow extra rigidity.

Your roll cage supplier will be able to offer advice as to how a turret brace can be fitted to your particular model to best effect. In our opinion, the ideal arrangement is one in which it can be slipped directly onto the bolts which protrude up through the turret tops from the shock absorber mountings, as this imparts maximum rigidity (the Honda Civic is one model which facilitates this arrangement). If that isn't feasible on your particular model, another highly effective fitting method is one in which the turret brace is bolted to the top wishbone mounts, at the points where they poke up through from the wheelwells.

Of course, the suspension units won't be on your car at this stage, so the actual task of bolting the turret brace to them must be undertaken later. On many models, it's simply not possible to bolt the turret brace directly onto the suspension units. If this proves to be the case, it's perfectly acceptable to weld a bracket onto each turret top and bolt the brace to those. Alternatively, there's a turret brace design which features a circular flange at each end: after drilling three holes in each turret top to correspond to holes pre-formed in the circular flanges, you just bolt it on.

In rare cases, the turret tops aren't sufficiently strong to take the additional stresses and strains fed in by the front

Triangulating the front turret tops with the roll cage bestows much greater rigidity, resisting the tendency of the forward part of the shell to distort under heavy cornering loads. It's sometimes necessary to weld a lug to each turret top before bolting the front triangulation struts to them.

triangulation struts and the turret brace. Rare, because modern cars tend to have a high degree of strength built into those regions. In some championships, the rulemakers allow the turret tops to be reinforced by means of additional material welded to the suspension mounting points, provided it conforms to the contours of the standard panel. If your roll cage supplier says your particular model benefits from local strengthening of the turret tops, and the regulations permit this, start by seam welding all the joints around the upper suspension mountings to add rigidity: the required method is detailed overleaf. After that, buy a pair of replacement turret top panels (these are available for most models) and weld them over the existing turret tops to create the necessary reinforcement.

Alternatively, many competitors prefer to seam weld steel plates to the *inside* of the wheelwells, at the points where extra rigidity is required – and this certainly looks tidier. Again, provided the reinforcing material conforms to the shape of the original panel, tech inspectors won't make waves.

It is disadvantageous to have to reinforce the turret tops in this – or any other – manner, so only add the minimum amount of material. If you have to weld extra material to the shell to create the necessary strength, you'll be carrying more weight than those who didn't need to take such drastic measures.

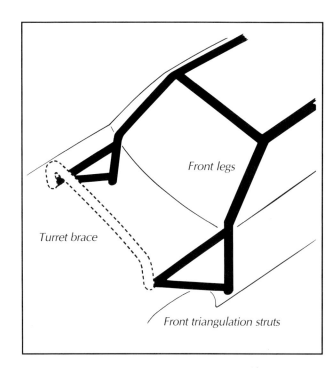

This diagram depicts a typical front triangulation arrangement extending out from the roll cage.

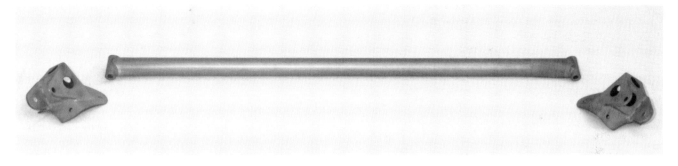

A typical turret brace: a detachable strut which runs transversely across the engine compartment, linking the turret tops (even in a welded-in cage this has to be a bolt-on element, to facilitate engine removal).

Seam welding

As many as 30 percent of the spot welds on bodyshells assembled by robots do not 'take', because the trend towards galvanizing bodypanels and employing zinc paint in the mass production process reduces the effectiveness of spot welding. For road use, a 30 percent failure rate in bodyshell spot welding is considered acceptable, but for competition applications, where the rigidity of the shell is of paramount importance, all of the welds should be made good – assuming the rulemakers permit it.

This latter point is important, as the regulations for some championships specifically prohibit seam welding.

On close inspection, you'll find that there are a multitude of spot welds throughout the shell. By upgrading them, you'll increase its overall rigidity by as much as ten percent, measurably improving your car's performance. If you employ a roll cage manufacturer to weld-in a cage, they're also likely to offer seam welding services for an extra fee. However, the vast majority of privateers do it themselves, which is fine provided one vital point is observed. Do not undertake any seam welding until your roll cage is securely installed, as an unsupported shell is particularly prone to distortion when heat is applied to a

Seam welding is illustrated to good effect here. A series of 'stitches' are being placed in overlap joints on the propeller shaft tunnel. The 'stitches' are approximately 1in long and are being placed at 2-3in intervals.

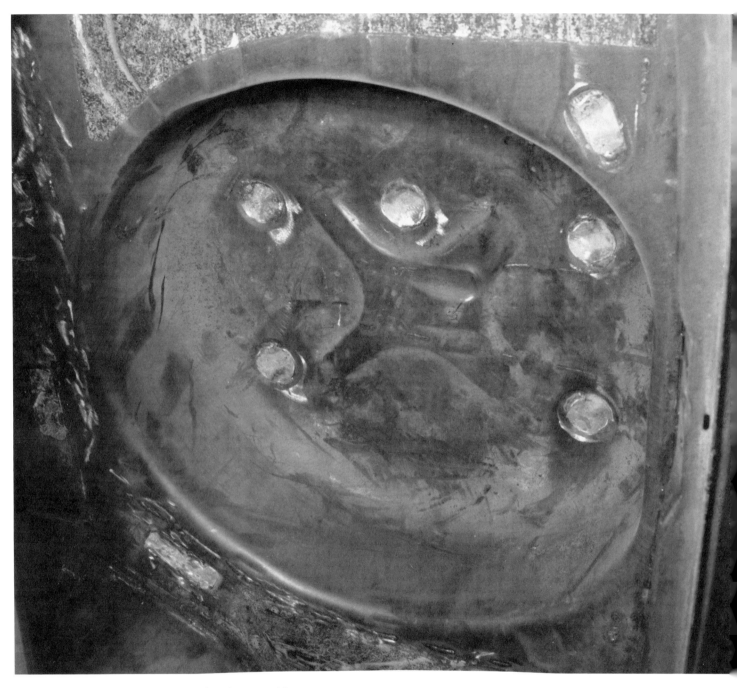

Cover the multitude of little drainage holes found in most bodyshells – these are in the spare wheel recess – by welding circular patches of 0.04in (1mm) thick sheet steel into each of them. This prevents foreign objects from getting in, and can introduce a little extra rigidity to the shell.

localized area. A certain amount of surface wrinkling is almost inevitable – it can be filled before the shell is repainted – but warping of the shell caused by concentrating heat on one area for too long is less easy to remedy.

It's important, when seam welding, to have good access to awkward areas – including the underside, where the shell derives a lot of its strength. Obviously, you can't weld upside-down, so it's necessary to turn the car over to get at the seams underneath. We strongly advise that you go to the trouble, and moderate expense, of fabricating a pair of spit-type body jigs, as described in Chapter 1. This will allow the shell to be rotated by hand through 360 degrees and locked at any angle, providing all-round access.

Locate the seams between panels and deal with them systematically, one by one. Place 'stitches' approximately 1in long, with 2-3in intervals, along the edges of all the joints. Pay particular attention to the flange joints around the door apertures, which are typical bodyshell weak spots. Only weld small lengths at a time, moving from one area of the shell to another to minimize the risk of distortion. If your car has welded-on fenders, reinforce the seams around them. If your car has bolted-on fenders, don't be tempted to weld them on, as the rulemakers usually prohibit this.

A revolutionary method of 'stitching' panels together has been pioneered in the USA, and some companies in Britain and Continental Europe are currently exploring its potential. The new technique is tradenamed Tog-L-Loc. A device not unlike a rivet gun is positioned at each successive joining point. Without adding any additional material, the gun pushes a neat, button-like feature about the size of a pencil tip through the two sheets and dovetails it.

In some models, there are dozens of narrow vertical slots in the driver and passenger footwells. We recommend that you fashion two sheets of 0.04in (1mm) thick aluminium large enough to cover all of them, and fix them into place with 1/8in rivets or self tapping screws.

As well as saving weight by not adding welding material, the Tog-L-Loc technique is good for getting into awkward areas.

Besides seam welding, this is an appropriate time to deal with the multitude of little drainage holes found in most bodyshells by welding circular patches of 0.04in (1mm) thick sheet steel into each of them. This prevents foreign objects from getting in, and can introduce a little extra rigidity to the shell. Some prefer to fashion patches from aluminium and glue them on with high-strength industrial adhesive.

In some models, there are dozens of narrow vertical slots in the driver and passenger footwells. We recommend that you fashion two sheets of 0.04in (1mm) thick aluminium large enough to cover all of them, and fix them into place with 1/8in rivets or self tapping screws. Some prefer the alternative method of placing two sheets of adhesive-backed aluminium film over these slots. This keeps foreign objects out and saves a little weight, but it doesn't contribute any stiffness.

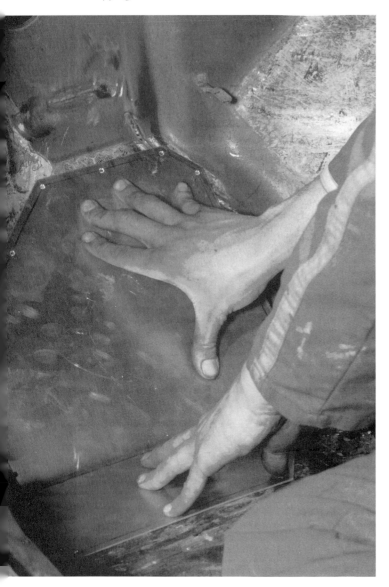

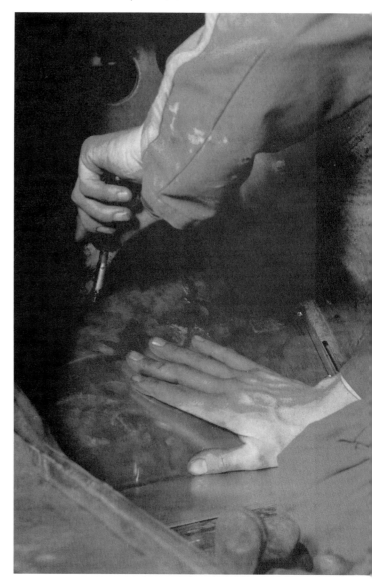

Towing eyes

Universally, the rulemakers demand that cars be equipped with towing eyes, so they can be flat-towed to safety in the event of an off-circuit excursion. A lot of manufacturers duplicate the towing eyes to cater for all circumstances, fitting two at the front and two at the rear. In that case, you may be able to save some weight by removing one from each end, as the regulations usually only specify that there should be one eye at the front and one at the back.

The standard towing eyes are likely to be adequate for competition use, although it's often a good idea to reinforce all the seams in and around them. Even if seam welding of the bodyshell is prohibited in the championship you intend entering, an exception will likely be made in the case of towing eyes. Of course, if seam welding of the shell *is* permitted, reinforce the towing eye seams at the same time.

One other point: the regulations usually specify a minimum internal diameter for the towing eyes, to ensure compatibility with racetrack rescue vehicles. Check now to see if your towing eyes conform. If they don't, remove them and cut a new pair of eyes from a thick plate of steel or aluminium sheet, then weld or bolt them onto the underside of a chassis rail to bring your car up to the regulatory specification. To avoid problems with tech inspectors later, ensure that the eyes will be accessible without removing or manipulating the bodywork, as this is a mandatory requirement.

The standard towing eyes are likely to be adequate for competition use, although it's often a good idea to reinforce all the seams in and around them. Also check that their internal diameters comply with the regulations..

Seat harness anchors

No matter which championship you plan to contest, the regulations stipulate that the standard belts on the driver's seat must be replaced with a race-specification safety harness. Although the harness won't be going in until later, you must decide at this time where the harness anchors will be located. Consult the regulations as to the minimum requirement. A four-point, five-point, or even six-point anchor layout may be specified. The regulations also specify which mounting methods are acceptable, and govern where the anchors are located.

In the case of the lap straps, employ the car's standard seatbelt attachment points as anchors. Usually, these anchors comprize two high tensile steel eyes screwed into captive nuts on a plate welded to the car's underside. The eyes for the lap straps protrude up through the floor at points directly behind the driver's seat: seam weld around the plates to strengthen them, and check that the captive nuts are firmly attached.

It's perfectly acceptable to anchor the shoulder straps to the standard rear seatbelt mounting points. These are identical to the front seatbelt anchors, and are located beneath the rear seats. You can get at them easily with the seats removed. Safety harness shoulder straps are very long, and the further back you can attach them, the better, because the nearer they are to the horizontal, the more effective the restraint they offer the wearer.

Alternatively, if your roll cage is to feature a rear strut brace, the shoulder straps can be attached to that. Consult your roll cage supplier and seat harness supplier first.

Regardless of the minimum regulatory requirements, some competitors want the added reassurance of crotch straps, although the upright seating position drivers adopt in the majority of models means it's unlikely he will 'torpedo' under the lap straps in the event of a heavy frontal impact. If you do wish to fit crotch straps, the best place to anchor them is just behind the driver's seat, between the standard lap strap attachment points. Extra sets of the manufacturer's standard seatbelt anchors can be purchased readily. Attach them to the floor pan in the same manner as the other anchor points.

Extra sets of the manufacturer's standard seatbelt anchors can be purchased if you wish to fit crotch straps. Attach them to the floor pan in the same manner as the other anchor points.

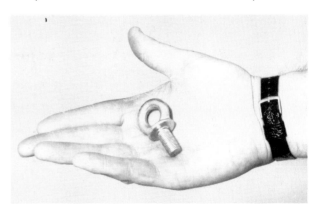

Fitting airjack tubes

In one of the British championships – the BRDC/BRSCC Saloon Car Championship – the rulemakers permit pneumatic jacking systems to be fitted aboard the cars, facilitating rapid tire changes. These are part of the standard procedure during endurance races, so if you plan to contest this championship you should definitely fit them or you won't be competitive. Airjacks can also be useful during conventional sprint races: if you sustain a puncture, you can make a rapid pitstop to replace the tire and might still be classified as a finisher.

In fact, airjacks can do more than just facilitate rapid wheel changes. In competition specification, the cars tend to have very limited ground clearance, so it can be awkward getting a standard floor jack under them. Airjacks simplify the whole operation by creating more clearance. If you fit them, you'll find you use them all the time, not just when you're in a hurry. They ease the workload during qualifying and test sessions.

You won't be fitting the airjacks until much later (Chapter 4), but you must make provision for them now.

When the rulemakers permit pneumatic jacking systems to be installed aboard cars, they modify their quoted minimum weight limit for each model to take into account the additional weight of the system: a typical maximum weight allowance is 6kg. The rulemakers also permit four holes to be cut in the underside of the shell, from which the jacks will protrude, and allow four short lengths of steel tube to be welded inside the shell to accommodate the jacks themselves. Bear in mind that these must not protrude beyond the rocker panel, as the regulations

Closeup view of a front airjack tube, showing how part of the fender has been cut away to accommodate it.

specifically prohibit anything from doing so.

When you cut holes to accommodate the four airjacks, there are three major points to bear in mind. The first is to ensure that the two rear jacks won't get in the way of the roll cage back stays. The second is to locate the jacks as close to the sides of the car as possible, to ensure that it can't topple over. The third is to ensure that there's sufficient vertical leeway to recess them thoroughly. The rulemakers permit the ends of the jacks to protrude from the underside of the car, but they shouldn't protrude more than absolutely necessary, as they will be susceptible to damage from kerbs and sand/gravel traps. Furthermore, the protruding ends may cause the car to infringe the minimum ground clearance regulations.

In our view, the best place to install the rear airjacks is just forward of the contoured feature in the floor of the shell to which the rear seat squab is mounted. Cut four lengths of steel tubing – of 0.15in (3mm) wall thickness – to accommodate the jacks, as propriety airjack tubes are not available. Then cut circular holes in the floor, with a diameter which matches the bore of the tubes. Weld the tubes into position directly above the four holes, using a bubble level to ensure that they're absolutely vertical.

Finally, cut two short 'straps' from 0.1in (2mm) thick sheet steel and weld one to the side of each tube, bracing them to the contoured feature where the rear seat squab goes, or to an adjacent area of the shell.

The best place for the front airjacks is under the fend-

The same airjack tube seen from a slightly different angle. Note how the tube has been welded to a bracket, which is in turn welded to the side of the bodyshell, tight against the engine compartment bulkhead.

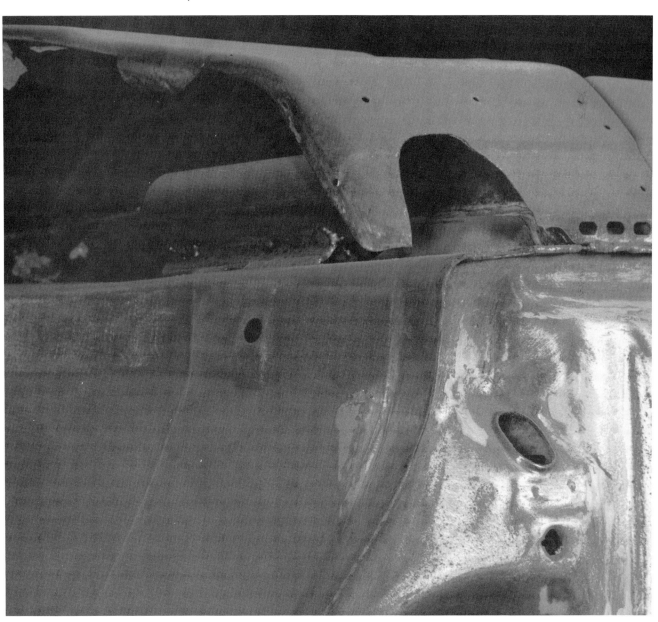

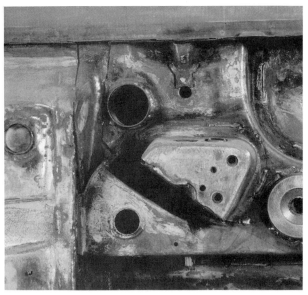

ers, just behind the wheels. Again, each airjack tube should be welded in vertically, to a bracket which is in turn welded to the side of the shell, tight against the engine compartment bulkhead. If your car has welded-on fenders, the best way to gain access to these areas is to remove the spot welds from the lower halves of the fenders and prise them aside. Once the tubes have been welded-in, renew the seam welding on the fenders.

That's all you need to do at this stage. The airjacks themselves shouldn't be installed until after the shell has been repainted, as you don't want to get paint on their very fine adjustment threads.

Closeup view of a rear airjack tube, showing how it is set into the underside of the car.

To reinforce the rear airjack tubes, cut two short 'straps' from 0.1in (2mm) thick sheet steel and weld one to the side of each tube, bracing them to the contoured feature where the rear seat squab goes, or to an adjacent area of the shell.

Making provision for a fuel cell

This is the time to consider your fuel system requirements. In many cases, the regulations state that competitors can either retain the car's standard tank, or fit a race- specification fuel cell. In cases where the rulemakers offer no choice in the matter, they will either have deemed fuel cells mandatory on safety grounds, or outlawed them on account of their high cost. Fuel cells are flexible bladders which deform in the event of an accident, rather than rupturing with potentially disastrous consequences. Besides their inherent safety, they offer a rapid fill/rapid vent capability – essential for endurance races.

Should you decide to retain your car's standard tank, there's nothing more you need do at this stage. If, on the other hand, you intend to fit a fuel cell – as the Dane Motorsport team did with our 'guinea pig' Ford Sierra Sapphire Cosworth – you must make some degree of provision for it now, even though the tank itself won't be going in until much later (the fuel system is dealt with in detail in Chapter 4). The first decisions you must take are: what type of fuel cell to fit, and where to locate it. The regulations sometimes stipulate that it must be positioned as close as possible to the site of the original fuel tank.

In our opinion, the best place to locate a fuel cell is inside the car, in the vacant spare wheel recess. As well as simplifying the task of installation, this helps to lower the car's center of gravity. A few competitors prefer to fit the cell *underneath* the car, just ahead of the rear axle, to keep as much weight as possible within the wheelbase. It's certainly true that if there's too much weight behind the rear axle, the car's handling qualities will be adversely effected. On the other hand, most competitors feel that it's best to have the weight of the fuel cell well behind the rear axle to help counterbalance the weight of the

If your car has a trunk, cut a sheet of aluminium which fits snugly against the bulkhead behind the rear seats. Consult the regulations as to the mandatory firewall thickness for the championship you're planning to contest: typically, it's in the 0.04-0.06in (1-1.5mm) range.

Before attaching the firewall, apply a propriety household silicon sealant along the edges to assure airtightness.

Self tapping screws (as shown here) are an ideal fitting method, or 1/8in pop rivets. With the shell mounted on axle stands, you can clamber around inside it in perfect safety.

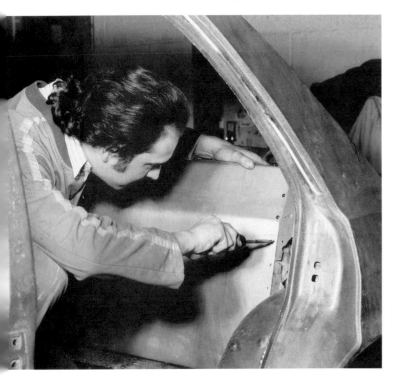

engine, most of which is concentrated ahead of the front axle.

Experienced campaigners explore the complexities of weight distribution, attempting to achieve the optimum balance, front to rear. They do so by making a succession of detailed weight calculations and locating items of equipment accordingly – within the limited scope allowed by the regulations: they verify their calculations with cornerweight scales (more details in Chapter 4). This is perfectly acceptable, provided the regulations aren't infringed, but it's advisable for newcomers to install a form-fitting, circular cell which conforms to the shape of the spare wheel recess, as this is by far the simplest solution.

A circular cell located in the spare wheel recess will not require any structural supports. It will simply be bolted in and covered with a steel or aluminium plate. If, on the other hand, you opt for a rectangular cell – which will be less expensive than a circular one – it's likely to require some type of structural support: either a length of angle steel (welded in), or angle aluminium (bolted or riveted in). The cell will then be affixed to the support by means of built-in fittings.

Discuss the matter with your fuel cell supplier first. If you opt for a design which requires some type of structural support, you may have to acquire the cell now and position it in the spare wheel recess to ensure that the supporting members won't get in the way of other items of hardware, such as elements of the roll cage. If the supports require welding in, this should be done now. If the supports are to be bolted or rivetted in, this should be undertaken after the shell has been repainted.

To ensure that there's adequate protection for the driver in the event of a fire in the vicinity of the fuel cell, the regulations stipulate that a firewall must be installed. The precise form it takes depends on whether your car is a hatchback, or has a trunk. If your car has a trunk, cut a sheet of aluminium which fits snugly against the bulkhead behind the rear seats. Consult the regulations as to the mandatory firewall thickness for the championship you're planning to contest: typically, it's in the 0.04-0.06in (1- 1.5mm) range. Self tapping screws are an ideal fitting method, or 1/8in pop rivets.

Mount the shell on axle stands before fitting this type of firewall, then you can clamber around inside it in perfect safety. Before attaching the firewall, apply a propriety household silicon sealant along the edges to assure airtightness.

Depending on the model you're working on, there may be several small apertures on either side of the rear seat bulkhead. The trunk will not be fully isolated unless these are covered, so cut little aluminium plates to fill the gaps. Use an angle grinder to help fashion the correct shape, incorporating cutouts if necessary to accommodate the roll cage back stays. These little plates must be of the same thickness as the primary firewall, and should be fitted in the same manner, then surrounded by silicon sealant.

If you have a hatchback, the only practical way to isolate the fuel cell from the cockpit is by fitting a propriety, form-fitting firewall directly over the cell and boxing the associated pipework in with 'tunnels' fabricated from aluminium sheet. Although these tasks won't be undertaken until much later, hatchback owners do have one job to undertake at this time: installing liquid-tight bulkheads in the rear fender flare cavities. The shell should be mounted on the 'spits' for this, to provide adequate access.

As stated earlier, a fuel cell must have a rapid fill capability for speedy pitstops. However, it must be able to vent as rapidly as it is filled, or an airlock will build up in the tank. In Chapter 4, we suggest that you specify combined fill/vent pipes and fit one on each side, as this will allow you to fill from either side, as variations in pitlane configurations dictate. Hatchbacks must have liquid- tight bulkheads installed in the cavities between the inner and outer fender flare walls, immediately above the wheel-wells, through which these combined fill/vent pipes will pass. This is to prevent leaking fuel or fuel vapor from making its way through openings in the inner wall and entering the cockpit, where it could accumulate and pose a fire hazard.

Due to the restricted access to the fender flare cavities, you cannot expect to make perfectly form-fitting bulkheads: they will, of necessity, be rather crude. However, you can create an effective seal by fitting two parallel

Depending on the model you're working on, there may be several small apertures on either side of the rear seat bulkhead. The trunk will not be fully isolated unless these are covered, so cut little aluminium plates to fill the gaps. Use an angle grinder to help fashion the correct shape, incorporating cutouts if necessary to accommodate the roll cage back stays (as seen here).

bulkheads in each fender flare and filling the gap between them with polystyrene foam. You can use the same type of foam which builders use to insulate cavity-wall dwellings!

Start by cutting two card templates roughly shaped to fit within one fender flare cavity, about 6in (15mm) apart. By using both sides of the templates, trace the shapes of the four bulkheads on a sheet of 0.04in (1mm) thick aluminium with a pencil. When you cut the bulkheads out, incorporate several small lugs on their inner edges, then put the bulkheads in a vice and push the lugs over until they lie perpendicular to the outer faces. These lugs will provide points at which the bulkheads can be pop rivetted into the fender flares. There's no need to spoil the car's external appearance by pop riveting the bulkheads to the outer fender flare walls, as attaching them to the inner walls will suffice.

Once the bulkheads have been rivetted in, seal any gaps around the edges with household silicon sealant. This will dry hard in about three hours. To insert the foam, drill a small hole through one inner wheelwell wall, push a plastic tube through to the cavity between the fore and aft bulkheads and simply squirt the foam in. The foam will expand to fill the cavity, plugging any gaps: it will soon harden. Repeat this process on the opposite side.

If you plan to fit a fuel cell into a hatchback, you must install liquid-tight bulkheads in the rear fender flare cavities, immediately above the wheelwells, through which the combined fill/vent pipes will pass. This is to prevent leaking fuel or fuel vapor from making its way through openings in the inner wall and entering the cockpit, where it could accumulate and pose a fire hazard. Due to the restricted access to the fender flare cavities, you cannot expect to make perfectly form-fitting bulkheads: they will, of necessity, be rather crude. However, you can create an effective seal by rivetting two parallel bulkheads into each fender flare and filling the gap between them with polystyrene foam.

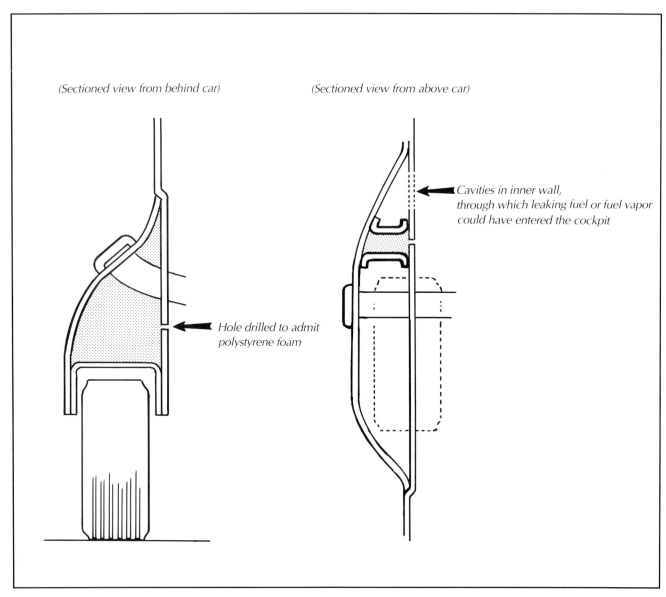

Flattening the wheelwell flanges

Another modification which should be undertaken at this time, if it appears necessary, is the flattening of any flanges on the outer edges of the front wheelwells. This will prevent them fouling a tire during heavy braking and cornering (the rear wheelwell flanges don't usually pose a problem, but it's worth checking). Usually, the regulations state that the production contour of the wheelwells must not be altered, and that any flanges within them must not be removed. However, provided you don't actually file the flanges off, safety considerations render it perfectly acceptable for you to flatten them back on themselves so they won't pose a threat to the tires.

Using a flat-faced hammer, gently tap each flange back. If your car had plastic dirt shields set into each wheelwell, you must leave the sections of the flanges which served as attachment points for them protruding down, otherwise there'll be no way of reattaching them after the shell's been repainted. There are usually between three and five attachment points on each flange, and they can be flattened back once the dirt shields have been reinstalled (see Chapter 4).

This is also the time to check that the bodyshell of your particular car conforms to the mandatory width regulations, which usually are based on the manufacturer's production specification. Carefully measure the distance across the shell between the outer edges of the front wheelwells (fender flares), then do the same at the rear wheelwells. You may find that your particular shell is fractionally under the permissable width, in which case you can gain a slight advantage by tapping the shell out to the maximum permissable measurement with a soft-faced hammer.

Such a small increase in the width of the bodyshell may seem insignificant, but for some drivers this has proved to be the difference between sustaining a puncture and winning a race!

To prevent the small flanges on the outer edges of the wheelwells causing punctures, use a flat-faced hammer to gently tap each flange back on itself.

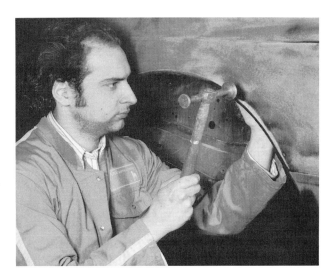

Other bodyshell modifications

Double check that there are no more structural modifications to make before the bodyshell is repainted. Carefully examine the regulations as they apply to your model to ensure conformance, as it will be awkward to make structural alterations afterwards.

Generally speaking, the regulations demand that the bodyshell's original, production-standard constitution and appearance must be maintained. It is sometimes permissable to add bolt-on reinforcement bars (Chapter 4), but the welding of additional gussets or crossbraces to the shell is universally prohibited. In very rare circumstances, the rulemakers permit the standard body panels to be replaced with lightweight versions, in which case the unwanted panels should be removed now (the lightweight panels won't be fitted until much later).

In the American championships, airjacks are prohibited, but the regulations for SCCA Pro Racing's World Challenge state that competitors may *"attach a plate or pad under the car to provide for jacking"*. Imaginative interpretation of this concession has resulted in cars being fitted with two 'plates', each so positioned as to lift three wheels off the ground simultaneously when a floor jack is raised under them!

For the benefit of readers interested in that particular championship, a brief explanation is in order.

One plate is welded onto each side of the car. Raising a jack under the plate on the left side lifts all but the right rear tire off the ground, while raising a jack under the plate on the right side lifts all but the left rear tire off the ground. In each case, the tire which the crew leaves on the car is the tire which receives the least wear: the right rear tire tends to get the least wear on racetracks with a predominance of right hand corners, while the left rear tire tends to receive the least wear on racetracks with a predominance of left hand corners.

If you're planning to contest the World Challenge series, try to watch this ingenious method at work from close quarters (the pit crew members use a rapid lift floor jack to save time). Closer inspection reveals that the 'plates' are actually steel tubes recessed into the underside of the car. They are fixed at an angle which ensures that they're perpendicular to the top of the jack when the car is in the fully raised position, causing the jack to hook into place. This is a precaution against the car slipping off the jack, as it's rather precariously balanced when three wheels are off the ground. The tech inspectors have been persuaded that 'tubes are plates' because tubes clearly present less opportunity for a car to slip than flat steel plates would.

The method for fitting such tubes to a car is virtually identical to that described earlier for fitting airjacks. The correct locations can only be found by trial and error, as they vary considerably from car to car, depending on the precise weight distribution front to back and left to right. Most teams use 1.5in (4cm) steel tubes of 3mm (0.15in) wall thickness, and cut the bottom of the tubes at an angle so that they lie flush with the underside of the car.

Repainting the car

At this point, the bodyshell is essentially race-prepared. However, it must be repainted to protect it from corrosion and make it look good (the latter is a mandatory requirement). Depending on your level of funding, you can either take the shell to a local paintshop to have it repainted professionally, or you can repaint it in your own workshop with hired equipment. The Dane Motorsport team took advantage of its parent company's comprehensive paintshop facilities to make a first class job of its Ford Sierra Sapphire Cosworth. However, for the purpose of outlining the required tasks, we'll assume that you're going to repaint your shell with only limited facilities at hand.

While standards of presentation vary from one competitor to another, the general rule is to make the car as attractive as possible. Not only will this make a good impression on casual onlookers (and that may include potential sponsors), but it will also promote a positive attitude within the team. Applying paint with a brush ruins the look of a car. A spray gun is essential, and doesn't cost much to hire.

The color, or colors, applied to your car will reflect your own particular circumstances: whether you have to cater for a sponsor, for example. If you have a free choice, we strongly advise that you opt for an overall white color scheme initially, then add other colors as necessary when the car has been fully race-prepared. You can't predict now when you'll want to sell the car, but that day will

After going over all the welds with an angle grinder to remove any sharp edges and high spots, apply a wire brush to the entire shell, from top to bottom, to dislodge any burrs and swarf left over from your cutting and grinding activities.

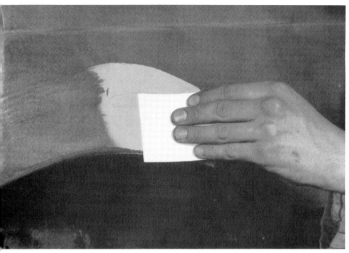

almost certainly come, and – human nature being what it is – cars painted a 'neutral' color, particularly white, tend to sell more readily than those bearing highly individualistic color schemes. If a sponsor enters the picture, the exterior surfaces can be colored accordingly, leaving the cockpit, roll cage, engine compartment, trunk and undersides plain white. Most sponsorship deals are for one season only, so this approach – 'white is right' – offers maximum flexibility.

There's the added benefit that white cars stay cooler

This is the time to effect repairs to any minor dents which may have been inflicted on the shell, and any minor surface wrinkling caused during seam welding. Apply automotive isoponic filler with a spreader, then allow it to harden thoroughly before reshaping the area with 40/80-grit production paper and giving it a finishing rub with 240-grit wet-or-dry paper.

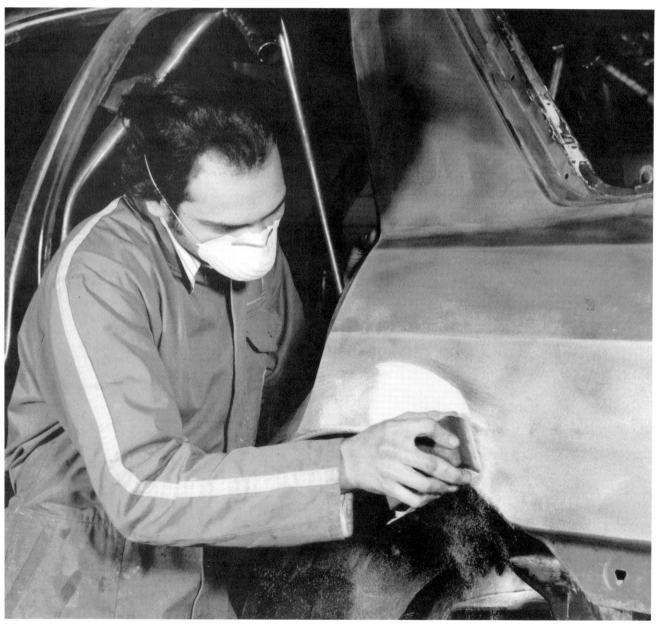

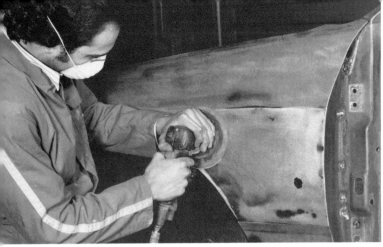

Once the dents are repaired, rub the rest of the shell down with an electric- or air-powered orbital sander. Use an 80- grit disc first, then go over everything again with a 240- grit disc. This will make the surface nice and smooth, but will leave a sufficient key for the first primer coat.

Throughout most – if not all – phases of the repainting process, it's best to have the shell mounted on spits. When applying successive coats, position the shell on one side, so the undersurfaces and the inside of the roof can be painted first. Apply the paint from one side, then rotate the shell through 180 degrees and apply the paint from the other side, to ensure that you cover any obscure areas you might otherwise miss.

on hot days.

For the preparations for repainting, the shell should be mounted on spits for easy access to awkward areas. Start by going over all the welds with an angle grinder to remove any sharp edges and high spots. Next, apply a wire brush to the entire shell, from top to bottom, to dislodge any burrs and swarf left over from your cutting and grinding activities.

This is the time to effect repairs to any minor dents which may have been inflicted on the shell, and any minor surface wrinkling caused during seam welding. Apply automotive isoponic filler with a spreader, then allow it to harden thoroughly before reshaping the area with 40/80-grit production paper and giving it a finishing rub with 240-grit wet-or-dry paper. Once the dents are repaired, rub the rest of the shell down with an electric- or air-powered orbital sander. Use an 80-grit disc first, then go over everything again with a 240-grit disc. This will make the surface nice and smooth, but will leave a sufficient key for the first primer coat.

Finally, seek out any gaps in seams (particularly in the floor pan) and fill them with silicon sealant to prevent water, grit and dust from entering the shell.

Before applying any paint, ensure that the workshop is

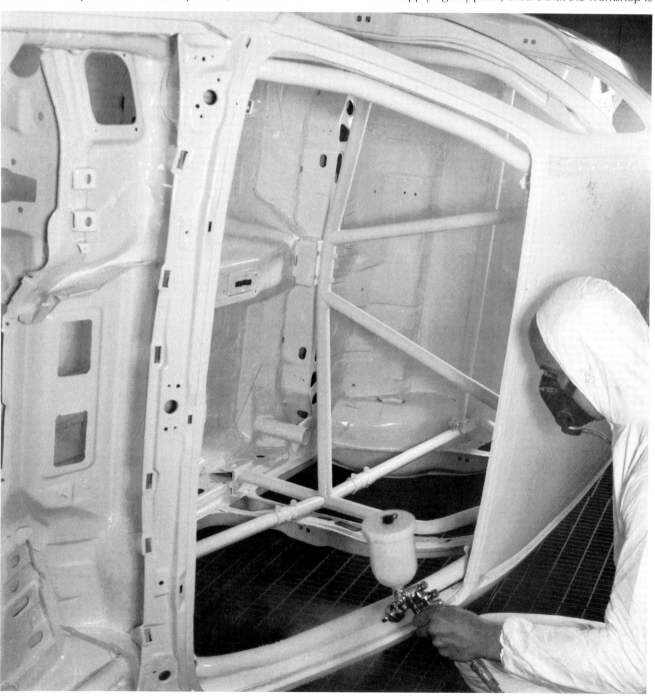

amply ventilated and as free of dust as possible. Dampen the floor with water, if necessary, to keep dust particles down. Throughout most – if not all – phases of the repainting process, it's best to have the shell mounted on the spits. When applying successive coats, position the shell on one side, so the undersurfaces and the inside of the roof can be painted first. Apply the paint from one side, then rotate the shell through 180 degrees and apply the paint from the other side, to ensure that you cover any obscure areas you might otherwise miss. After that, 'right' the shell and paint the rest of the exterior, the engine compartment, the trunk, the remaining interior surfaces, and the wheelwells.

Paint everything! No masking is required, unless of course you wish to apply more than one color. It doesn't matter if you overlap an area slightly, but don't smother the car. You may find it difficult to spray behind parts of the roll cage which lie snugly against the shell, so be doubly careful not to leave any bare patches.

It's not advisable to use ordinary primer on bare metal.

When the shell has been 'righted', paint the rest of the exterior, the engine compartment, the trunk, the remaining interior surfaces, and the wheelwells.

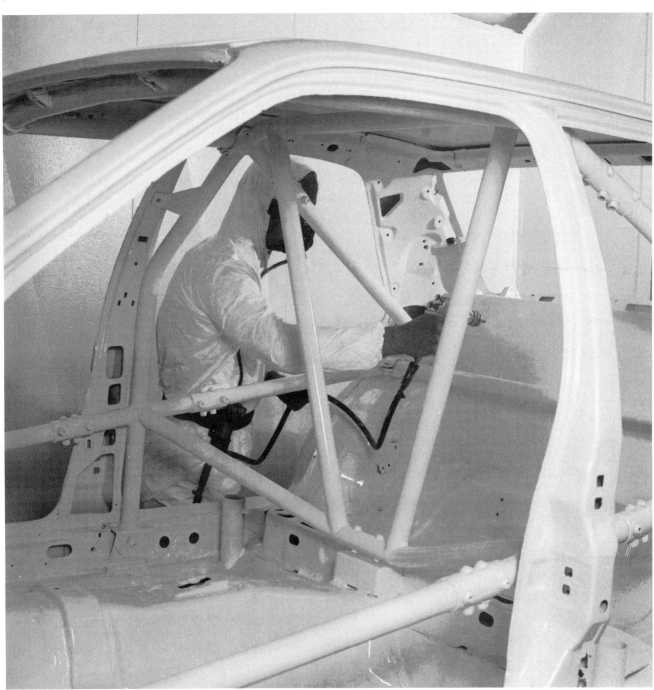

Etch-prime it first, if you can, using an epoxy primer. When that has dried, go over everything with another coat, then apply a coat of ordinary primer. Go over the entire shell with an orbital sander after each coat has been applied, to create a good key for the next coat. For awkward areas, where the orbital sander won't go, use a scurfing pad (such as Scotchbrite). A professional bodyshop would oven-bake the shell between coats, but if you're painting it in your own workshop you'll just have to leave it to dry naturally.

If you're a stickler for detail, hand-flat the shell inside and out with 600-grit wet-or-dry paper as a prelude to applying the finishing coats. Then use an air line to blow off any little pieces of dirt, and simultaneously rub solvent (RM Panel Clean) on to remove any greasy hand prints.

Use a reputable high-gloss paint for the final coats. Cellulose, which was applied to race cars for many years, is giving way to versatile two-pack paints which harden as a result of chemical action, rather than exposure to air. It is imperative that the manufacturer's recommended safety precautions are observed when using two-pack paints, as incorrect use can be fatal. If you can't get the proper breathing equipment, don't use two-pack.

Go over the entire shell with an orbital sander (above) after each coat has been applied, to create a good key for the next coat. For awkward areas, where the orbital sander won't go, use a scurfing pad – such as Scotchbrite, as seen here (below).

The professionals mix a flexing agent into the paint, to make it more durable. That's particularly good for the undersides of race cars, which get peppered with flying debris. Applying finishing coats to the underside of the car may seem overly fastidious, but it has several very practical advantages. A smooth, all-over finish (particularly if it's white) makes it easier to spot small leaks – oil from a differential, for example – and even tiny cracks which might develop during the lifetime of the car. It also makes it easier to wash the car down after races.

Apply two coats of gloss to the entire shell, inside and out. After the first coat has dried thoroughly, give the surface a rub with a soft, solvent-soaked cloth held in one hand, and wipe it off immediately with a lint free cloth in the other hand. Again, a professional paintshop would oven-bake the shell at this stage. When the final coat has dried thoroughly, perfectionists 'de-nib' the exterior with very fine grain wet- or-dry paper (1200-grit), just to remove any little surface blemishes, then apply some polishing compound and machine polish the whole shell with a buffer. Finally, wax the car.

Other components should be repainted separately, using the same techniques applied to the shell. These include bolted-on fenders, any lightweight replacement body panels if these are permitted, mirror covers, the hood, the trunk lid, the doors, and any spoilers or air dams. All of the fittings should be removed from these components and carefully put to one side before any paint is applied. Suspending larger components from the ceiling on lengths of chain or wire often makes repainting them easier. Smaller components, such as the mirror covers, can be suspended on lengths of string.

Some people prefer to deal with the roll cage in the

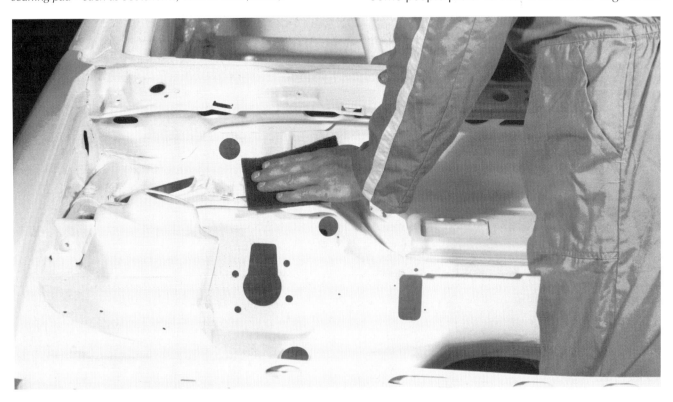

Before applying the first gloss coat, use an air line to blow off any little pieces of dirt, and simultaneously rub solvent (RM Panel Clean) on to remove any greasy hand prints.

Apply two coats of gloss to the entire shell, inside and out. After the first coat has dried thoroughly, give the surface a rub with a solvent-soaked soft cloth held in one hand, and wipe it off immediately with a lint free cloth in the other hand.

same manner – unless it's a welded-in cage, of course – removing it before the shell is repainted and stringing the individual lengths of tubing from the ceiling to be painted separately. However, it's difficult to reassemble a cage in a repainted shell without scratching the paintwork. Furthermore, if your car has a trunk, there'll be complications where the roll cage back stays pass through the airtight firewall – unless you remove the firewall, too, prior to repainting the shell.

On balance, therefore, it's easier just to paint the roll cage *in situ*. Of course, this only applies to a bolt-in cage with a bare metal finish. If the cage already has a powder coated finish, applied by the manufacturer, it's better just to leave it as it is.

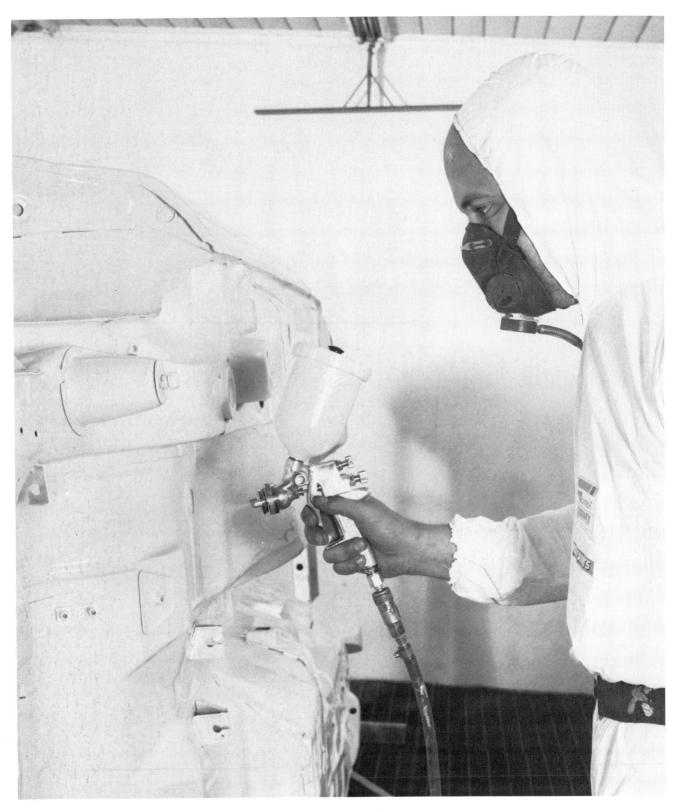

Applying finishing coats to the underside of the car may seem overly fastidious, but it makes it easier to spot small leaks – oil from a differential, for example – and even tiny cracks which might develop during the lifetime of the car. It also makes it easier to wash the car down after races.

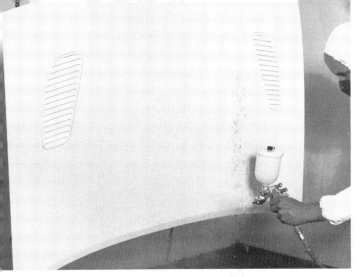

Other components should be repainted separately, using the same techniques applied to the bodyshell. These include bolted-on fenders, any lightweight replacement body panels if these are permitted, mirror covers, the hood, the trunk lid, the doors, and any spoilers or air dams. Suspending larger components from the ceiling on lengths of chain or wire often makes repainting them easier. Smaller components, such as the mirror covers, can be suspended on lengths of string.

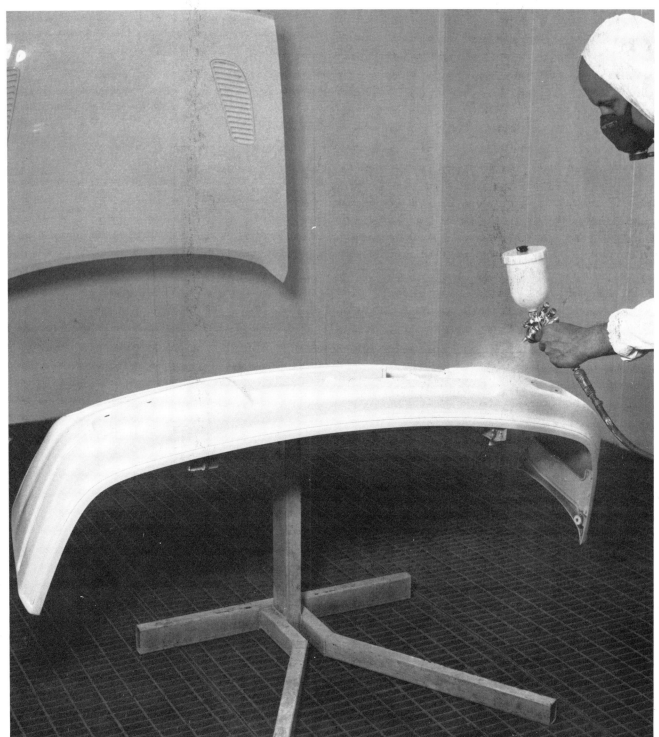

Apply some polishing compound, then machine polish the whole shell with a buffer. Finally, wax the car.

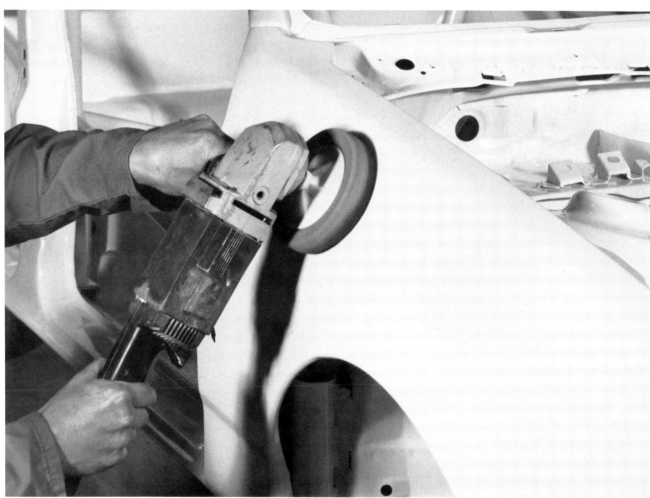

3
Engine preparation

Once the bodyshell is race-prepared, you can focus your attention on the rest of the car, starting with the engine. This chapter differs from the others. It explains what *someone else* will do – rather than what you should do for yourself – because race engine preparation should definitely be entrusted to a specialist. The information contained in this chapter should prove useful when dealing with an engine-tuner, as it provides an insight into what happens when an engine goes behind closed doors!

If you've worked on engines in the past, you'll certainly be capable of taking one to pieces and putting it back together, weighing various components and checking clearances as you go. But that's not enough. Many specialist engine-tuners have between ten and twenty years of continuous development work behind them, accumulating experience at every stage.

The difference between a specialist race engine-tuner preparing a standard engine, and a highly-competent individual undertaking the task himself, might be as little as 5hp – but that makes a world of difference in this category of motorsport.

When it comes to selecting an engine-tuner, there are several factors to consider. Tuners tend to specialize in certain types of engine, or even particular makes or models. Cost is another important factor, of course – as is the logistical element. If you need to pick up a rebuilt engine at short notice, it's better if the journey's short, too. Furthermore, it's worthwhile maintaining personal links with the engine shop, and that's easier if geographical factors are conducive.

Consult the list of engine-tuners in the Directory at the back of this book. This is a starting point, although the list is by no means exhaustive. While the engine is away, turn your attention to the tasks outlined in Chapter 4.

Due to its complexity, more regulations apply to the engine than any other element of the car. For the same reason, more work goes into preparing an engine for competition than any of the other elements. The regulations in this category of motorsport are intended to preserve a close relationship between race cars and their roadgoing counterparts. For this reason, lightweight blocks, special pistons and so on are universally prohibited. Nevertheless, there's still scope for increasing the power output.

Comprehensive technical details of the eligible models are contained in documents specified by the relevant sanctioning body, and they're closely allied to the original roadgoing specification. When your engine passes into the hands of a specialist tuner, he'll completely disassemble it, then painstakingly rebuild it to extremely fine tolerances to ensure that the weights and dimensions of all the key components, and the clearances between them, reflect the most favorable interpretation of the published specifications.

This process is known as 'blueprinting', because the tolerances in question are detailed in the manufacturers' 'blueprints'.

The host of minute alterations the engine-tuner makes to your engine as he skillfully interprets the acceptable tolerances, will result in smoother running and extra horsepower.

If experience is one key to a race engine specialist's superior capabilities, another is undoubtedly the tools he has at his disposal. The top tuners have sophisticated equipment for balancing and grinding, and computer-controlled honing equipment. They run the engine on a dynamometer to assess its performance – quantifying its power output and obtaining feedback from equipment clustered around the dyno. This enables the specialist to study the behavior of gases flowing within the engine: through an inlet manifold, for example.

By analyzing the results, he can make subtle changes here and there, introducing improvements and constantly refining his engines. Parameters such as torque levels at different areas of the rev range are measured as a matter of course, as is the amount of fuel given to the engine in return for its power output. The specialists also measure the engine's emissions, manifold pressures, blow-by on the piston rings, exhaust temperatures: the list goes on and on.

Turbocharged engines have their own list of requirements: engine-tuners are particularly interested in monitoring the charge temperature (the temperature of the air entering the engine), because if this is excessive, cavitation occurs and the engine performs less efficiently.

It will be clear why a privateer can't hope to better the efforts of a specialist race engine-tuner. It's not too expensive to get an extra twenty horsepower out of a standard engine, but wringing the last three or four horsepower out can cost a small fortune if you don't know where to find it. Therefore, cash-in on the hard won experience of a reputable specialist.

The tasks undertaken to race-prepare an engine vary considerably from one make to another. The engine-tuner's two most important objectives are to bring tolerances as close as possible to the optimum, and to make up for some of the standard engine's deficiencies. There are a

If experience is one key to a race engine specialist's superior capabilities, another is undoubtedly the tools he has at his disposal. The top tuners have sophisticated equipment for balancing and grinding, and computer-controlled honing equipment. This is a computerized valve seat cutter.

lot of gray areas when it comes to defining what is legal and what is illegal. The good engine-tuner will almost always be in the gray, but never in the 'black' territory of outright cheating.

Some engines require less attention than others, because they've been built to such exacting tolerances to start with. This is particularly true of the latest, higher-performance engines, which benefit from the enormous advances in metallurgy and engine management system technology over recent years. The engines in Honda's Civic VTEC and General Motors' Nova GSi, for example, are truly outstanding. The Honda Civic VTEC engine develops a lot of power for a small (1.6-liter) capacity: 140hp in standard form. This compares extremely favorably to the 2.8-liter Ford V6 engine, which develops 145hp in its standard form.

Once the specialist tuners get to work on an engine that's excellent to start with, the figures become *very* impressive. Some 1.6-liter Honda Civic VTEC engines prepared for Britain's BRDC/BRSCC Saloon Car Championship develop over 180hp.

In the following (alphabetical) listing of engine preparation tasks, note the different approach taken when optimizing an engine for the racetrack, as opposed to the road. It's very much a case of 'Same meat, different gravy!'

Balancing: One of the most important aspects of blueprinting an engine is bringing all the reciprocating components into balance, whilst at the same time reducing their weights to the lowest permissable values, thereby alleviating the losses attributable to inertia. All engines are balanced by the original manufacturer, but they're seldom balanced to the degree that they need to be for competition use.

All of the reciprocating components are balanced indi-

The engine is run on a dynamometer to assess its performance – quantifying its power output and obtaining feedback from equipment clustered around the dyno. This enables the specialist to study the behavior of gases flowing within the engine: through an inlet manifold, for example.

vidually, so that the whole assembly will be in balance when everything is put back together.

Engine-tuners employ two methods to achieve balance: 'batch- loading' and machining. When machining, engine-tuners must employ the same methods as the original manufacturer, or they will infringe the regulations. 'Batch-loading' entails searching through a large stock of standard components – conrods, pistons, crankshafts, and so on – selecting components which will complement each other.

Some shops specialise in balancing, and do nothing else. It's a relatively inexpensive service. In-line engines are generally the easiest to balance, because a greater number of weight-distribution calculations are necessary with a V- configuration unit – due to the fact that the relative motions of the reciprocating components are more complex.

Bearings: Replacing the standard bearings with more capable ones is contrary to the regulations in this category of motorsport, but as part of the blueprinting process, engine-tuners try to match the largest shell bearing diameters with the smallest crank pin diameters, in an effort to reduce frictional losses.

Cooling system: See Chapter 4.

Cams: One of the engine-tuner's aims is to achieve the optimum cam timing. He is severely limited in many respects. The rulemakers prohibit engine-tuners from altering the standard cam profile: the blueprints specify the dimensions of the cams and their parameters of movement. Tech inspectors have been known to remove a cam from a race car, and compare it to a cam taken from the same model in a showroom!

In other categories of motorsport, engine-tuners change the lift and/or duration of the camshaft, dramatically alter-

One of the most important aspects of blueprinting an engine is bringing all the reciprocating components into balance. When machining, engine-tuners must employ the same methods as the original manufacturer, or they will infringe the regulations. Here, a conrod is receiving attention.

ing the performance characteristics of the engine by influencing the point in the rev range where the power comes in.

Automobile manufacturers design their engines to perform within a wide speed envelope, and to ensure long life and good serviceability. The criteria when preparing an engine for competition are entirely different. A good production cam will be designed for a wide speed range, minimum emissions, and low-speed torque, so that the car can be driven effectively in heavy traffic. These parameters are less important in competition.

Interestingly, the Honda Civic VTEC has a variable-cam system, so that, above 5,000rpm, another lobe comes into effect. This gives the driver the best of both worlds: bottom-end torque and top-end torque.

Combustion: Bore clearance represents another point of departure from standard practice. The original manufacturer may well have specified a bore which will perform effectively for 100,000 miles. The race engine-tuner has an altogether different outlook. Where the original manufacturer will have specified a very tight bore clearance, the engine-tuner will opt for a wider clearance. He doesn't

Another of the race engine-tuner's aims is to ensure that the combustion chamber volumes are equalized. Otherwise, one cylinder will perform more efficiently than the others, creating a mechanical imbalance. Here, the volume of a combustion chamber is being measured with a burette: a graduated glass tube with a stopcock at one end for dispensing and transferring known volumes of liquids.

mind if, when the engine is started from cold, you can hear the pistons rattling. He's only interested in optimizing its running performance under racing conditions.

Another of the race engine-tuner's aims is to ensure that the combustion chamber volumes are equalized. Otherwise, one cylinder will perform more efficiently than the others, creating a mechanical imbalance. The combustion chamber volumes are measured with a graduated glass tube known as a burette.

When an engine-tuner bores or hones a block – especially a cast iron one – he fits a device known as a 'deck plate', which is torqued down onto the block to simulate the structural effect of the cylinder head being in place.

Conrods: Engine-tuners attempt to match the lengths and weights of the conrods, and to assemble a set with the minimum permissable weights. In terms of length, it's usually desirable to obtain the longest permissable conrods, then match them with the tallest pistons and the shortest block, thereby creating the highest compression ratio.

Manufacturers drill holes in the reciprocating parts to bring them into balance, and engine-tuners employ the same technique – but to a more precise degree. Deeper drilling takes place if more material needs to be removed. There are generally little areas of extraneous material – webs, for example – where drill holes can be inserted. In the case of a conrod, there's generally one machined face (as opposed to a cast finish) into which the tuner can drill a lightening hole.

Crankshaft: While tech inspectors will certainly take exception to a *lot* of lightening holes – because this would indicate that the crank has actually been lightened beyond the acceptable limit, rather than just balanced – the odd hole drilled here and there is perfectly acceptable. The precise location of the drilling depends upon where weight must be removed in order to achieve balance.

As part of the blueprinting process, engine-tuners try to obtain a crankshaft with equal strokes and equal centers.

Manufacturers drill holes in the reciprocating parts to bring them into balance, and engine-tuners employ the same technique – but to a more precise degree. Deeper drilling takes place if more material needs to be removed. There are generally little areas of extraneous material – webs, for example – where drill holes can be inserted. This crankshaft was balanced by this method.

Cylinder head: Work undertaken on the cylinder head tends to go hand in hand with work undertaken on the pistons. The engine-tuner often planes material off the head until he achieves the smallest permissable combustion chamber volumes, which translates into the highest possible compression ratio. That said, the highest compression ratio isn't *always* the best way to improve the overall performance.

Whatever the case, the cylinder head is planed in order to achieve a specific compression ratio, be that high or low.

Emissions: Specialist engine-tuners monitor NOX, hydrocarbon, and carbon dioxide content to ensure that complete combustion is taking place. They also listen for detonation (premature combustion) when the engine is run on the dynamometer.

Engine management system: These days, this tends to be the single most important performance-related element of an engine, regardless of whether it's a normally-aspirated unit, or turbocharged. Indeed, it can account for up to 90 percent of the total performance gain in this category of motorsport. The regulations almost always permit the engine management system to be reprogrammed, as this is the only way the full benefits can be gained from the other adjustments made to the engine.

At the core of the system is its 'brain' – the engine control unit, or ECU. To modify the engine management functions, engine-tuners alter the internal resistances and physically replace the standard microprocessor (chip)

To modify the engine management functions, engine-tuners alter the internal resistances and physically replace the standard microprocessor (chip) within the ECU. The replacement chip – it's known as an EPROM (Erazable Programable Read Only Memory) – will be the same shape, with the same interfaces, but will have a different configuration.

within the ECU. The replacement chip – it's known as an EPROM (Erazable Programable Read Only Memory) – will be the same shape, with the same interfaces, but will have a different configuration. The parameters of greatest importance are emissions, fuel economy, driveability, and starting performance. Reprogramming can also control detonation (by automatically retarding the ignition), and can even account for differences in climate from one country to another, and variations in fuel quality.

Although, in most championships, it's permissable for an aftermarket rev-limiter to be fitted, this is generally a function of the ECU, so the engine-tuner may reprogram it accordingly. If the car has a cruising-speed control mode, the regulations invariably state that it must be disabled: again, this tends to be a function of the ECU, so some reprogramming may be necessary.

In a few cases, the engine management system is also linked to an antilock braking system (ABS) – and even a traction- control system. The latest General Motors Astra GSi, for example, has both of these fitted as standard, both governed by the engine management system.

Exhaust system: Time was when all cars in this category of motorsport had to run with their standard exhaust systems. In a few championships, they still do, but this tends to diminish the entertainment value for spectators. The cars just don't *sound* as though they're racing! For this reason, the rulemakers generally adopt a more liberal approach.

It's usually permissable to fit a modified exhaust system aft of the manifold element, provided it doesn't exceed the production diameter, and provided the tailpipe exits in the same position as the production model. Depending on the precise wording of the regulations, you can either have catalysts and other non-essential internal fittings removed to lighten the standard exhaust and improve its performance, or upgrade to a race-specification exhaust system.

Regardless of the exhaust configuration, the mandatory national competition decibel limit must be observed. Noise limitations are a recurring source of frustration for engine- tuners and competitors alike, but with the Green Lobby gaining support year by year, it's something the motorsport fraternity is having to come to terms with – and rightly so.

External detailing: When the engine is returned to you, there will be external evidence of the tuner's eye for detail. The engine will be spotlessly clean, and may even have been painted. This isn't just a cosmetic improvement. The intention is to help competitors to detect oil leaks and other faults.

In addition, a lot of the fasteners will be lockwired to aid reliability.

Fuel economy: Unlike the original manufacturer, the race

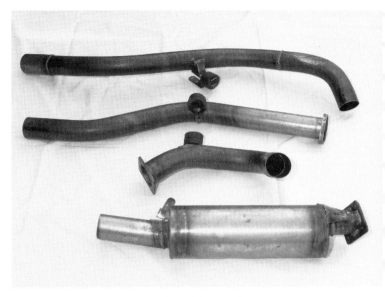

Depending on the precise wording of the regulations, you can either have catalysts and other non-essential internal fittings removed to lighten the standard exhaust and improve its performance, or upgrade to a race-specification exhaust system prepared (as seen here).

engine-tuner doesn't have to concern himself unduly with fuel economy. If a four door sedan only returns 8mpg, that's perfectly normal in racing, but it certainly wouldn't be acceptable for roadgoing use.

Ignition system: Usually, there are so many regulatory constraints on the ignition system that all an engine-tuner can do is replace the standard spark plugs with platinum-tipped versions, which are more resistant to extreme temperatures.

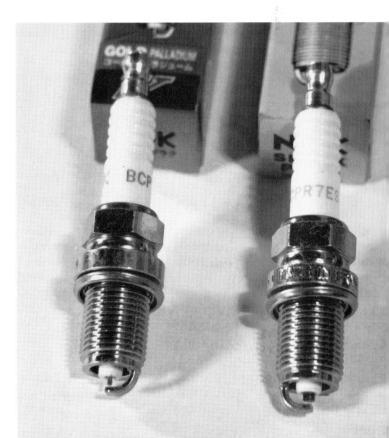

Usually, there are so many regulatory constraints on the ignition system that all an engine-tuner can do is replace the standard spark plugs (right) with platinum-tipped versions (left), which are more resistant to extreme temperatures. Note the difference in the size of the electrodes.

Induction system: The regulations generally state that carburetors, or parts of fuel-injection systems which regulate the rate at which fuel enters the engine (injectors, carburation jets, and so forth), may be modified or replaced, provided there's no influence on air admission.

Good atomization is critical to engine performance, and it is certainly a more important factor in this category of motorsport than, say, fuel consumption. That said, it's no good if fuel is just dripped into the bore, because it won't ignite. The rate at which fuel enters the engine is usually governed by the engine control unit (ECU), which may be reprogrammed to open the pintle nozzle for fractionally shorter, or longer, time intervals in order to obtain better atomization under racing conditions.

In most cases, an engine-tuner will opt to fit improved fuel injectors and reprogram the ECU accordingly. Injectors are generally color-coded, according to their size, with each manufacturer having its own color-coding system. For example, injectors fitted to British Ford Sierra Sapphire Cosworths are readily identifiable by their green or gray tops.

Turbocharged/supercharged engines offer greater potential for extracting extra performance than normally-aspirated engines, as increases in performance can be found within the turbocharger unit itself. It is not permissable, within this category of motorsport, to supercharge the engine with anything other than standard production components.

A Calibration Certificate for a digital pop off valve controller box.

The rulemakers reserve the right to alter boost limits to achieve performance parity between the various models. They employ one of two methods to regulate the boost: a turbo pressure dump (pop off) valve governed by an electronic black box, or a straightforward baffle on the turbo compressor air intake, limiting its maximum diameter. The latter is known as a restrictor.

Restrictors are virtually tamper-proof, but electronic regulating devices have, on occasion, been the subject of cheating. For example, in Britain's BRDC/BRSCC Saloon Car Championship, the Ford Sierra Sapphire Cosworth was approved to run with 12.8lb of boost. Clever competitors discovered that if the 12-volt electrical supply to the black box was reduced to, say, nine volts (by means of a resistance wire), the dump valve would not be triggered at the preset level. Instead, it was possible to go to 20lb of boost before the valve would be activated – and get away with it by running fractionally below that level.

It took the rulemakers some time to find out what was happening.

Lubrication system: Standard roadgoing cars weren't designed to be driven around corners on the limits of tire adhesion in the way they are on the racetrack. Powerful cornering forces drive the engine oil to one side of the sump or the other, and hard acceleration and deceleration drive it fore and aft, drastically diminishing the efficiency of the oil pickup pipe, situated in the bottom of the sump. If this is starved for even a brief moment, the

In most cases, an engine-tuner will opt to fit improved fuel injectors and reprogram the ECU accordingly. Injectors are generally color-coded, according to their size, with each manufacturer having its own color-coding system. The color-code feature is pointed out here.

Sealing

It is a common occurrence for tech inspectors to disassemble an engine and examine it thoroughly to ensure that it complies fully with the regulations. The competitor is informed at the end of the race, when the top-placing cars enter the inspection area – but the actual examination takes place elsewhere, at a later date.

To prevent unscrupulous individuals from tampering with the engine before it has been examined, tech inspectors have the right to 'seal' it in a manner analogous to the sealing of legal documents. A typical sealing method they employ is to lockwire the cylinder head to the block, then apply a special, snap-shut lead seal that cannot be released without causing visible damage. In addition to this time-honored practice, an infinitely more advanced sealing method is gaining acceptance. Tech inspectors apply a special type of paint to certain key areas of the engine at the time they impound it. Just before they disassemble the engine for inspection, they apply a reagent to the painted areas, whereupon the paint should turn a particular color. If it doesn't change color in the prescribed manner, it's a clear indication that the engine in question has been tampered with, and that paint which *looks* official – but isn't – has been applied in an effort to mask the indiscretion.

At that point, the competitor concerned, and his engine-tuner, have a lot of answering to do...

This snap-shut lead seal was lockwired to a turbo restrictor by an RAC MSA tech inspector.

bearings can be ruined.

The rulemakers, recognizing that dozens of broken cars at the trackside would spoil the racing, permit sumps to be freely modified. However, dry sumps are prohibited in this category of motorsport, and it is not permissable to increase the oil capacity by adding 'wings' to the bottom of the sump. Consequently, the only option open to race engine-tuners is to fit baffles within the sump to eliminate oil surge. Certain sump designs are more resistant to surge than others: some require hardly any attention at all – particularly those in the latest, higher-performance models.

The baffling engine-tuners fit within the sump also prevents the retention of oil up inside the engine, which could otherwise cause drag. They might well fit a plate just above the throw of the crankshaft, to prevent flying oil from accumulating beneath the pistons and on the crankshaft weights – a potential source of the type of drag known as 'viscous coupling'. Fitting such a plate has the secondary effect of retaining most of the oil down in the sump area.

Your engine-tuner may recommend that you run the engine half way between the manufacturer's recom-

Dry sumps are prohibited in this category of motorsport, and it is not permissable to increase the oil capacity by adding 'wings' to the bottom of the sump. Consequently, the only option open to race engine-tuners is to fit baffles within the sump to eliminate oil surge.

mended minimum and maximum oil levels, so that the oil does its job as a lubricant, but doesn't become a source of drag.

As the engine oil gets progressively hotter during the course of a race, the oil pressure can drop. To ensure that no part of the engine is starved of oil, the specialists usually increase the oil pressure by 10-20 percent: the exact amount depends what pressure the engine normally operates at (the Honda Civic, for example, runs at comparatively high pressures). Placing spacers behind the oil pressure relief valves, and replacing the original springs with externally identical, higher-tension versions, increases the oil pressure in a manner the rulemakers consider acceptable.

Pistons: Engine-tuners try to select a set of pistons of the minimum permissable weight, and also want the weights of the pistons to be equalized. In addition, they attempt to match the tallest piston with the longest conrod and the shortest block, thereby creating the highest compression ratio.

Power band: In this category of motorsport, the power band is critical. With a lightweight single-seater, torque is nice to have, but not essential. With a comparatively heavy sedan, on the other hand, torque is imperative – because once the car's been slowed down, there's a lot more weight to accelerate back to speed again.

This vitally important factor, which is sometimes overlooked by those engine-tuners who engage in a blinkered quest for more horsepower, is known as 'driveability'.

Rev band: The rev counter might typically bear a red line at 7,000rpm. In road use, an engine very rarely revs at this rate, but on the racetrack it will run almost constantly in the 5,000-7,000rpm range, and will seldom spend any time below 3,000rpm. Consequently, specialists optimise the engine for the highest region of the rev band.

Placing spacers behind the oil pressure relief valves, and replacing the original springs with externally identical, higher-tension versions increases the oil pressure in a manner which the rulemakers consider acceptable.

Of course, a tuner must consider whether the engine can withstand sustained operation at higher revs than the original manufacturer intended. Here, conrods tend to be the 'weak link'. Engines are subjected to enormous stresses during a race, but never moreso than when the driver mistimes a down shift, generating excessive revs. A car can be hurtling along the straightaway at a perfectly acceptable 6,000rpm, then its driver will brake for a corner and shift down far too early. Suddenly, the engine revs to 8,000rpm – and conrods start popping out the sides.

Engine-tuners try to select a set of pistons of the minimum permissable weight, and also want the weights of the pistons – as with all the other reciprocating parts – to be equalized.

Rev-limiter: Although this function is usually undertaken by the engine control unit (see *Engine management system*, above), there's nothing in the regulations to prevent an aftermarket rev-limiter from being fitted in most championships – but it won't help on downshifts.

Tolerances: Engine-tuners aim to get *cumulative* benefits from their manipulation of the various tolerances. Furthermore, they don't just blithely go to the maximum or minimum stated tolerances. On one parameter, they might lean toward the 'minus' end of the tolerance band, while on another they might go to a 'plus'. On yet another parameter, they might aim right for the middle of the tolerance band. Their overall intention is to ensure that the bias in each tolerance stacks up to a performance

gain, not a performance loss.

Take a cylinder bore, for example. There might be an optimum bore clearance for roadgoing use, but another for competition use: one which strays on the larger side, to create greater clearance for pistons operating at higher temperatures. This will tend to reduce frictional losses, and will lessen the risk of seizure. That said, engine-tuners must be careful, particularly with a turbocharged engine, that they don't go so far as to lose power due to excessive blow-by. It's another of those tradeoffs.

Valves: Engine-tuners are concerned with valve train inertia. Whether an engine has eight valves, sixteen valves, or more, they aim to ensure that they are all of the same weight, and that the valve springs are in equal tension. Manufacturing tolerances result in springs of slightly unequal tensions. Their fitted length has a significant effect on this, so the traditional way engine-tuners match all the spring forces is to shim the valve springs to equalize their fitted length (thin washers are packed beneath them).

It's customary for an engine-tuner to 'true' the valve seats, then verify this with a vacuum test.

Ascertaining the fitted length of a valve spring. Manufacturing tolerances result in springs of slightly unequal tensions. Their fitted length has a significant effect on this.

Measuring a valve spring on a spring tension tester.

The traditional way engine-tuners match all the spring forces is to shim the valve springs to equalize their fitted length: thin washers are packed beneath them.

Conducting a vacuum test on a valve seat to verify that it has been successfully 'trued'.

4
Rebuilding the car

Brake, fuel and air lines

With your engine being attended to at the tuning shop, you can devote all your attention to rebuilding the car. It's best to mount the bodyshell on axle stands after repainting it, and install as much of the internal equipment as possible before lowering the car onto its wheels. It's much easier to work on it when it's in an elevated position: you can climb into the cockpit in perfect safety, and enjoy excellent access to the undersides. When preparing this book, we had the Dane Motorsport Sierra Sapphire Cosworth mounted on its wheels as soon as it returned from the paint shop. This was purely for technical reasons: *our* priority was the photographer's lens!

The first hardware you should install is the pipework for the brake and fuel systems – and for the pneumatic jacking system if you plan to fit one. In some cases, the standard rigid piping must be reinstalled, but if the rulemakers permit it (they sometimes *demand* it), it's better to replace the original pipework with lengths of flexible aviation-specification armored piping. This is far superior from the safety standpoint: it's more robust than conventional automotive piping, being specifically designed for operation in demanding environments.

Aviation-specification piping is fairly expensive, but it's highly versatile. It can carry hydraulic fluid as part of a brake system, gasoline as part of a fuel system, or compressed air as part of a pneumatic jacking system. Joined by threaded connectors (unions), it has an outer braid which is resistant to abrasion, corrosion and flame. There are several excellent brands on the market: the top suppliers are Aeroquip, Earl's and Russell.

The rulemakers normally permit competitors to route flexible piping anywhere they wish, provided it isn't going to get in the driver's way or chafe against anything. Generally speaking, trim items don't represent a chafing threat, so you can route sections of the piping under them if necessary. When running a length of flexible piping from the rear of the car to the front – a fuel line, for example – an excellent route is along the tunnel, as there's usually plenty of room there. You should certainly try to get as much of the piping as possible inside the car, where it will have the maximum protection. Any piping routed along the underside of the car will be susceptible to damage from high curbing – or sand/gravel traps, if you're unlucky enough to slide off the racetrack. The regulations often stipulate that fluid pipes *must* be routed internally, in the interests of safety. Aviation-specification piping is easy to install, but you should ask your supplier for advice on which unions to use for particular applications. The car's manufacturer will likely have used clips of some sort to retain the original pipework to the bodyshell. For our purposes, there's an infinitely better fixing method – saddles and tie wraps – as these facilitate easier removal. If you need to effect repairs at a later date, or wish to repaint the shell at some stage, you can simply cut the tie wraps and remove the pipes. Saddles and tie wraps offer an added benefit: they allow you to reroute a length of pipe

If the rulemakers permit it, replace the original pipework with lengths of flexible aviation-specification armored piping. Joined by threaded connectors (unions), it has an outer braid which is resistant to abrasion, corrosion and flame. It can carry hydraulic fluid as part of a brake system, gasoline as part of a fuel system, or compressed air as part of a pneumatic jacking system.

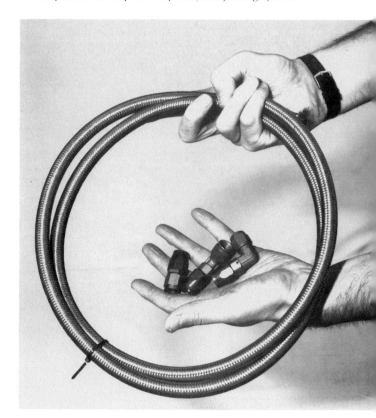

The rulemakers normally permit aviation-specification piping to be routed anywhere, as long as it isn't going to get in the driver's way or chafe against anything. Here, a fuel line is being routed through the engine compartment bulkhead.

at will and tie it down firmly somewhere else if you find that it's chafing against something.

Saddles are simply riveted into holes drilled along the desired route. The tie wraps are then looped under them.

You'll need about 30ft (9m) of piping for the brake system and the fuel system – more if the car has a fuel-injected engine, as a return pipe must be routed back along the length of the car to the fuel source. If you intend to fit air-jacks, you'll require a further 25ft (7.5m) or so.

Here are some general guidelines for installing aviation- specification flexible piping.

Brake lines: Although the regulations for most championships permit cars to be fitted with aviation- specification flexible piping, the incorporation of dry-break couplings is often prohibited. For those unfamiliar with them, dry-break couplings 'compartmentalize' the brake system, reducing the extent to which air bubbles are introduced during repairs and maintenance. This can save a great deal of time, particularly during endurance races.

The regulations generally stipulate that pipes carrying hydraulic fluid must meet specified minimum burst-pressure requirements and be capable of withstanding extreme temperatures – a precaution against the consequences of fire. The top brands easily exceed all of the mandatory requirements.

If the rulemakers permit a brake proportioning valve to be fitted, this is the time to do it, using aviation- specification piping (see *Brake system*).

Fuel lines: If you intend to retain the car's standard fuel tank, the rulemakers generally offer the option of either reinstalling the original fuel pipes and fittings, or installing aviation-specification piping. If you plan to fit a fuel cell, on the other hand, there's no choice: the rulemakers demand that you upgrade to aviation-specification piping. A feed pipe should be routed between the engine compartment and the point where the fuel cell will be mounted, via the point where the standard fuel pump is to be refitted. If your engine is fuel-injected, install a return pipe directly between the engine compartment and the planned fuel cell site.

Inspired by NASCAR's Smokey Yunick, some competitors run with extra-long fuel lines in endurance races, enabling additional fuel to be carried. This can be a neat way of bending the rules, without actually breaking them, but check the precise wording of the regulations first, to ensure that the car will be legal.

Again, the regulations stipulate that lines carrying fuel must meet, or exceed, a regulatory minimum burst-pressure and be capable of resisting specified high temperatures.

Air lines: If you're planning to fit a pneumatic jacking system, aviation-specification pipework will be an essential element of it. High pressure unions are also essential, to cope with the approximately 500psi operating pressure required to lift a typical car. You must decide where the air inlet is to be located: see *Airjack system*. There's no potential for weight saving in terms of the amount of pipework you fit, as wherever you site the inlet, it must run to a multipoint union at a central point within the car. Working outwards from that, route two lengths of flexible piping to the front of the car and two to the rear, then divert them right and left to each airjack.

When running a length of aviation-specification piping from the rear of the car to the front – a fuel line, for example – an excellent route is along the tunnel, as seen here. This photo was taken at a later stage in the rebuild sequence, to show how lengths of flexible piping (and electrical wiring) can be routed under trim items.

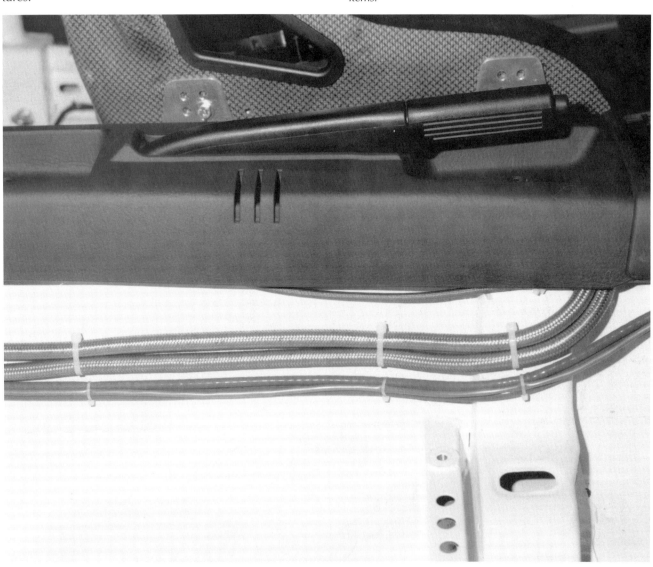

Wiring harness

When all the pipework is in place, you can turn your attention to the wiring harness. Rewiring, and even the replacement of the existing harness with a non-standard version, is permitted in a few championships, but in most cases the original harness must go back in.

These days, manufacturers aim for commonality: wiring harnesses in the majority of models have a standard layout, with little or no variation between a basic-specification vehicle and de luxe version. As a result, there's likely to be some wiring you don't need: typically, wires associated with electric windows, an electric sunroof, a rear screen wiper, the roof courtesy light, and any door-mounted warning lights. Check the regulations to ascertain which, if any, of these items must remain in working order, and which are potentially dispensable. For example, it's generally permissable to substitute electric window mechanisms for manual ones, so identify the extraneous wires and remove them as a weight saving measure.

Modern wiring harnesses are designed for commonality, with little or no variation between a basic-specification vehicle and de luxe version. As a result, there's likely to be some wiring you don't need. Study the regulations to ascertain which wires are potentially disposable. For example, it's generally permissable to substitute electric window mechanisms for manual ones, so identify the extraneous wires and remove them as a weight saving measure.

When reinstalling the wiring harness, replace it in its original configuration. If you don't, there's the risk of it fouling the interior trim and other items of original equipment when they're mounted back in the car later.

Some of the better financed competitors hire an electrical specialist to lay the wiring harness out and identify all the non-essential wires. While researching this book, we encountered a Ford RS2000 race-preparation project in which this highly professional approach was adopted. The RS2000 has a standard Ford Escort harness, applicable to the entire range, so the team found they were able to remove 9lb (4kg) of unnecessary wiring from the car!

This is often a gray area from the legality standpoint. The regulations seldom state that you can't delete sections of wiring, and many of these wires are in no way essential. Nevertheless, tread carefully.

When reinstalling the wiring harness, replace it in its original configuration. If you don't, there's the risk of it fouling the interior trim and other items of original equip-

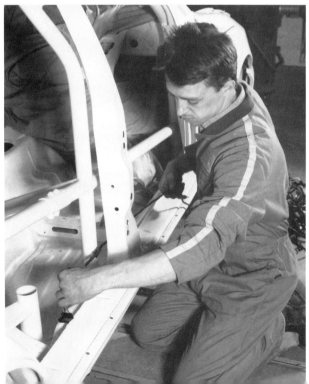

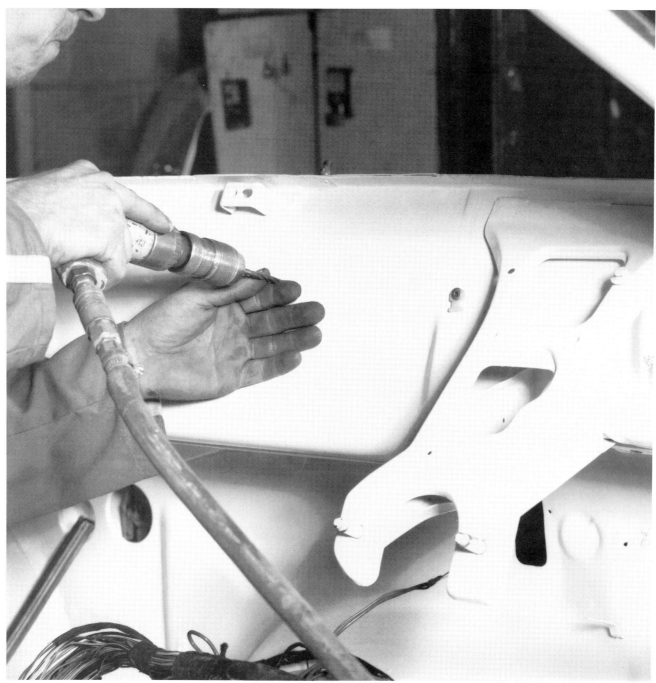

Use saddles and tie wraps to hold the loom in place, so that if you need to effect a repair or wish to repaint the bodyshell at a later date, you can just cut the tie wraps and lift out the entire harness. Saddles are simply riveted into holes drilled along the desired route, as demonstrated here. The tie wraps are then looped under them. Employ the same method to retain aviation-specification piping in the car.

ment when they're mounted back in the car later. Use saddles and tie wraps to hold the loom in place, so that if you need to effect a repair or wish to repaint the bodyshell at a later date, you can just cut the tie wraps and lift the entire harness out.

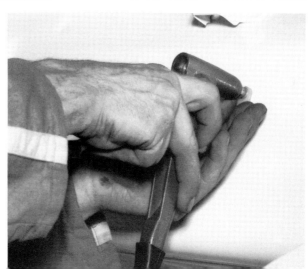

The regulations may state that extra fuses, relays – and sometimes even voltage regulators – can be added to the electrical system. In fact, though, you need only modify the electrics if you decide to fit additional external lights for certain endurance races (see *External lights*).

Usually, the rulemakers stipulate that cars must be fitted with internal and external ignition system cutoff switches. These can employ the same type of T-shaped handles used to activate the on-board fire extinguisher. The internal switch should be sited on the dashpanel within easy reach of the driver, while the external switch is best located immediately forward of the windshield, on the cowl. An ignition system cutoff can either be a single-switch device which isolates the battery, or – if the car is equipped with an alternator – a double-switch device which both isolates the battery and breaks the alternator charging circuit.

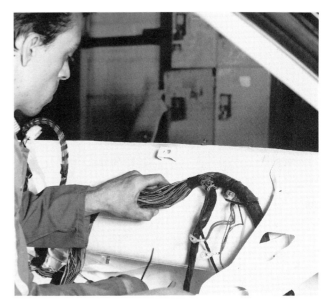

Most of the wiring harness is concentrated behind the dashpanel.

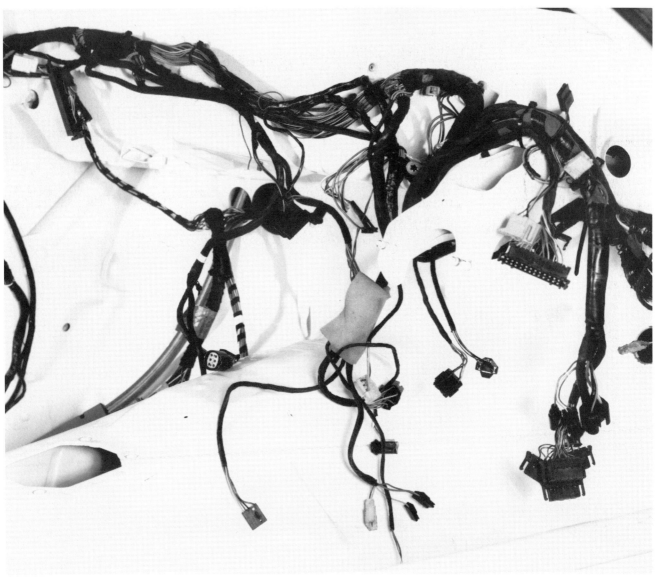

Light units

If you're planning to compete in conventional sprint races, which only take place during the hours of daylight, chances are you can simply reinstall the car's original light units and leave it at that. This is what the Dane Motorsport team did with the Sierra Sapphire Cosworth. However, you should still read the regulations carefully to ensure that the light units on your car are in full compliance.

In some championships, the rulemakers require protective headlight covers to be fitted in fine weather (these must have no influence on the car's aerodynamics). In other championships, competitors must stick strips of adhesive tape over the headlights to prevent shards of glass being scattered in a collision.

For races scheduled to run after sunset, and/or before sunrise, a limited amount of supplementary lighting may be fitted to improve the driver's visibility. Obviously, 24-hour races do, but so do certain other endurance races. It's usually permissable to fit driving light mounting bars – or aerodynamic light pods, which are even better – as the rulemakers do not allow supplementary lights to be housed within the bodywork. Where alterations to the standard lighting layout are permitted, the original headlights can usually be rendered inoperative. However, with the exception of one series (IMSA's Bridgestone Supercar Championship) lights cannot be removed simply to provide holes for brake ducts – or, for that matter, to enhance engine cooling.

Most of the commonsense rules applied to lighting

If you're planning to compete in conventional sprint races, which only take place during the hours of daylight, chances are you can simply reinstall the car's original light units and leave it at that. This is what the Dane Motorsport team did with our 'guinea pig' Ford Sierra Sapphire Cosworth.

on roadgoing cars also apply to race cars: for example, cars are not permitted to have forward-facing red lights. Usually, the regulations state that headlights and other external lights must be arranged in pairs. Lights which are movable while the car is in motion are prohibited.

Sometimes, modification of the existing lighting is limited to the fitment of aftermarket bulbs and lenses. In many championships, however, any of the lights accepted by the rulemakers as being part of the model's standard array may be exchanged for similar lights: spot lights or fog lights, for example.

There are certain minimum lighting requirements for cars racing at night – and by day, in poor visibility – and competitors who don't comply can be disqualified. For night racing, it's customary for the rulemakers to allow cars to be fitted with special lighting to aid identification by pit crew members. Identity lighting, as it's called, must

not impair the vision of other competitors, nor compromize circuit safety by resembling the lights on emergency and rescue vehicles. In other words, they must burn continuously, not flash, alternate or rotate – nor may they be used for car-to-pit signalling purposes, which is strictly prohibited. Identity lights need not be fitted in pairs.

If you wish to install identity lightning, choose a distinctive color or combination of colors, and a prominent position for the lights: perhaps one side of the roof, or the center of the hood. Believe it or not, the best lights to use for this purpose are the type you see fitted as nocturnal decorations on trucks!

This car, competing in an endurance race, has strips of adhesive tape over the lights to prevent shards of glass being scattered in a collision, and supplementary lighting (with protective covers fitted during the hours of daylight).

A typical identity light installation.

Bumpers and exterior fittings

This is a good time to reinstall the exterior trim items, together with any aerodynamic surfaces: also the trunk lid, the bumpers and the wiper blades. In most championships, all items of exterior trim must be retained. Similarly, the standard bumpers must go back on in their original positions, though it's often acceptable for the bumper brackets to be reinforced.

Standard front and rear spoilers/air dams delivered on the model by the manufacturer can be refitted. The regulations sometimes state these these may be reinforced, but not modified. All of the standard hood and trunk fasteners should be removed, and replaced with quick-release fasteners. Do this now, but don't actually fit the hood until the car is back on its wheels.

The original windshield wiper mechanisms must be retained, but the blades may usually be substituted with aftermarket parts of a different design. The same applies to a rear screen blade, if one is fitted as standard.

Fitting quick-release fasteners (for the trunk lid) to a trim panel and reinstalling the panel on the car.

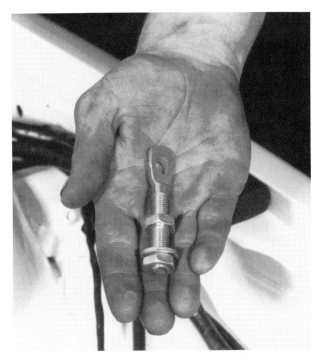

Clockwise. This sequence shows an alternative quick-release fastener installation being implemented (on the hood).

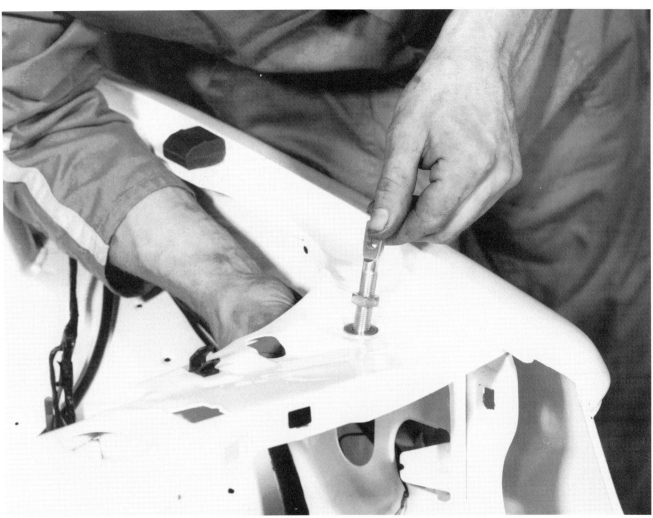

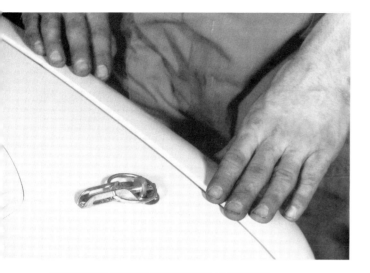
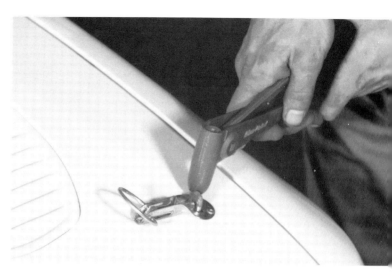

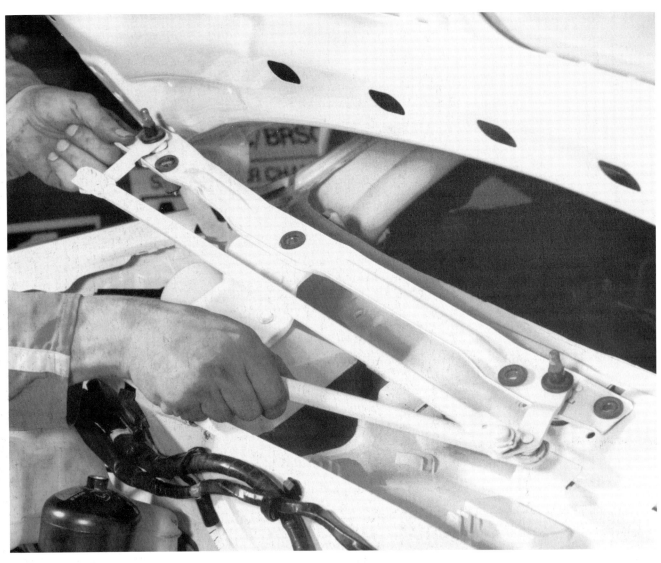

The original windshield wiper mechanisms must be retained, but the blades may usually be substituted with aftermarket parts of a different design. The same applies to a rear screen blade, if one is fitted as standard.

The standard bumpers must go back on in their original positions, though it's often acceptable for the bumper brackets to be reinforced.

Standard front and rear spoilers/air dams delivered on the model by the manufacturer can be refitted. The regulations sometimes state these these may be reinforced, but not modified.

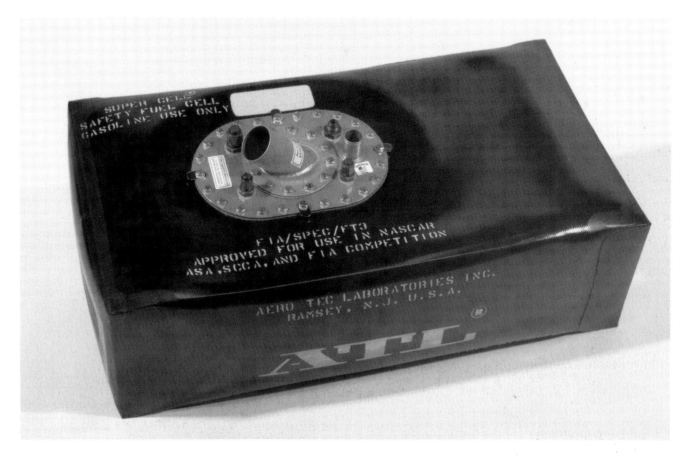

This is the least expensive type of flexible fuel cell. As a general rule: the more complex the shape, the higher the cost.

Fuel system

In some championships, the rulemakers allow competitors to either retain the car's standard fuel tank, or fit a race- specification flexible fuel cell: that choice should have been made earlier (Chapter 2). If you've opted to retain the car's standard fuel tank, have it steam cleaned. Then, after ensuring that any residues of moisture have dried out, mount it back under the car using the standard saddle straps.

If you've elected to fit a fuel cell, as Dane Motorsport did, there's a little more work to do. A circular fuel cell can be bought 'off the shelf', ready to drop straight into the spare wheel recess: that's the easiest way. Alternatively, some competitors go to the expense of designing their own fuel cell and send the required dimensions to the manufacturer, who fabricates it to that specification. If you haven't already done so, scrutinize the regulations thoroughly to ensure that the fuel cell of your choice will satisfy the tech inspectors. The rulemakers specify a minimum fuel cell capacity, which includes the capacity of all the filler pipes and necks, and in some cases demand that the cell incorporates a drain hole through which the contents may be completely evacuated.

The siting of the fuel cell is important from the point of view of weight distribution. Theoretically, the lower the mass is sited the better, which is one reason for fitting a cell in the vacant spare wheel recess. Alternatively, a fuel cell can be fitted *atop* the spare wheel recess, mounted on a sheet of steel or aluminium. This provides scope for positioning it in accordance with your weight distribution goals. Remember, when making your weight calculations, to allow for the weight of fuel within the cell. This can be altered in the interests of weight distribution: provided the car meets the mandatory weight requirements, you need only carry the minimum quantity of fuel necessary to complete the race distance.

Wherever you elect to site it, the fuel cell should be installed in accordance with the instructions supplied. If the regulations specify that the cell must be equipped with a drain hole, drill a hole in the underside of the car and insert a short length of pipe in the appropriate position. If not, the standard fuel pump can be used to drain the cell.

The cell must be held in position with two straps. These can either be made of steel or aluminium – with rounded edges, so they won't cause any chafing – or even of a hardy fibrous material. In terms of thickness, the straps should be adequate to support the weight of the cell in the event of a rollover. Retain them to the bodyshell with bolts.

Fitting the necessary (aviation-specification) pipework should present no problems. The feed pipe, and the return pipe if your car is fuel-injected, should have been installed earlier, so all you need do now is plug it/them into the cell. The combined fill/vent pipes are supplied, and should simply be routed between the appropriate points atop the

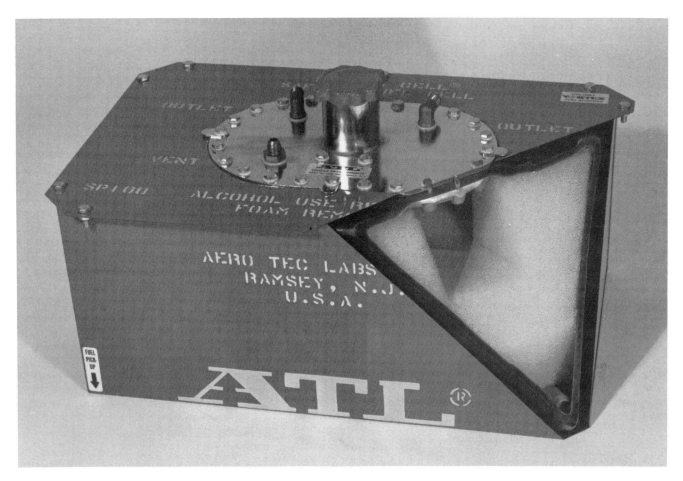

(Above) Fuel cells are filled with foam baffling, as revealed in this sectioned example. The baffling prevents fuel from surging from one side of the tank to the other – the inertia would upset the car's handling – and ensures that the fuel pickup is constantly fed. It also gives the cell its resistance to explosive combustion. If a spark were to enter the cell, the foam and gasoline would burn, but the flame couldn't travel fast enough through the foam to cause an explosion. Although the foam baffling is dispersed throughout the cell, it only displaces 3-5 percent of the internal volume.

(Below) A fuel cell like this can be bought 'off the shelf', ready to drop straight into the spare wheel recess. The fill/vent pipes are situated on either side, and the orifice for the fuel pipe to the engine can be seen on the far side. Scrutinize the regulations thoroughly to ensure that the fuel cell you purchase will satisfy the tech inspectors. The rulemakers specify a minimum fuel cell capacity, which includes the capacity of all the filler pipes and necks.

Closeup view of a fuel cell fill neck. These feature dry-break connectors for use in conjunction with overhead rigs mounted in the pits, and there are regulations governing where they are sited. They cannot be located in window panels, for example, nor must they protrude from the bodywork: they must be mounted virtually flush with the surface.

cell and the points where the necks will be located in the bodyshell. The necks feature dry-break connectors for use in conjunction with overhead rigs mounted in the pits (more details in Chapter 5).

There are regulations governing where the necks are sited on the car's exterior. They cannot be located in window panels, nor must they protrude from the bodywork: they must be mounted virtually flush with the surface. Check the regulations to ensure that the necks will be sited legally, then cut holes of the appropriate diameter in the bodywork and fit them.

If your car has a trunk, you'll have already installed a firewall to isolate the fuel cell from the cockpit. If your car is a hatchback, you should by now have fitted liquid-tight bulkheads in the rear fender flares, through which the fill/vent pipes will pass, thereby preventing leaking fuel or vapor from accumulating in the cockpit.

If your car is a hatchback, you must isolate the fill/vent pipes from the car's interior. Using aluminium sheet, fabricate two vertical tunnels (shoulders) and two horizontal tunnels to link those to the shield which shrouds the fuel cell. The shoulders and tunnels should be pop riveted to the shell and rendered airtight with silicon sealer. Both tunnels should have an inspection panel set into them, which in turn should incorporate a gasket to maintain airtightness.

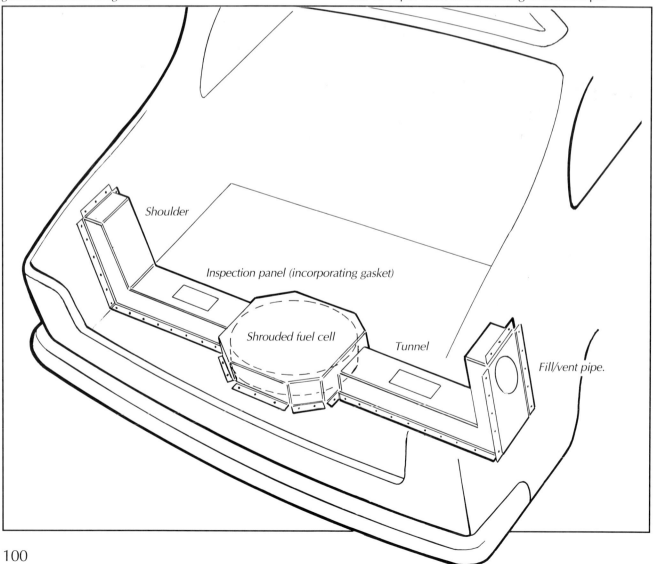

The regulations state that the fuel cell must be shielded with aluminium or steel sheeting, so that if the cell is crushed in an accident, the shielding will bend and the flexible bladder will deform harmlessly, rather than rupturing with potentially disastrous consequences. Whether the shielding shrouds the cell completely, or merely acts as a 'lid' on top of it, depends on whether the cell is located in a separate compartment from the cockpit. If it's located in a compartment already isolated from the driver, you only need cut and fit a plate atop it. If it's in the same compartment as the driver, you must cut and shape the sheeting so as to fully enclose the cell, then render it airtight with domestic silicon sealer. The regulations are specific as to the thickness of the aluminium or steel employed for this purpose.

If your car is a hatchback, there remains the task of isolating the fill/vent pipes from the car's interior. Using aluminium sheet, fabricate two vertical tunnels (shoulders) and two horizontal tunnels to link those to the shield which shrouds the cell. The shoulders and tunnels should be pop riveted to the shell and rendered airtight with silicon sealer. Both tunnels should have an inspection panel set into them, which in turn should incorporate a gasket to maintain airtightness.

In the unlikely event that you opt to fit the fuel cell *underneath* the car, the rulemakers stipulate that it must be covered by a (carbonfiber) shroud. These are available from good motorsport equipment stores.

As an alternative to fitting the fuel cell in the spare wheel recess, it can be mounted atop *the recess on a sheet of steel or aluminium. This provides scope for positioning it in accordance with your weight distribution goals. The cell shown here is fully enclosed in steel sheeting, for maximum protection.*

Airjack system

In one British series – the BRDC/BRSCC Saloon Car Championship – the regulations permit a pneumatic jacking system to be fitted aboard cars, to facilitate rapid tire changes. If you are going to fit airjacks, you'll already have welded four tubes into the shell to house them (Chapter 2). The principle upon which airjacks operate is straightforward: the volume of compressed air fed into each airjack body displaces the pistons, raising the car off the ground. When the supply is discontinued, the air escapes back through the piping and the car settles down on its wheels again.

Installing an airjack system isn't difficult, although the instructions provided don't always explain things very well. Start by measuring the length of the travel of the airjack – the maximum length that the piston extends – then measure how high the car needs to be raised before all four wheels leave the ground. These measurements govern the extent to which the airjacks will be adjusted vertically when they've been installed.

One at a time, guide each airjack body up into the tube with one hand, and hold it securely with the other hand when it reappears. Then screw the threaded collar down to the required level, in accordance with the earlier measurement. When all four airjacks have been installed, screw a high-pressure union into the hole atop each one to create the necessary interface for the aviation-specification piping you installed earlier. The compressed air supply required to activate the airjack system (a minimum of 500psi) must be contained in an external cylinder, because the rulemakers do not allow compressed air cylinders to be carried aboard the cars for safety reasons. To raise the car onto its jacks, an external air line is plugged into a valve protruding from the bodywork.

Opinions as to where this valve should be sited vary considerably. It's not easy to avoid potential impact areas, as the car is as likely to be struck from the rear as it is to sustain a frontal impact. On most cars, the airjack valve either protrudes from the rear valance, or from the front spoiler/air dam (sometimes offset to one corner). If a car has been equipped with a fuel cell, the airjack valve

One at a time, guide each airjack body up into the tube with one hand, and hold it securely with the other hand when it reappears. Then screw the threaded collar down to the required level. When all four airjacks have been installed, screw a high-pressure union into the hole atop each one to create the necessary interface for the aviation-specification piping you installed earlier.

can be fitted under the original filler cap flap, conveniently at waist level. Alternatively, we know of competitors who've fitted the valve near the exterior mirror on the driver's side. It's very much a matter of personal preference.

Bear in mind that the BRDC/BRSCC grant a weight allowance for the airjack system: 6kg.

Fire extinguisher

Almost universally, race cars must be equipped with a fire extinguisher. The regulations relating to fire extinguishers define a minimum permissable cylinder capacity, which varies considerably from one championship to another. Typical mandatory capacities are 5lb and 10lb in the United States, and 2.5kg, 5kg and 10kg in Europe. The rulemakers also specify the number of activation points. Usually it's two: an internal point for use by the driver, and an external point for use by racetrack personnel when the driver is either incapacitated or is unable for some other reason to activate the system himself. Before ordering a fire extinguisher system for your car, check the mandatory requirements.

While conventional domestic fire extinguishers are designed for hand operation, a race-specification fire extinguisher is mounted in a fixed position and remotely operated. Another fundamental difference between a conventional domestic fire extinguisher and a race-specification unit is that the latter is designed to discharge all its contents in a single operation, without interruption. The extinguishant is piped directly from the cylinder to a nozzle in the engine compartment. In some cases, a second pipe carries a simultaneous flow of extinguishant into the airtight compartment containing the fuel cell.

If the regulations state that a nozzle should also be located within the cockpit, this must not point directly at the driver.

Race-specification fire extinguishers are activated either manually by means of a pull-cable, or electrically by means of a push-button. Some systems employ a combination of the two, with – for example – the internal activation point being of the electrical type, and the external activation point being of the manual variety. The rulemakers don't normally stipulate whether the system has to be manually or electrically activated: they merely specify how many activation points there must be, and require them to be readily identifiable and accessible.

BCF (Halon 1211), pressurized with nitrogen, is the standard extinguishant employed for motorsport applications. It has a low toxicity, leaves no residue, and is highly effective. Fire is, in effect, a very rapid process of oxidation, to the point where both light and heat energy are emitted. It's believed that Halon interferes with the chemical chain reaction by which fire propagates, inhibiting it.

Competition-specification fire extinguishers are designed to operate in any orientation, because in an accident the car is quite likely to come to rest inverted, or on its side. One leading manufacturer, Lifeline, has patented a flexible gravity bias mechanism known as a Dip Tube to ensure that, irrespective of the vehicle's orientation, the entire contents of the cylinder are discharged.

Full fitting instructions will be supplied with the fire extinguisher, together with a wiring diagram if it's an electrically-operated system. The steel cylinder, which can be supplied either epoxy powder coated or with a natural aluminiumized finish, should be bolted firmly to the floor pan – or to a roll cage member – using the light-

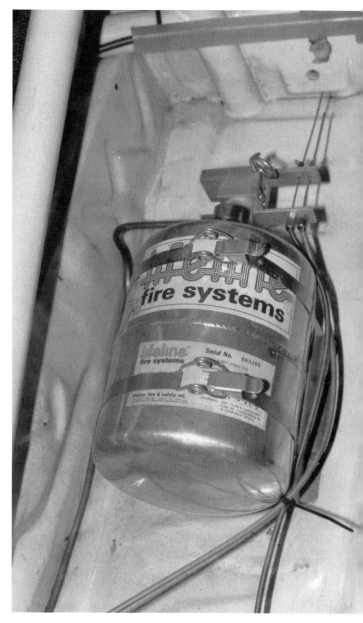

weight brackets provided. Ensure that the extinguisher cylinder is secured and protected in accordance with the regulations. The rulemakers specify that fire extinguishers should be mounted in such a manner as to be readily removable for the purposes of weight verification. They also require the contents gauge to be easily readable.

Fire extinguisher kits usually include the necessary pipework: typically, thin-walled aluminium tubing, polythene-coated, with push-in connectors at either end. Electrically-activated systems operate totally independent of the car's electrical circuit, employing a simple series loop circuit interrupted by a switch. Polarity is immaterial. Fireproof wiring is supplied, and more can be ordered if required. Typically, the power pack is a high-amperage manganese alkaline battery with in-built test facilities for both the battery and the wiring circuit. All of the electrical components are supplied with the extinguisher.

Three alternative fire extinguisher installations: one mounted on the cockpit floor (left), one mounted on a roll cage element, also within the cockpit (below), and one mounted in the trunk (right). Electrically-activated systems operate totally independent of the car's electrical circuit, employing a simple series loop circuit interrupted by a switch. All of the electrical components are supplied with the extinguisher.

Check the regulations thoroughly to ascertain which items of original equipment must be reinstalled. It's usually easiest to start outfitting the cockpit at roof level and work your way downwards, as this provides more room to maneuver. Replace the original head liner first – unless you have a sunroof to fit, in which case that takes priority.

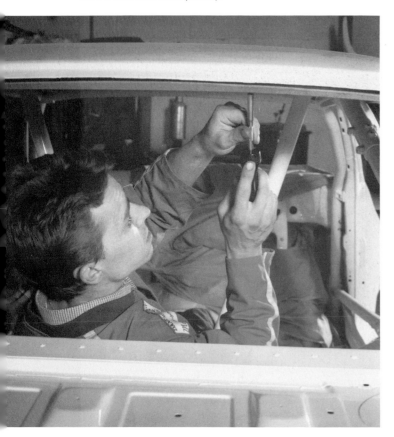

Outfitting the cockpit

The degree to which the car's interior must adhere to the original specification varies considerably from one championship to another. In the most extreme cases, virtually all of the interior materials, such as the head liner, carpeting, carpet pad or insulation, sound proofing, leather/plastic/fabric interior panels and the like may be discarded, and substitute interior panels may be fabricated and painted to match the original panels. More often, however, most of the original trim items and other hardware must be reinstalled in an unmodified condition: only the carpeting may be discarded, as this could pose a fire hazard if it became saturated with fuel.

Competitors are permitted to modify or remove items of interior trim to accommodate the roll cage elements, and cage elements which the driver could come into contact with in the event of an accident must be swathed in protective padding of a specified minimum thickness.

Check the regulations thoroughly to ascertain which items of original equipment must be reinstalled. It's usually easiest to start outfitting the cockpit at roof level and work your way downwards, as this provides more room to maneuver. Replace the original head liner first – unless you have a sunroof to fit, in which case that takes priority. Don't reinstall any of the sunroof winder mechanisms, be they manual or electrical, as these represent unnecessary weight. Instead, introduce extra rigidity to the bodyshell by fitting a small bracket to each side of the sunroof, and to corresponding points in the roof, and bolting them firmly together to render the sunroof panel permanently closed. The rubber weatherstripping should be replaced in the original manner, to create a proper seal.

In the unlikely event of a tech inspector taking exception to this, tell him you've fixed the sunroof to the roof in the interests of driver safety, to prevent it bursting open in an accident.

Cars fitted with an *electrically operated* sunroof as original equipment – the Porsche 911 is one – are, in certain circumstances, permitted to run with the sunroof in the closed position and the relevant electrics disconnected.

Glass sunroofs aren't permitted on the racetrack, for obvious reasons. If your car had a glass sunroof, you must replace it with a steel one: we're assuming that the manufacturer offers an aftermarket steel version, or the problem will already have been dealt with (Chapter 1). To keep the cost down, acquire a sunroof from an auto breaker, then fit it in the manner described above.

Generally speaking, the rulemakers do not permit fabric-top convertibles to race. However, there are some championships in which a competitor may enter such a car if prior approval has been granted: in such cases, a removable hard-top must be securely mounted in place of the original fabric top assembly. Note that removable roof panels – T-tops and targa tops, for example – must be installed aboard the car and securely fastened.

Turn your attention next to the heating and/or cooling system. Under some sets of regulations, the standard components can be deleted, but in the majority of championships they must be reinstalled. If the car has an air conditioning system, the rulemakers almost always permit it to be discarded. Do so, because it represents unnecessary weight and complexity.

Next, deal with those elements of the steering system which reside in the cockpit. The steering column lock must be disabled for competition use. The easiest way is to remove the lock, grind away the mortice with a bench grinder and a rotary file, then put the lock back on. That will leave the driver with a means of switching the electrics on and initiating ignition. Alternatively, you can disable the lock by removing the fuse – or discard the lock altogether, if the wording of the regulations allows it.

Under most sets of regulations, competitors are free to replace the standard steering wheel with a race-specification version. In championships where this is not permitted, competitors may fit an approved aftermarket steering wheel. In both cases, wood rim steering wheels are prohibited on safety grounds.

In some championships, competitors are permitted to replace the key start with a push button.

Reinstall the windshield, the rear-quarter windows, and the rear screen next. Only very rarely do the regulations permit anything other than the original glass to be fitted (standard location and angles), and excessive tinting is prohibited. In some championships, the rulemakers permit a specified number of metal safety clips to be bolted or riveted to the bodyshell and cowl to help retain the windshield at the top and bottom. In some championships,

Under some sets of regulations, the standard heating and/or cooling system components can be deleted, but in most cases they must be reinstalled. If the car has an air conditioning system, the rulemakers almost always permit it to be discarded. Do so, because it represents unnecessary weight and complexity.

the original rear screen can be replaced by a lightweight version made from clear plastic material of a specified minimum thickness. It must be of the same size and shape as the standard screen, and must be located in precisely the same position.

If you elect to fit a lightweight rear screen, you must secure it with two additional straps of specified dimensions, bolted or riveted to the bodywork at the top and bottom of the rear window frame.

In most cases, competitors are free to replace the standard steering wheel with a race-specification version. In championships where this is not permitted, competitors may fit an approved aftermarket steering wheel. In both cases, wood rim steering wheels are prohibited on safety grounds.

Reinstalling the steering column. The steering column lock must be disabled for competition use. Either grind away the mortice with a bench grinder and a rotary file, remove the fuse – or discard the lock altogether, if the regulations permit it.

In all probability, the regulations you're working to will stipulate that the standard dashpanel and instruments must be replaced as before. In that case, you should do so now. Regulations governing the layout of the dashpanel are more liberal in a few championships: while the instrument panel must remain essentially 'stock-appearing', the original instruments may be replaced or supplemented with additional engine monitoring gauges. The rulemakers normally permit the car's standard audio system to be removed – often specifying that the hole in the dashpanel be covered with an aluminium panel.

As far as the interior mirror is concerned, in some championships it's permissable to replace the standard mirror with a multi-plane version, improving the driver's visibility when he's defending his position against potential overtakers.

Under some sets of regulations, the installation of a two-way radio is permitted, facilitating driver-to-pit communications during races (the frequency must not interfere with emergency networks at the racetrack). In other cases, radios are only permitted if the race in question holds International status, or if it's a driver-change event. The receiver may replace the standard radio/cassette player. Two-way radios optimized for competition use are available from all good motorsport accessory stores. If licenses are required by law, race officials may request to inspect them prior to the event, so make sure you're in possession of the necessary paperwork.

If there's to be television coverage of races, it's often a mandatory requirement for competitors to install an in-car camera and video recorder if requested to do so. Competitors are prohibited from installing any camera other than those of the official film producer. The rulemakers lay down stringent conditions as to what lies in the camera's field of view, in terms of advertising. In the case of a forward-facing camera, the rulemakers specify which logos must be displayed inside the car, particularly on the dashpanel, and may place restrictions on other advertising within the cockpit. They may even limit the logos carried on the driver's helmet and overalls.

Video recorders are usually mounted on brackets, firmly affixed to the back cage.

Consult the regulations as to the disposal of any on-board tools, including the standard jack. It's usually acceptable for competitors to remove them, and in a few cases this is a mandatory requirement. Also ascertain the status of the spare wheel/tire. In some championships, the regulations state that this must be removed. In others – particularly those featuring endurance races – carriage of the spare wheel/tire is optional (note that it must comply with the regulations applying to the other wheels/tires).

In all probability, the regulations you're working to will stipulate that the standard dashpanel and instruments must be replaced as before. Regulations governing the layout of the dashpanel are more liberal in a few championships: while the instrument panel must remain essentially 'stock-appearing', the original instruments may be replaced or supplemented with additional engine monitoring gauges. Note the T-shaped cutoff devices for the ignition systems and the fire extinguisher.

Seats and safety harnesses

In most championships, the standard driver's seat must be replaced with a race-specification version. In cases where this isn't mandatory, the rulemakers still grant competitors the *option* to do so. As far as the other seats are concerned, in some cases the front passenger seat, and the rear seat and seat backs, may be removed. In others, the original seating positions must remain, and the front passenger seat must be replaced by a race-specification version – which offers a considerable weight saving, of course.

Check the regulations to ascertain what the mandatory seating requirements are.

Race-specification seats differ from conventional seats in many ways. Strength is obviously an important factor.

Practically everybody who's serious about racing uses seats with a hybrid Kevlar/carbonfiber shell. These are strong, but very light. The shape of the seat is also important: it needs to be more than just a 'bucket seat'. Increasingly, over recent years, rulemakers are demanding that seats have high backs, in order to support the dri-

This seat has a hybrid Kevlar/carbonfiber shell, which is strong but very light. The shape is very important. Increasingly, rulemakers are demanding that seats have high backs, in order to support the driver's head in the event of a rear-end impact. To help counter high cornering loads, the sides of the seat curve upwards to support the driver's hips and thighs, and the top of the seat is contoured to support his shoulders.

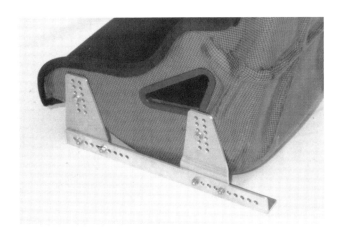

A very important factor is the manner in which the seat is attached to the aluminium subframes, and the subframes attached to the floor pan. The structural integrity of a seat is only as good as its anchorage. Aluminium subframes are supplied with the seat. They will already be attached to threaded bolts bonded to the seat shell, so all you need do is ensure that the subframes are fixed securely to the floor pan.

ver's head in the event of a rear-end impact. To help counter high cornering loads, the sides of the seat curve upwards to support the driver's hips and thighs, and the top of the seat is contoured to support his shoulders.

On a race-specification seat, fire resistant material is employed for the padding and covering. Amazingly, this is not a mandatory requirement in some championships – merely a recommendation on the part of the regulatory authority.

A very important factor is the manner in which the seat is attached to the aluminium subframes, and the subframes attached to the floor pan. The structural integrity of a seat is only as good as its anchorage. If a tech inspector suspects that a seat is not securely attached, he'll push and

It's usual for the standard seat belts to be replaced with a race-specification safety harness. Consult the regulations as to whether a four-, five-, or even six-point harness must be fitted (this is a four-point version). The rulemakers often specify which materials the straps should be made from: typically, nylon or dacron polyester. They also lay down rules governing the type of buckles employed: quick-release buckles are essential.

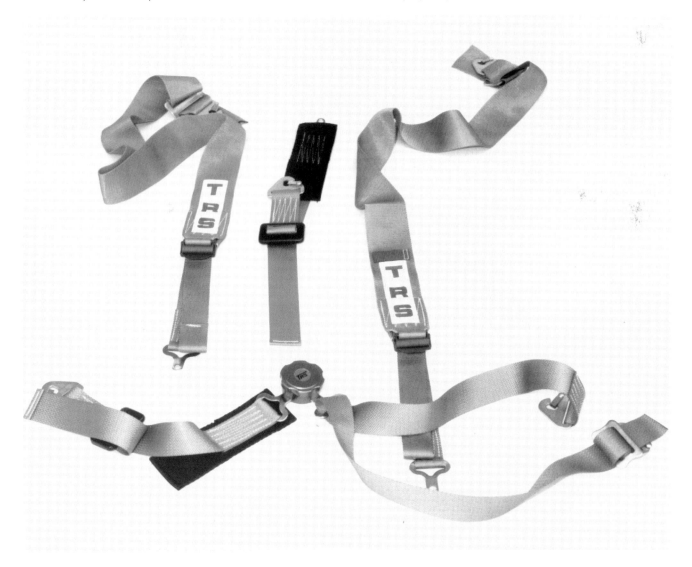

pull the top of the seat to see if it rocks back and forth. Aluminium subframes are supplied with the seat. They will already be attached to threaded bolts bonded to the seat shell, so all you need do is ensure that the subframes are fixed securely to the floor pan.

Note that a race-specification seat must be fitted within the parameters of adjustment of the original seat – though the regulations permit the standard mountings to be modified, in order to provide room for the lightweight subframes. Under no circumstances should the original runners be employed: the new seat should be fixed in one position, even though this can create difficulties in the case of multi-driver events.

The fitting method varies from car to car. Some competitors weld supporting brackets to the floor pan first, then bolt the seat subframes onto them, but we feel that's overkill. Indeed, in some championships this is illegal, because the tech inspectors then consider the brackets to be a part of the bodyshell, and adding material directly to the shell is usually contrary to the regulations. That said, there's been some softening of official attitudes in this direction of late, so assess the latest regulatory situation

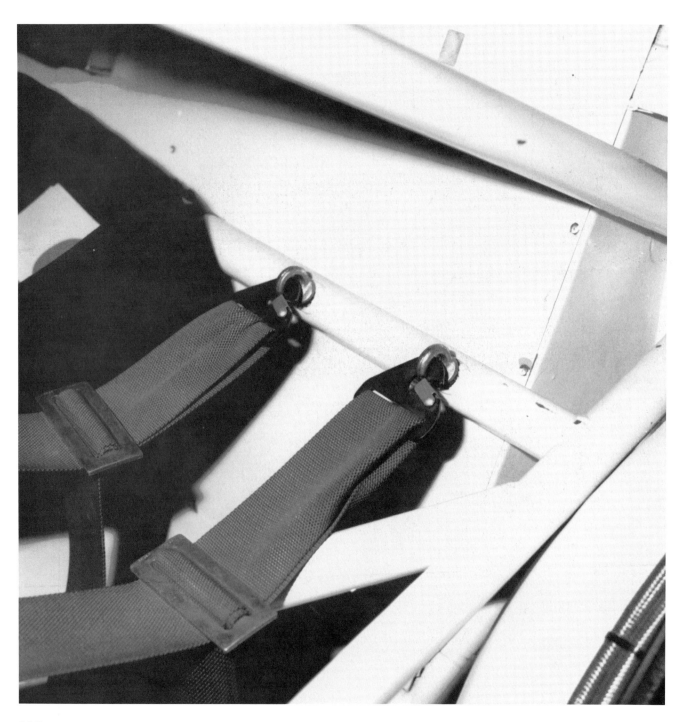

before committing yourself.

In some championships, the regulations stipulate that the back of the driver's must seat be secured to the roll cage main hoop, or to its cross bracing, so as to provide additional anchorage in the event of an accident.

With the other seats, it's usually permissable for competitors to position the seat backs as they please. The ideal configuration, in our view, is to have the back of the passenger seat pushed back as far as it will go, and the rear seat backs pushed fully forward, to lie almost flat, as this arrangement facilitates rapid evacuation of the car in an emergency.

If a race-specification driver's seat has been fitted, you can replace the standard seat belts with a safety harness. Race- specification seats feature five slots to accommodate alternative safety harness installations: there are two slots near the top for the shoulder straps, two at the sides for the lap straps, and one near the front, should the competitor wish to fit crotch straps. You should already have reinforced the attachment points (Chapter 2), and will also have consulted the regulations as to whether a four-, five-, or even six- point harness must be fitted. The rulemakers often specify which materials the straps should be made from – typically, nylon or dacron polyester – and usually stipulate what width they should be. They also lay down rules governing the type of buckles employed: quick-release buckles are essential.

Installation of the harnesses should present no difficulties. Take care to ensure that the straps aren't twisted. If you're attaching the shoulder straps to the rear strut brace of the roll cage, as opposed to the floor pan, consult your harness supplier and roll cage supplier for advice as to the safest fitting method.

Two alternative shoulder strap installations: attached to the floor pan (below), and attached to the rear strut brace of the roll cage (left). Consult your harness supplier and roll cage supplier for advice as to the safest fitting method.

There are two slots near the top of the seat for the shoulder straps, two at the sides for the lap straps, and one near the front to accommodate crotch straps.

Weight watching

One of the most difficult tasks in race car preparation is achieving an equitable weight distribution when rebuilding the car. Seasoned campaigners have elevated this aspect of race preparation to the level of an art form, giving them an edge over their less experienced opponents.

A car will perform better on the racetrack if it is well balanced. In a perfect world, all four tires would bear an equal proportion of the car's weight, allowing them to perform with equal efficiency. In the real world, of course, that's virtually impossible to achieve. With most cars, the position of the engine concentrates weight on the front wheels. The position of the driver has a similar effect, except that he is also positioned asymmetrically, concentrating more weight on one side of the car than the other.

Whilst recognizing that you can't achieve perfection, you can attempt to improve the car's weight distribution as much as possible.

The nature of the regulations is such that most of the car's fittings must remain in their original positions. Nevertheless, the rulemakers offer some latitude with respect to a handful of items. For example, the manner in which a fuel cell is installed offers scope for altering the car's weight distribution, there being cells of different shapes to fit in a variety of locations. In some championships, the position of the battery can be altered. This may only represent a minor weight shift, but every little helps.

In some championships, the regulations state that ballast may be fitted to bring the car up to a specified minimum weight. In these circumstances, the rulemakers don't specify where the ballast should be mounted: they merely stipulate that it should be located in a safe and readily identifiable position. Therefore, the siting of ballast provides yet more scope for improving a car's weight distribution – but check the regulations first, as carrying ballast is strictly illegal in many championships.

Among the other items of hardware which can be sited with a view to improving the overall weight distribution is the fire extinguisher.

Whether you take weight distribution into account or not, always be diligent about *reducing* the weight of the car. This is one of the gray areas in this category of motorsport, and some competitors reduce the weight of their car by leaving certain items of equipment out – those which are not readily apparent. In doing so, they run the very real risk of detection and stiff penalties. Some unscrupulous competitors 'graduate' from gray areas into black, engaging in such practices as removing material from the insides of the doors, which is highly illegal. There's no shortage of ways to break the rules, but we strongly recommend that you stick to the straight and narrow.

That said, it's perfectly legal to look at every single part of the car and decide if the regulations allow it to be left out. If your car has twin-tone horns, for example, you may be able to take one off. Depending on the wording of the regulations, you may be able to take them *both* off.

If you want to get serious about reducing the weight of your car, and wish to experiment with redistributing the weight to best effect, you must invest in some specialized equipment. You'll need a set of cornerweight scales – in order to quantify how the weight is being redistributed as you build the car – together with a sturdy set of domestic scales.

Assuming you're starting with a complete car, take it to a weighbridge before disassembling it: alternatively, ascertain the manufacturer's published weight. Also check the cornerweights. This provides two baselines from which to work: the overall weight, and the weight bias. It's impractical to keep going back to the weighbridge while the car is being reassembled, as it isn't mobile. However, now that you know how much weight you need to add or lose in certain areas, you can weigh the various items of equipment the regulations allow you to relocate and position them accordingly.

Conduct this exercise on paper initially. Later, when the car is back on its wheels, you'll be able to verify your calculations on the weighbridge and cornerweight scales. Always make cornerweight measurements with the driver on board, to allow for the asymmetric weight bias.

Domestic scales will allow you to make an ongoing series of weight calculations, adding and subtracting known weights. For example, the regulations allow the car's standard seat to be replaced by a race-specification bucket seat. Weigh the original seat when you remove it, and deduct the weight of the new bucket seat that's going in, thereby obtaining an aggregate figure.

The rulemakers generally allow the floor carpet to be removed. Weigh the carpeting that comes out and deduct that from the overall weight of the car. The same applies to the other things that won't be reinstalled.

Bear in mind the allowances the rulemakers have prescribed for items of safety equipment: specifically the roll cage and the fire extinguisher. In a typical championship, there might be three weight allowances for three different levels of roll cage sophistication, and a uniform weight allowance for the fire extinguisher. In Britain, there may also be a weight allowance for an airjack system.

When you make your calculations, start with the approved – or known – weight of your particular model. Add the appropriate allowances to arrive at an interim figure, then deduct from that the various aggregate weight savings you intend making during the course of the rebuild. This produces the theoretical 'dry' weight of your car. The rulemakers usually specify a 'wet' weight, which must include the weight of the oil in the engine, and possibly even the screenwash water.

It's a complicated business!

The degree to which you engage in 'weight watching' depends entirely on how much confidence you have in your ability to make accurate weight calculations, and – based on those – meaningful alterations to the car's overall weight and its weight distribution.

Doors, windows and mirrors

The regulations usually specify that both the driver door and the passenger door must be capable of being opened from either inside the vehicle or outside, for safety reasons. In some cases, the inner door panels may be replaced, and additional pockets added to them.

Electric windows, a 'luxury item' in roadgoing use, aren't particularly desirable when a car is destined for competition. The problem is that electric window mechanisms tend to be fairly heavy, so its better to remove them. However, the regulations usually state that the windows must be capable of being opened and closed by some mechanical means, so you must acquire and install another set of doors fitted with conventional window winder mechanisms (corresponding 'as standard' mechanisms from the same model).

Acquire these from an auto breaker, if at all possible, as brand new doors – or new mechanisms and replacement door trim panels – will cost you dear.

In some championships, the regulations state that a car cannot compete unless the driver and passenger windows are either open, or removed altogether. This is to aid access by racetrack rescue personnel in the event of an accident.

In both cases, a window net must be securely firmly across the driver window to prevent the occupant's arms from flailing out in an accident. The rulemakers lay down requirements for the fitting of the window net – stipulating that it must be attached to the roll cage, for example – and also place constraints on the materials used: plastic buckles and elastic straps are prohibited.

Many of the comments we ascribed to electric windows apply to electrically adjustable mirrors. Their mechanisms are fairly heavy, so they are definite candidates for removal. That said, some drivers prefer to have one on the passenger side, as adjusting it during the course of the race allows them to counter overtaking threats!

In a few championships, race-specification external mirrors may be fitted in place of the standard mirrors.

Reinstalling the manual window winder mechanism into a freshly painted door panel. If your car has electric winder mechanisms, and the regulations you're working to permit them to be replaced with manual mechanisms as a weight saving measure, it's best to acquire these from an auto breaker, as brand new doors – or new mechanisms and replacement door trim panels – will cost you dear.

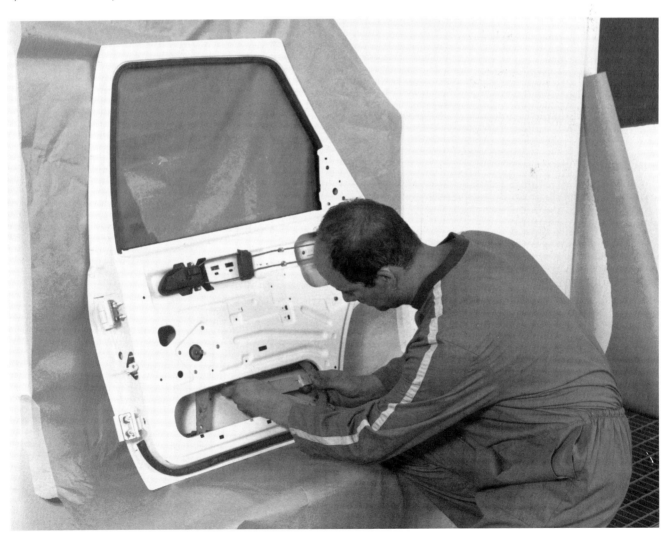

Engine compartment/steering system
Start by reinstalling all of the periphery hardware around the engine compartment: the water reservoir, air box, and so on. All of these items should be checked carefully for damage, then cleaned, beforehand. Most items of equipment within the engine compartment will be reinstalled in their original state, as the rulemakers do not permit much in the way of modifications.

In all but a few championships, the battery can be replaced with a more capable equivalent, the make and capacity of which are unrestricted. That being the case, fit a reputable race-specification unit – but bear in mind that the rulemakers often require the siting of the battery, and its voltage, to conform to the roadgoing specification. If you *can* move the battery, pay attention to the impact this will have on the car's overall weight distribution. Also ensure that the fixing method conforms to the regulations: the rulemakers usually state that the battery must be secured by a tie-down bracket and covered to prevent accidental sparking.

If the regulations permit the battery to be replaced, the associated cabling also can be freely altered. Note that hot leads must be insulated.

The rulemakers generally permit the generator to be replaced by a more powerful unit, to support any supplementary external lights. If you plan to undertake endurance races, you should definitely fit a more capable generator.

At this stage, reinstall the front subframe. Modifications are not permitted.

In virtually every championship, the rulemakers permit the material from which the engine mounting bushes are composed to be altered. This allows the standard bushes to be replaced with equivalent bushes made from a firmer compound. It is not, however, permissable to *increase* the number of engine mounting bushes. There's sound logic behind the concession to fit firmer bushes. Production mounting bushes are a compromize between the need to achieve long-term serviceability and the requirement for effective isolation of engine vibration. In a motorsport environment, the priorities change: long-term serviceability takes second place to durability, and the driver must learn to live with higher vibration levels.

When an engine is being driven hard, powerful torque reactions and considerable inertia forces exert themselves on the mountings. Firmer bushes can help keep these forces in check, and are capable of withstanding the excessive stresses and strains of vigorous driving. Coincidentally, firmer bushes make a contribution to the overall rigidity of the car, reducing the tendency of the bodyshell to flex under heavy cornering loads.

In most cases, the regulations state that replacement engine mounting bushes must bear a recognized serial number, proving that they are genuine aftermarket versions and not 'demon' parts.

Once the new bushes are in place, hoist in the freshly race-prepared engine – with the gearbox attached, if required. When the engine has been tightened down, systematically remove the small plastic caps the engine-tuner has inserted in each orifice. Then, unless the rulemakers specifically prohibit it, fit lengths of aviation-specification flexible piping and unions in place of the standard rubber hoses and hose clips. You'll be applying this formula to almost all of the engine/car interfaces: the lines to oil coolers, the water connections, and lines to gauges and senders. Upgrading these to a higher specification offers protection from excessive heat and vibration, enhancing reliability.

Recognizing the strains to which it will be subjected, the rulemakers normally allow the standard accelerator cable to be replaced with one more suitable for competition use, or doubled by another cable.

Usually, the regulations stipulate that the standard engine ducting must be retained. It's very important – particularly with a turbocharged engine – that all of the ducting is properly routed, in order to give the intercooler the best possible chance of performing efficiently. Attention should be paid to clearances between the ducting and the hood, to ensure that under-hood temperatures don't rocket. You should also exercise care when siting wires, or the turbo might melt them.

The regulations usually permit sheets of aluminiumized, quilted matting to be placed over vulnerable items: those that might either fail due to excessive heat, or simply catch fire. Falling into that category are the alternator, the distributor, parts of the wiring harness, the throttle and clutch cables, and those parts of the fuel system which might

116

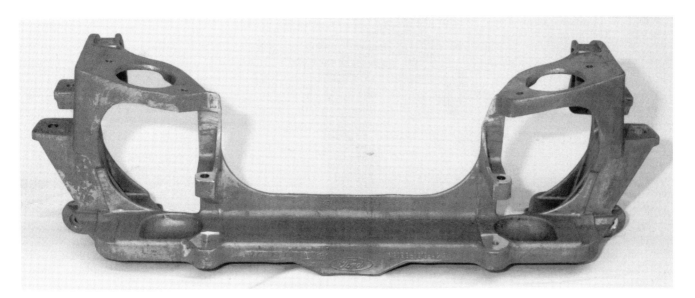

suffer from vaporization problems if subjected to excessive heat. You should also employ heat-resistant quilting to isolate heat sources. Lag the exhaust manifold, for instance.

A most effective way to protect large items from thermal distress is to fabricate an aluminium shield and pop rivet it to the engine compartment wall with brackets, positioned so as to lie between the heat source and the item you wish to protect. Line the shield with the foil matting, and you'll find that this type of shield lasts almost indefinitely.

Attention to detail in preventing thermal distress within the engine compartment is a significant aid to reliability, and is consequently of major importance.

Reinstall all of the periphery hardware around the engine compartment: the water reservoir, air box (as seen at right), and so on. All of these items should be checked carefully for damage, and then cleaned, beforehand. Most items of equipment within the engine compartment will be reinstalled in their original state, as the rulemakers do not permit much in the way of modifications.

The front subframe should be refitted in an unmodified state.

There isn't much scope for improving the engine cooling capability. Extra water radiators aren't usually permitted in this category of motorsport, but extra *oil* radiators can be fitted in some cases. The best location varies from one model to another, but tends to be directly in front of the standard water radiator. Under most sets of regulations, the temperature at which the cooling fan cuts in can be adjusted. Thermostats operate on electrical resistance, so all you need to do is put a resistor in line, or fit a different sender switch.

While you're working in the vicinity of the engine compartment, reinstall those elements of the steering system which reside there. Modifying these is prohibited. Therefore, if power steering was standard equipment, it must remain fitted and functioning. Also fit the trackrod ends, track control arms (renew the bushes first) and front wheel hubs.

Fit the exhaust system at this point: either the standard exhaust, or a race-prepared version, depending upon

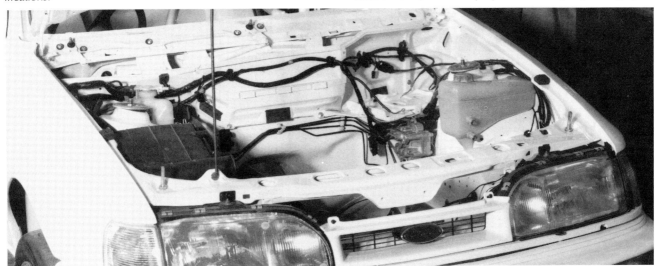

If the regulations permit it, remove the standard engine mounting bushes and replace them with equivalent bushes made from a firmer compound. When an engine is being driven hard, powerful torque reactions and considerable inertia forces exert themselves on the mountings. Firmer bushes can help keep these forces in check, and are capable of withstanding the excessive stresses and strains of vigorous driving.

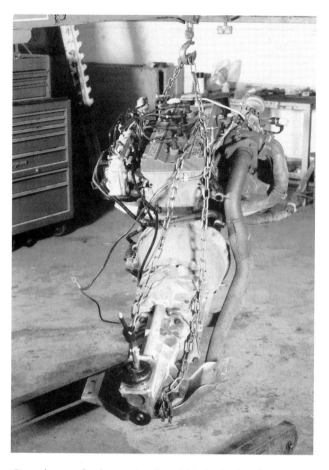

There isn't much scope for improving the engine cooling capability. Extra water radiators aren't usually permitted in this category of motorsport, but extra oil radiators can be fitted in some cases. The best location varies from one model to another, but tends to be directly in front of the standard water radiator.

Once the new bushes are in place, hoist in the freshly race-prepared engine – with the gearbox attached, if required. When the engine has been tightened down, systematically remove the small plastic caps the engine-tuner has inserted in each orifice.

Also fit the trackrod ends, track control arms (renew the bushes first) and front wheel hubs.

what the regulations permit. A race-prepared exhaust can be equipped with sturdier mountings than the usual rather flimsy rubber and wire ones. Specify the 'cotton reel' type, which are threaded at both ends, enabling the exhaust pipe to be bolted under the car in a much more positive manner. It's a good idea to loop a length of lockwire under the exhaust pipe at various points, to prevent it dragging along the racetrack if it happens to break free for any reason. This is a very worthwhile precaution against a guaranteed black flagging offence.

Finally, if you're going to fit a turret brace, wait until the engine compartment has been fully outfitted, or it'll get in the way.

If you're going to fit a turret brace, wait until the engine compartment has been fully outfitted, or it'll get in the way. The installation seen here is on a Honda Civic VTEC.

Transmission

Before turning to the transmission elements, deal with the rear beam. In most championships, this must be reinstalled in an unmodified state – though it's usually permissable to mount it on firmer bushes. That being the case, check it carefully for signs of damage and clean it thoroughly before refitting it. There are some championships in which the rear beam can be reinforced with steel plates, welded on, provided they conform to the shape of the standard beam and are in total contact with it. The places requiring reinforcement are those where flexing takes place: obviously, this varies from one model to another.

Although the build quality of transmissions in modern roadgoing cars tends to be very high, they weren't designed for the rigors of racing. As a result, they represent the weak link in this category of motorsport. The rulemakers prohibit competitors from exchanging the standard transmission components with those of other models, and ban the use of alternative gear ratios and special materials. Consequently, there's limited scope for improvement. However, provided the regulations you're working to don't specifically prohibit it, there *are* certain steps which can be taken to improve not only the reliability of the transmission, but also its performance.

The art of blueprinting, described in the Introduction and Chapter 3, is applied almost exclusively to the contents of the engine compartment, but certain elements of the transmission – particularly within the gearbox – can also benefit. The techniques involved are highly specialized, and should be entrusted to an expert. By paying fastidious attention to detail, he can improve on the standard build quality of gearboxes, differentials and CWPs – always working within the manufacturer's published tolerances, so as not to infringe the regulations.

A key facet of blueprinting a drivetrain is ensuring that all of the clearances are correct: the backlash between the teeth, for example. Excessive pinion preloads and side loads can sap engine power, so these are controlled by shimming. This minimizes frictional losses while at the same time ensuring that there is sufficient preload to keep the bearings running correctly in their outer cases under all circumstances. The transmission specialist will also seek to ensure that the selector mechanism functions properly, and has the correct amount of travel.

Gearbox: Typically, when a specialist conducts a thorough examination, he'll find that 90 percent of the gears and final drive ratios require deburring. Using a rotary file, he'll carefully remove all the minute rough edges, thereby reducing those power losses attributable to friction. The specialist will also shot peen the gears and final drive ratios to 'stress relieve' them: this has the effect of hitting them with millions of tiny hammer blows, dimpling what was previously a smooth surface. As a result, there'll be no stress lines along which cracks can develop.

Almost by accident, shot peening also provides a surface finish which is more conducive to oil retention.

In the past, specialists would 'lap in' the gears, running them in against each other with a very fine abrasive paste to remove any minute high spots. This is rarely necessary with modern production gears, which are manufactured to much more exacting standards. Once a gearbox has been run on the open road for a half hour or so, any high spots that were present will have disappeared anyway.

The quality of the lubricant you use is vitally important: as important as anything you can do to improve the performance of the transmission. Replace the standard oil with the best hypoid gear oil available: TQF or ATF. These are very high temperature, low viscosity oils (less drag in the gearbox) which also provide better coverage on the gears than conventional lubricants.

Drivetrain: The clutch unit must remain as standard, with one exception: in most cases, it's permissable to replace the standard clutch disc with one better suited to the high

In most championships, the rear beam must be reinstalled in an unmodified state – though it's usually permissable to mount it on firmer bushes. There are some championships in which the rear beam can be reinforced with steel plates, welded on, provided they conform to the shape of the standard beam and are in total contact with it. The places requiring reinforcement are those where flexing takes place: obviously, this varies from one model to another.

In this category of motorsport, the rulemakers do not permit the driveshafts to be modified – only balanced – but standard driveshafts usually cope very well with the stresses and strains of racing and it's unlikely you'll have any trouble with them.

wear rate experienced in competition use, provided its surface area does not exceed that of the original item. Before you fit the replacement clutch disc, carefully measure its thickness to provide a baseline for monitoring its wear rate. The thickness should then be measured after every three events, as detailed in Chapter 5.

In this category of motorsport, the rulemakers do not permit the driveshafts to be modified, but standard driveshafts usually cope very well with the stresses and strains of racing and it's unlikely you'll have any trouble with them. Likewise, the standard driveshaft couplings must be retained. What *can* help is hiring a specialist to ensure that the driveshafts are perfectly balanced, using small weights. He can also dismantle the driveshaft CV joints and polish all the grooves and edges in the tracks using a rotary file with wet-or-dry paper. This 'eases' them, improving their performance by ensuring that they run freely.

Matching of compatible components is rare but we do know of some specialists who select elements from several drivetrains to obtain components with complementary weights. For competitors with virtually unlimited finances and an obsessive approach to preparation, this is fine – provided the manufacturer's published tolerances are observed at all times.

Certain elements of the transmission, particularly within the gearbox, can benefit from blueprinting. The techniques involved are highly specialized, and should be entrusted to an expert. By paying fastidious attention to detail, he can improve on the standard build quality of gearboxes, differentials and CWPs – always working within the manufacturer's published tolerances.

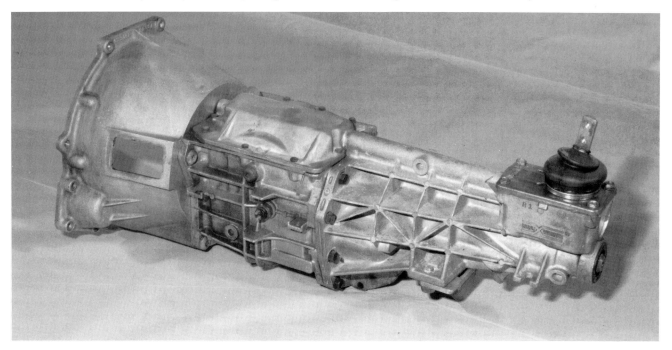

If a model features a torque-biasing differential as either standard equipment, or as a manufacturer's available option, this may be retained. In a few championships, competitors are permitted to fit one in any case, provided no modification to any standard part or housing takes place. If your car has a limited slip differential (LSD) fitted as original equipment, this may be retained, but the rulemakers generally prohibit race-specification units.

If a model features a torque-biasing differential as either standard equipment, or as a manufacturer's available option, this may be retained. In a few championships, competitors are permitted to fit one in any case, provided no modification to any standard part or housing takes place. Check the regulations to ascertain if the differential may be locked, if that's your preference. Very little can be done to improve its performance, but it should certainly be inspected to ensure that it's in tip-top condition if you can't afford to have it blueprinted. If your car has a limited slip differential (LSD) fitted as original equipment, this may be retained, but the rulemakers generally prohibit competitors from fitting a race- specification unit.

In a perfect world, steps would be taken to ensure that all of the drivetrain elements are properly aligned, one to the other, in rear-wheel-drive cars. Unfortunately, the vast majority of modern production cars offer no means of adjusting the alignment of the propeller shaft elements. These are installed on rubber bushes on the production line – end of story.

Note that, in some championships, the rulemakers specify that two 360-degree steel loops should be fitted as close as possible to the front and rear universal joints, of sufficient strength to prevent the propeller shaft from dropping in the case of a failure in either joint.

Suspension

The rulemakers limit the degree to which modifications can be made in this area: part of their policy of upholding the roadgoing pedigree of the cars. In championships where only minimal modifications are permitted, the suspension must remain totally standard and competitors can do no more than adjust the factory suspension settings within the normal range. In the majority of championships, however, there's some scope for modifications. It's usually permissable to replace the standard dampers and springs with race-specification versions, provided they are fitted in the original positions: that is to say, the springs must be mounted in the standard spring cups.

Installing these is no different from fitting the original parts.

Race-specification dampers and springs are designed for rigidity, combined with an ability to compress and extend progressively. They should also provide a realistic 'feel' to the driver, and perform consistently – behaving the same on the first lap as they do on the last, with no appreciable degeneration. Heat is the primary enemy of consistency. As the damper does its work, heat builds up within it. In a roadgoing car, this heat dissipates very rapidly, as the damper workload is seldom excessive in street use. Another contributor to the heat build up in dampers in a racing environment is the brakes, which are in close proximity and transmit their heat through the wheel hubs. The temperature of the dampers typically will rise from ambient to 210degF (100degC) during the course of a race.

Needless to say, this heat build up has an effect on the oil within the dampers: its viscosity tends to degrade. Special synthetic-based oils (damper fluids) have been developed for racing dampers. Their viscosity remains stable over a wide temperature range, ensuring consistency of performance.

The type of dampers you fit will depend very much on your budget. There's an approximately four-fold price increase between the two types of damper available for this category of motorsport. One is an upgraded version of the standard roadgoing damper, with new internals, valving and oil, but no structural alterations. The other is a dedicated race- specification, gas-pressurized damper. The latter is adjustable, by means of a 'key', so the driver can have the damper rate altered to suit his own particular technique, as well as the prevailing racetrack conditions.

Damper manufacturers offer three alternative adjustment modes: one in which the rate the damper is both compressed and extended is adjustable; one in which the rate of compression can be adjusted in relation to the rate of extension, which remains constant; and one in which the rate of compression remains constant, while the rate of extension is adjustable. The most expensive of the three designs is the one which facilitates 'two-way' adjustment. Of the other two, there's little to choose between them in terms of cost.

Like the dampers, race-specification springs are much more robust than their roadgoing counterparts. The reg-

In championships where only minimal modifications are permitted, the suspension must remain totally standard and competitors can do no more than adjust the factory suspension settings within the normal range. In the majority of championships, however, it's permissable to replace the standard dampers and springs with race-specification versions, provided they are fitted in the original positions.

Race-specification dampers and springs are designed for rigidity, combined with an ability to compress and extend progressively. They should also provide a realistic 'feel' to the driver, and perform consistently – behaving the same on the first lap as they do on the last, with no appreciable degeneration.

ulations generally state that they must be of the original gauge, but the spring-rate can be altered to improve the car's handling. Spring-rate is expressed in poundage: typically, it might be 700-800lb (320-360kg), but it can be as high as 1500lb (680kg).

The ways in which suspension adjustments can be made to improve the car's handling are described in Chapter 5.

Rulemakers normally permit the suspension to be lowered considerably, to reduce the car's center of gravity, but a minimum ride height is also specified. Of course, this is only possible if the standard dampers and springs have been replaced with much shorter, race-specification versions. However, the car must be capable of being pushed over a wooden block of the specified height, clearing it without anything on the underside making contact. Reinforcing the suspension is prohibited in most championships, but where exceptions are made there's scope to increase the length, width, thickness and vertical curvature of leaf springs and the diameter of torsion bars.

In most cases, the standard antiroll bars must be retained, but all the rubber bushes in the rear axle and in the front suspension can be replaced with race-specification versions. These are very hard, and therefore flex less, making the car more stable under high cornering, braking and acceleration forces.

When reinstalling the suspension, replace any dirt shields back into the wheelwells, reattach them to the small steel tabs, then tap the tabs back on themselves with a flat-faced hammer so that there's no risk of them fouling the tires (see Chapter 2).

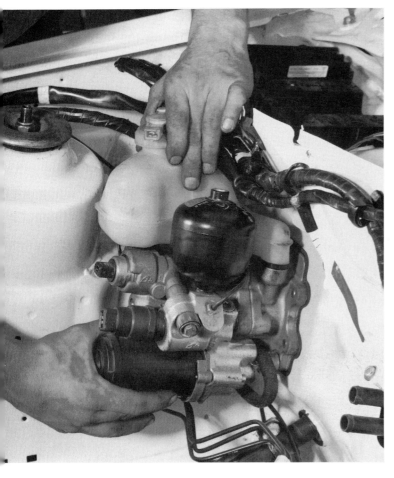

Reinstalling an ABS. It can be engaged or disconnected to suit the driver. However, the rulemakers rarely permit an ABS to be removed from the car altogether – which is a pity, because they're very heavy!

Brake system

Antilock braking system (ABS): Cars are prohibited from running with an ABS in some championships, but in most – provided it's an 'optional extra' on the model concerned – the car can run with it. If your car is equipped with an ABS and the regulations you're working to don't specifically prohibit them, you have the choice of either racing the car with the system functioning, or disconnecting it. The rulemakers rarely permit an ABS to be removed from the car altogether – which is a pity, because they're very heavy!

Whether you disconnect the ABS, or opt to use it, is entirely a matter of personal preference. It depends a lot on the competitor, and his level of experience. Some drivers are of the opinion that they can brake better without it – getting a better 'feel' for the corners – but an increasing number of competitors these days are using ABS. They find they're less likely, in a panic situation where they stamp on the brake pedal, to flatspot their tires if the ABS is functioning.

There are limitations, of course. A roadgoing ABS isn't as effective as one optimized for racetrack use. In certain conditions – especially on the bumpier circuits, or if the car is driven over kerbs or 'rumble strips' a lot – the ABS sensor becomes saturated and will then operate intermittently. Such unpredictability would be dangerous under any circumstances, but in the competition environment it is especially hazardous. You can't avoid this problem by operating the master switch during the course of the race, disengaging then reengaging the ABS, because that's prohibited.

If you opt to disconnect your ABS, simply locate the sensors and unplug them.

Brake proportioning valve: In many championships, it's permissable to fit a race-specification brake proportioning valve, so that the braking bias, front-to-rear, can be altered. A brake proportioning valve reduces the hydraulic pressure to the rear brakes, but doesn't effect the front brakes: if it altered all four units, that would only increase the pedal effort required. The same amount of pressure is inherent in the system, but differently proportioned, back to front. Think of it as a 'check' in the brake system which allows the effectiveness of the pair at the rear to be adjusted in relation to the pair at the front as an aid to balanced braking.

In a few cases, brake proportioning valves are only permitted if the model in question already had one in its original production form. Check the regulations carefully to ascertain the status of brake proportioning valves in the championship you intend to contest.

A brake proportioning valve, if fitted as standard, is normally 'hidden' about two feet aft of the handbrake, and is only adjusted during maintenance. In this category of motorsport, there are tight restrictions on its use: the driver cannot alter the braking bias during the course of the race. To ensure that this ruling is observed, the rulemakers generally stipulate that the brake proportioning valve must be located out of the driver's reach, so adjustments can only be made in the pits or the paddock.

Different groups of rulemakers go to varying lengths to ensure that the driver can't alter the braking bias out on the racetrack. Some sets of regulations even state that the bias-adjuster must be situated in a separate compartment from the driver. In most cases, however, the regulations simply state that the valve must be fitted in the same compartment area as the standard proportioning valve, and in the *approximate region* of the standard unit.

If you're going to fit a brake proportioning valve, do so at the same time as you install all the aviation-specification piping, using the same type of unions. The valve should be set into the length of piping which connects the front brake units to the rear, and be bolted firmly to the floor pan.

Calipers: The standard brake calipers must be retained. Check the original units carefully for damage or excessive wear before reinstalling them, then either reconnect them to the original pipework, or fit the appropriate unions and connect them to the aviation-specification piping if you installed that earlier.

Cooling: Almost universally, competitors are permitted to fit racing-type cooling ducts in place of the original ducting, but usually only to the *front* brakes. In most cham-

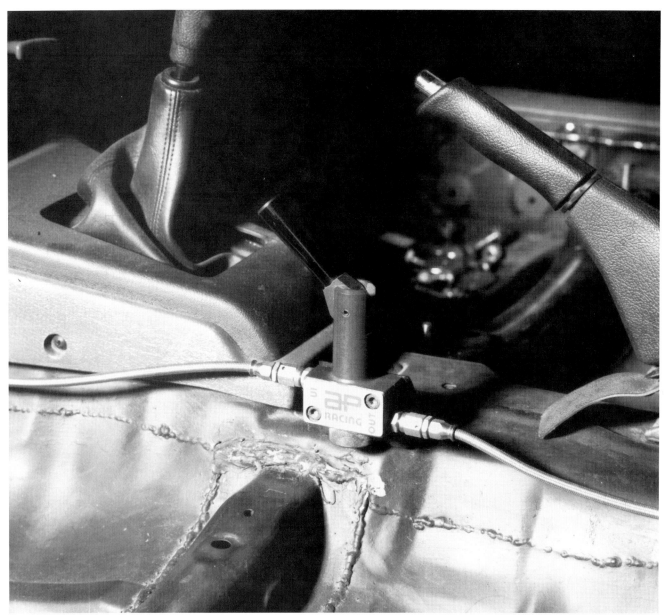

It's sometimes permissable to fit a race-specification brake proportioning valve, so the braking bias, front-to-rear, can be altered. Fit this at the same time as you install all the aviation-specification piping, using the same type of unions. The valve should be set into the length of piping which connects the front brake units to the rear, and bolted firmly to the floor pan.

pionships, the bodywork must not be modified to accept the ducts, nor may the ducts protrude beyond the planform (the car's outline as viewed from directly above). Usually, the regulations state that there can be no more than one pipe per wheel, and specify a maximum diameter and cross- sectional area. However, it's permissable to have a split duct arrangement, in which a single pipe branches into two pipes, provided the cumulative diameter of the two pipes does not exceed the regulatory maximum. This arrangement can be adopted if you wish to direct cooling air to the disc and the caliper simultaneously.

Fit as much ducting as the regulations permit, as the brakes will need all the help you can give them. The ducting can be purchased from any good motorsport accessory supplier, but you'll have to fabricate the adaptors which fit at either end. Cut 0.06in (1.5mm) thick sheet steel or aluminium into shapes which can be folded and welded or pop riveted to fit your particular vehicle. It's a time-consuming and somewhat arduous task taking the various measurements and fabricating the rather intricate shapes, but it's well worth the effort.

Attach the adaptors to the hubs, or to the uprights: the rulemakers do not permit you to physically add brackets to these elements, so you must attach the adaptors to the existing pinch bolts, or to the locking nuts, the track control arms, or the caliper bolts. Use saddles and tie wraps, pop rivets, or hose clips to attach the adaptors to the plastic ducting, and fix the ducting to the bodywork with saddles and tie wraps.

Depending on the specific brake cooling requirements of the model concerned, ducting arrangements can vary considerably. That said, you should always ensure that the air is aimed directly at the very center of the inner surface of the brake disc, right next to the hub. The vanes on the disc will carry the cooling air from the inside outwards to best effect. Well-funded competitors can afford to experiment, trying different ducting layouts then making a series of comparative measurements with a temperature gauge. Unfortunately, these are expensive, and beyond the means of the average privateer.

There's further scope for cooling the brakes if the regulations you're working to permit protection plates and dust shields to be ventilated, bent, or even removed altogether (the rulemakers rarely permit material to be added here). In very rare cases – only, to our knowledge, in Class A of SCCA Pro Racing's World Challenge series – wheel fans may be fitted.

Water cooled brakes are universally prohibited.

Discs: To maintain the roadgoing nature of the cars, the regulations usually stipulate that the standard brake discs must be retained. Race-specification discs – carbonfiber ones, for example – are prohibited. However, if the original manufacturer produces ventilated discs for your particular model, it's permissable to run them in most championships.

Handbrake: In most championships, the handbrake must be retained in its standard form. Under some sets of regulations it may be removed, while in others, the mechanism of the handbrake lever may be adapted to facilitate instant locking: the so-called 'fly-off handbrake'.

Master cylinder: The master cylinder should be reinstalled at the same time as the pedal box, after checking and cleaning. It cannot be modified in any way.

Pads: Competitors can replace the standard brake pads with race-specification versions in every championship except SCCA Club Racing's Showroom Stock category. The pads can be either rivetted or bonded to the calipers, but the production disc-to-pad contact area must not be increased.

Race-specification pads are more hard-wearing than standard roadgoing pads, and aren't so prone to brake fade. The type of pads you fit depends very much on the nature of the circuit and the length of the race (more details in Chapter 5).

The ultimate pads are of the carbon metallic variety, but these are very expensive. Carbon metallic pads have

In virtually every championship, competitors are permitted to replace the standard brake pads with race-specification versions.

In most championships it is permissable to fit special race-specification foot pads in place of the standard rubber pads. They can be angled to suit the driver, have anti-slip surfaces, and are specially shaped to facilitate the 'heel and toe' technique.

lots of good qualities and very few drawbacks. They have a superior heat dissipation capability, excellent wear characteristics, and perform outstandingly at high temperatures, being virtually impervious to fading. If you decide to run carbon metallic pads, you may not be able to obtain them for your particular model, so you'll have to buy pads for a similar model and use an angle grinder to fashion them to the required shape. Place a standard pad from your car on the back of a carbon metallic pad, and use a can of spray paint to delineate the required shape.

Health and safety note: the rulemakers have steadily outlawed the use of asbestos-lined brake pads in recent years.

Pedal box: The pedal box itself cannot be modified – altering the pivot points to improve the braking efficiency, for example, is not acceptable – but in most championships it is permissable to fit special race- specification foot pads in place of the standard rubber pads. They can be angled to suit the driver, have anti-slip surfaces, and are specially shaped to facilitate the 'heel and toe' technique.

Servo-assisted brakes: If your car is fitted with servo-assisted brakes, the servos may be disconnected so as to provide the driver with more 'feel'. Disconnection is quite straightforward, although for obvious reasons you should exercise great care to ensure that the braking system has remained fully functional when altering the mode of operation of elements within it. To disengage the servo, simply disconnect the vacuum hose.

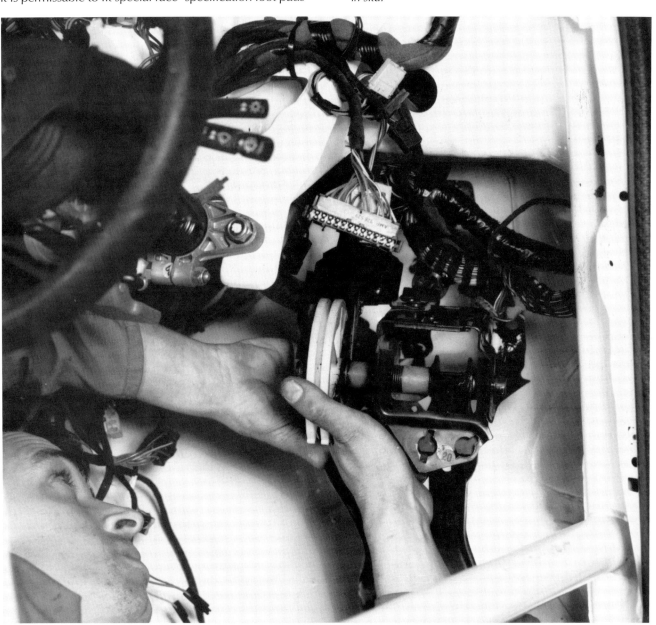

The pedal box itself cannot be modified. Altering the pivot points to improve the braking efficiency, for example, is not acceptable. Just refit it as before, with the race- specification foot pads in situ.

In many championships, the rulemakers permit race-specification wheels amd tires to be fitted. Racing wheels are lighter and better balanced than conventional roadgoing wheels, reducing unsprung weight. They also feature larger beads, for better tire retention, and they're designed to maximize the flow of cooling air over the brake discs.

Wheels/tires

By placing limits on wheels and tires, rulemakers influence the performance of the cars very considerably. Indeed, in certain championships, the regulators reserve the right to adjust the rules governing wheel/tire sizes to achieve equality in vehicle performance, though they usually employ other methods to achieve this goal.

In many championships, the rulemakers permit race-specification wheels to be fitted. However, they must not protrude beyond the car's planform and there are restrictions relating to the effect this has on the car's standard track measurement. Otherwise, rim widths tend to be unrestricted, but the wheel diameter must not exceed that of the standard model. Race-specification wheels are lighter and better balanced than conventional roadgoing wheels, reducing unsprung weight. Racing wheels also feature larger beads, for better tire retention, and they're designed to maximize the flow of cooling air over the brake discs.

In those championships which do not permit race-specification wheels, the standard wheels may be replaced with the manufacturer's aftermarket optional versions. Usually, the regulations state that any hub caps and trim rings must be removed, as they can be hazardous in an accident.

There are also regulations governing fixing methods. Usually, the standard, bolt-on method must be maintained, but in some championships it's permissable to switch to fixing by pins and bolts, provided the number of attachment points corresponds with that of the standard model and the diameter of the threaded part conforms to the production specification.

In most championships, it is permissable to replace the standard wheel bearings, which usually have plastic cases, with bearings featuring metal cases. These are better suited to the rigors of racetrack use, especially the higher wear rate to which bearings are subjected in endurance racing. When you acquire replacement wheel bearings, wash them out thoroughly – despite the fact that they're brand new – and repack them with grease of the highest quality (bearing manufacturers don't always use the best). Be careful not to overpack them, though, as this can lead to overheating or leakage.

It is not permissable to add air extractors to the wheels, and wheel spacers are prohibited.

We deal with the subject of tires in detail in Chapter 5, but you should double-check the regulations to confirm what the tire restrictions are in the championship you plan to contest. All you need at this point is one set of tires for the car to stand on. In several championships, the rulemakers specify that the cars must be fitted with roadgoing tires, though it's usually permissable in such circumstances for these to be of the 'special performance' variety. In other championships, the rulemakers permit the standard tires to be replaced with race-specification covers. As with the wheels, the tires must not protrude beyond the bodyshell planform.

You should already have ensured that the tires aren't going to foul the wheelwell flanges (Chapter 2).

Finishing touches

With the car now fully reassembled in race trim, the 'finishing touches' can be applied. The rulemakers require competitors to present their cars at race meetings in a neat and clean condition. All of the specified race numbers, decals and markings must be in place, either at the time of the pre-race technical inspection, or prior to the start of the first practice session. This isn't a mere nicety: the organizers reserve the right to forbid cars not meeting these requirements from taking part in the race.

Rulemakers specify where the race numbers should be displayed on the car, and there's a mandatory size, width and color for the numbers. It's usual for the organizers to supply the number panels and class identifying letters, while competitors obtain their own numbers. For championships in which the cars are divided into several classes, race numbers are often allocated in batches corresponding to the various denominations, and specific numbers are usually reserved for class winners in the previous season's championship.

The rulemakers also allocate spaces on the car where the logos of the series sponsors should be displayed, and ban other logos from being placed in those regions, thereby establishing a clear link between the sponsors and the series. Typical locations are the doors, the region where the rear license plate would normally be located, and along the top of the windshield. Contrast must be maintained between logos and their background.

Signwriting has become a thing of the past. These days, logos are applied to race cars in the form of 'vinyls': computer generated adhesive characters produced by specialist suppliers. They can be supplied in an infinite range of typefaces. If you've managed to sign a sponsor, the company in question will normally agree to supply its own vinyls and have them applied at the same place where their roadgoing vehicles are dealt with.

While paint schemes are unrestricted, organizers encourage multi-car teams to have slightly dissimilar paint schemes, to aid identification. If you're going to race as part of a team, perhaps pooling resources with a competitor/friend who's running the same model, it's a simple enough matter to spray your front spoiler/air dam a different color to his.

There's a safety dimension to paint schemes, too. The towing eyes should be painted in a contrasting color to aid identification. Dayglo red is good, as it makes them really stand out. Ideally, there should also be a clear visual indication as to where they're located. Paint some small arrows indicting their position – again, in dayglo red – and, if you want to add a really professional touch, have the legend *Tow* applied to each arrow. Traditionally, the regulations stipulate that the location of the external fire extinguisher trigger should be readily visible, and marked with a red symbol bearing the letter E.

Rulemakers specify where the race numbers should be displayed on the car, and there's a mandatory size, width and color for the numbers. It's usual for the organizers to supply the number panels and class identifying letters, while competitors obtain their own numbers.

5
At the racetrack

Having detailed the full race-preparation process, it's appropriate to outline activities at the racetrack. The intention of this short chapter is merely to provide some useful guidelines, as an in-depth description of how to go racing would constitute a book in itself!

Accommodation: The degree to which you'll require overnight accommodation depends on the format of the race meetings you're contesting, and the geographical circumstances. Bear in mind that, for one-day meetings, competitors usually have to arrive at the circuit early in the morning, in order to sign on. If you have to awake at some ungodly hour to get there, you're likely to be jaded by the time you actually drive on the racetrack, which is no way to achieve results.

Some of the better-funded teams have the luxury of motorhome accommodation and sleep at the racetrack, or stay overnight in a local hotel or motel. Members of less well financed outfits get good night's sleep by pitching a tent at the circuit, or improvising beds in the back of their support van.

Air cylinder trolley: Consider making your own four-wheeled 'air trolley', for use in both the workshop and the pits. You may be able to put one adaptor onto three compressed air bottles, thereby providing a supply sufficient to operate four airguns at once during tire-change pitstops.

Brake pads: The type of pads you fit depends very much on the nature of the circuit and the length of the race. For a typical 10-lap race, you'll want the pads to warm up quickly, and won't be particularly concerned if they aren't made to last. Harder-wearing pads will be needed for, say, a 4-hour race. Obviously, these won't be as efficient, but this is tolerable in the interests of having them last the distance.

The rate at which the brake pads should be replaced varies considerably. In SCCA Club Racing's Showroom Stock category, cars must run with their original pads, so the top competitors fit a new set before every outing. Brake pads *must* be bedded in before they're used on the racetrack. Therefore, always have a set of bedded-in pads available, ready to run. Deglaze them during practice, so they're ready for the race itself.

Checklists: Create a set of checklists, to avoid forgetting things in the heat of the moment. It's essential to list the equipment needed for race meetings. Also compile a post-race checklist, to include such items as a compression check.

Clutch disc: Measure the clutch disc prior to installation, then measure it every three events to monitor the wear rate.

Consumables: There's a constant need for adhesive racing numbers, duct tape, cleaning cloths, and so on. There's always at least one supplier's truck in the paddock at races, so you can purchase most of these items there. However, suppliers tend not to be present on test days, so you must carry an independent supply.

Crew clothing: Ensure that everyone who works on the car is suitably clothed. Take gloves, for example. Heat is

Consider making your own four-wheeled 'air trolley', for use in both the workshop and the pits. You may be able to put one adaptor onto three compressed air bottles, thereby providing a supply sufficient to operate four airguns at once during tire-change pitstops.

transmitted from the brake units to the wheels, then to the wheel nuts – which can become very hot indeed. The wheel nuts should be replaced during tire changes, as it's sometimes difficult to get them back on when they're hot. Asbestos- lined gloves provide the necessary protection (plastic ones melt!). The best gloves for the job are the type gardeners wear for pruning roses. These are available from garden centers and home improvement outlets. Alternatively, get a pair of drivers' fireproof gloves. These are more expensive, but offer greater dexterity.

Also wear heat-resistant gloves when changing brake pads, as these get *extremely* hot.

If you're planning to contest a championship which features endurance races, ensure that crew members assigned to operate the overhead refueling rig (see *Refueling*, below) are suitably clothed. They should wear a one- or two-piece suit, socks, hood, gloves and shoes made of approved flame-retardant materials, plus goggles or a full-face helmet equipped with a visor.

Engine oil: Synthetic oil is far superior to regular multi-grades. It's more expensive, but lasts longer. Bear in mind that synthetic oil isn't suitable for running-in, as there's insufficient friction.

Engine rebuilds: While the engine in a roadgoing car should be serviced at intervals ranging from 6,000 to 12,000 miles, the same engine in race specification must be rebuilt much more regularly if it is to deliver optimum performance. Maintenance intervals tend to be based on the number of hours the engine has run, rather than the mileage.

Establish a close liaison with your engine-tuner, and ensure that a strict build code is maintained.

Nutrition: Drivers should consider *themselves*, as well as their car. Precautions should be taken to avoid dehydration in hot conditions, and attention should be paid to diet quality.

Pitlane procedure: Race regulations also govern activities in the pitlane. Here, the emphasis is on safety, and there are stiff penalties for offenders. It is the driver's responsibility to maintain a safe speed in the pitlane, and there is often a mandatory upper limit. There are also regulations pertaining to cars reversing in the pitlane, if only for a short distance – whether they are under their own power or not.

If the rulemakers permit teams to erect temporary structures in the pits – such as timing stands – these must be constructed sturdily and sited safely. Awnings and light poles, and anything else which might extend over the pitlane work area, must be constructed of flame-retardant materials, and the rulemakers specify a mandatory minimum height.

Due to the possible presence of fuel vapor accumulations, gasoline-powered generators and air compressors must either be equipped with spark-arrestors, or sited outside the pit area. For the same reason, smoking and welding are strictly *verboten*, as are any other activities which might create sparks. Cars requiring such work must be moved to the paddock (often under the supervision of a tech inspector or another official).

Anything which extends over the pitlane work area – such as a light pole, as seen here – must be sturdily constructed, and the rulemakers specify a mandatory minimum height.

Further regulations apply to refueling of the car during the course of a race, in those championships where it's permitted: see *Refueling*, below.

Presentation: As well as being neat and clean, and carrying all the required race numbers, decals and markings, cars must not be presented bearing any 'old damage'.

Racewear: The rulemakers specify minimum requirements for the driver's clothing: helmet, suit, underwear, gloves and shoes. Requirements vary from one championship to another. In Britain's Dunlop Rover GTi Championship, racewear is supplied by the organizers. It's not free, however, as the cost is included in the fairly substantial series enrollment fee.

Tech inspectors scrutinize the driver's personal safety equipment at the same time they check his car.

Refueling: In championships featuring endurance races, cars can make pit stops to refuel. Pressurized refueling systems are banned, so overhead gravity-feed refueling rigs are the norm. These rigs are generally built by the teams themselves. They must be stationary (wheels and castors are prohibited), and the rulemakers specify a maximum capacity and overall height. Refueling rigs must be vented to the atmosphere, to prevent an accumulation of fuel vapor, and it's often mandatory for them to be grounded, with a metal stake driven into the ground.

One crew member should operate the dead-man valve at the overhead tank, while another stands nearby with a fire extinguisher at the ready. If fuel is spilled during refueling operations, it should be diluted immediately with water, then cleaned up with oil dry and a broom. The regulations usually stipulate that a pail containing water for this purpose must be readily at hand at all times.

Crew members operating refueling rigs must be suitably clothed: see *Crew clothing*, above.

Tech inspection: Inspection conducted *before* the event is primarily concerned with the safety aspects, to ensure that the car is fit to participate – though there's a certain degree of eligibility assessment, too. Inspection conducted *after* the event is almost wholly concerned with the technical aspects, to confirm eligibility, and the only safety check that's likely is one to ensure that the fire extinguisher is both full and functioning.

Tires: During race meetings, there's generally at least one tire supplier's truck in the paddock. In some championships, the rulemakers limit the quantity of tires assigned to each car at a race meeting, to help the less well financed competitors compete with the big-buck outfits, and generally to contain costs.

In cases where this system is applied, each car typically is limited to six tires per race meeting. If race-specification tires are permitted, those six covers can be of any compound, and the ruling does not apply to tires used in wet weather – nor does it apply to endurance races. At tech inspection, the six tires nominated by each competitor are marked with his race number, with indelible paint. No other dry-weather tires may be fitted, unless they're replaced under the supervision of a tech inspector in the event of a puncture.

Choosing tires when this system is in force can be a tricky business. Competitors must decide before qualifying which six tires they're going to use, and it's not always possible to predict what the weather and track conditions are going to be by the time the race itself starts. For example, if you've chosen dry-weather tires, and the track subsequently becomes a little damp – but not damp enough for wet-weather tires – then you've just got to live with the resultant poor handling.

The subject of tires is dealt with in greater depth in the accompanying sidebar.

Tools: Put tools and other items of equipment away after use, or they may get lost – or even stolen. Worse still, they could get left in the car and jam something during the course of a race.

Tuition: There's a trend towards increasing the general standard of competence amongst competitors. In Britain, for example, the RAC MSA has made it a mandatory requirement for competitors seeking their first competition license – or those who've allowed an earlier license to lapse – to attend an approved racing drivers' school for a special introductory course.

Drivers should consider their capabilities in a realistic manner before embarking on a new championship trail.

Wheel bearings: Apply the 'prevention is better than cure' philosophy. The wheel bearings should be checked every time the car is returned to the paddock, and regreased after every race meeting. Don't overpack them, though, as this could result in overheating, or cause seals to leak.

The frequency of wheel bearing replacements varies from one championship to another. In SCCA Club Racing's Showroom Stock category, even the top competitors change them just once a year: at the mid-season point. They repack them at least once between-times.

Windshield: Use anti-mist spray on the interior surface of the windshield if the heater can't do the job unaided.

It's not permissable to start a race with a damaged windshield. However, if you're unfortunate enough to sustain a broken windshield during qualifying, all is not lost. Contact one of the commercial emergency replacement services immediately, either by means of a cellular phone or the racetrack telephone facilities. All going well, they should be able to fit a new windshield in time for the race.

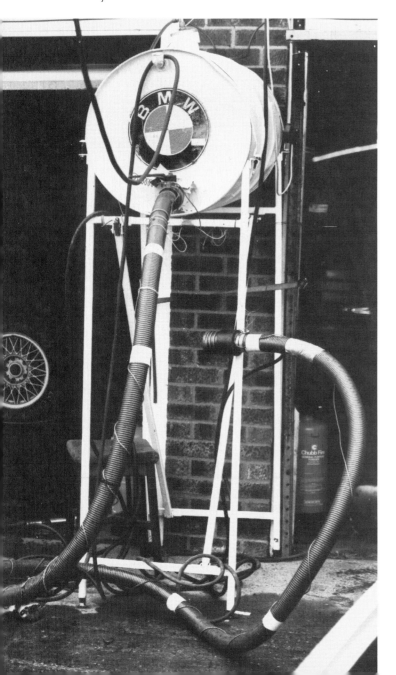

Pressurized refueling systems are banned, so overhead gravity-feed refueling rigs are the norm. These rigs are generally built by the teams themselves. They must be stationary (wheels and castors are prohibited), and the rulemakers specify a maximum capacity and overall height.

Tire talk

If you're going to contest a championship which limits competitors to roadgoing tires, your options are limited. The rulemakers usually specify a tire type (by serial number) for each eligible model. Get the treads of covers you earmark for use in dry conditions buffed down to reduce 'tread squirm'. The amount of tread that can be removed varies according to the championship regulations, but a typical tread depth after buffing is 1/8in (3mm).

Tires earmarked for use in wet conditions should be left as they are, because you need all the tread you can get.

It's essential to put several laps on new tires before they're used in a race – otherwise known as scrubbing the tires in. This does a lot more than just removing the smooth mould finish. Running the tire in an inflated state warms it through, permanently altering its molecular structure. The simple act of putting a few laps on a new tire 'conditions' it for the rest of its working life. It will then behave consistently.

This is achieved at the cost of a slight loss in outright speed capability – but during a race, it's consistency that counts. For qualifying sessions, when outright speed is the aim, use brand new tires (if you can afford them).

If you're contesting a championship which permits race-specification tires, as opposed to roadgoing covers, the car's performance will be greatly enhanced. A racing tire differs from its roadgoing counterpart in three main areas: construction, shape (sometimes called profile), and tread pattern. It's worth looking at each of these in turn.

Construction: The construction of a racing tire differs from a roadgoing tire in respect of both the material which comes into contact with the track surface (the compound) and the materials within the carcass itself.

Race tire compounds are formulated so as to heat up quickly, and to soften further than road tire compounds – reaching optimum grip at around 80degC (175degF). They can run safely at temperatures as high as 110degC (230degF), whereas a road tire seldom runs hotter than 50degC (120degF).

Generally speaking, the softer the compound, the better the grip. Test the different compounds which are available to you, to ascertain which ones suit your car best in a given set of conditions.

A race tire needs to be very stiff, for enhanced response and stability. Its carcass features reinforcing agents which maintain a high stiffness, even when running hot. This concentrates stress in a very localized region of the sidewall construction. Hence, the carcass of a race tire has a limited life before the construction begins to break down. For the same reason, extended running at reduced pressure is not possible.

A road tire, on the other hand, is designed for a long life – and, perhaps, retreading. The stresses caused by sidewall deflections are distributed more evenly, as passenger comfort takes precedence over response.

Shape: Racing tires have a different shape to roadgoing tires – even though, in this category of motorsport, they're to be fitted to wheels of standard, or near-standard, width. In their efforts to optimize this very restrictive mandatory envelope, race tire manufacturers must reconcile their desire to improve grip – by increasing the tire's area of contact with the racetrack (the footprint) – with the need to maintain sidewall stiffness.

Thus, while a typical roadgoing tire is rather 'round' in the area of the bead, a race tire tends to be somewhat slab-sided.

Tread: The tread pattern of a typical roadgoing tire comprizes 70 percent land (blocks) and 30 percent sea (grooves). In order to suit a wide variety of conditions, its design is a compromize between achieving grip on dry road surfaces and achieving grip on wet road surfaces. Greater groove content would lead to block instability – and, hence, a 'vagueness' in handling – while any less grooving would promote aquaplaning, due to the inability of the tire to displace surface water rapidly.

Race-specification tires, on the other hand, are more specialised. There are three basic types of racing tire, each optimized for specific conditions: Slicks have no tread pattern, and are designed for use in dry track conditions; Intermediates have relatively little grooving (representing approximately 20 percent of the total surface area), and are designed for use in damp track conditions in which surface water tends not to be prevalent; and Wets feature wide, deep grooves (representing up to 40 percent of the total surface area), to offer grip in conditions where surface water is prevalent.

Setting up

Setting up is the process of making a combination of adjustments to extract the maximum performance from a car on a particular racetrack. Because cars in this category of motorsport run with their original suspension arrangements, and either their standard shock absorbers and springs or race-specification shock absorbers and springs mounted in the standard locations, the process of setting them up is fairly limited by comparison with setting up a pure race car.

The adjustable parameters are summarized below.

Spring-rates: The car's handling is governed to a large degree by the spring-rates – provided the rulemakers permit race-specification springs to be fitted in place of the standard springs. You should acquire a selection of springs with different spring-rates, to suit specific racetracks and a variety of driving conditions.

Running high spring pressures reduces the tendency of the car to wallow in corners, but can create difficulties when turning-in to a corner, because instead of energy being absorbed by the action of the body of the car heeling over, the loadings are transferred almost directly to the tires, and the car becomes skittish.

Achieving the correct spring settings is a matter of compromize. As a general guideline: the stiffer the spring-rate at the front, the more understeer is induced; and the stiffer the spring-rate at the rear, the more oversteer is induced.

In wet conditions, 'softer' spring rates are required.

Damper-rates: Race-specification dampers can be adjusted by means of a 'key' device, as detailed in Chapter 4. The damper-rate should be adjusted in accordance with adjustments to the spring-rate. Again, the degree of adjustment depends on the prevailing racetrack conditions and the driver's personal style.

Geometry adjustments: By adjusting the angles of the wheels – both relative to the racetrack surface as viewed from the front (camber), and relative to the steering arc of the front wheels (caster) – a car's handling characteristics can be altered considerably.

To quantify the extent to which adjustments are made, a camber/caster gauge is required. This device incorporates a bubble level, and can be affixed to the face of a wheel. By rotating the wheel through 90 degrees with the gauge attached, the camber angle and the caster angle can be measured in turn.

It's important to be able to measure the relative alignments of all four wheels: whether they are toeing-in, toeing-out or parallel. This task is undertaken using a track alignment gauge, which comprizes two near-identical elements, affixed to the outer faces of the wheels on opposing sides of the car. One element bears a sight, while

Paul Chopping, of Mike Taylor Developments, demonstrates the use of a camber/caster gauge. One element of the track alignment ensemble – bearing a mirror – has also been positioned on the wheel, although this is not used in direct conjunction

On the opposite side of the car, the second element of the track alignment ensemble – which bears a sight – has been positioned on the wheel.

the other bears a mirror. By aligning them, the tracking measurement between the two front wheels, or the two rear wheels – they aren't necessarily the same – can be ascertained with great accuracy.

When *adjusting* the camber, caster and track alignment – as opposed to simply checking them – the rear wheels should be mounted on fixed platforms and the front wheels mounted on small turntables. These are normally supplied as part of the geometry equipment kit, and full operating instructions are provided.

By experimenting with geometry adjustments, a driver can arrive at a combination of settings which suit him, his car, and the prevailing racetrack conditions. If you have no prior experience of this process, here are some good settings to start with.

■ Rear-wheel-drive cars: about 1.5deg camber at the front, and 1deg camber at the rear; about 3deg caster; slightly toe-in tracking at the front; parallel tracking at the rear.

■ Front-wheel-drive cars: about 1.5deg camber at the front, and 0.5deg camber at the rear; as much caster as you can get; slightly toe-out tracking at the front; parallel tracking at rear.

■ Four-wheel-drive cars: about 1.5deg camber at the front, and 1deg camber at the rear; about 3deg caster; slightly toe-in tracking at the front; slightly toe-in tracking at the rear.

Tire pressures: The car's behavior can be significantly influenced by adjustments to the tire pressures. With front-wheel-drive cars, increasing the rear tire pressures tends to induce oversteer – because a smaller 'footprint' is in contact with the racetrack surface, reducing grip. Also, if the rear tire pressures are increased beyond a certain level, they heat up to the point where they actually generate *less* grip.

By increasing front tire pressures, understeer can be induced. Lowering the front tire pressures tends to make the car turn-in better – but, obviously, you can only go down so low before it has the reverse effect. And so high, too. If tire pressure is excessive, there's the risk of exceeding the maximum design temperature (particularly with roadgoing tires).

Cornerweights: Cornerweight scales should be used to obtain the optimum balance. It's surprising how far a car's weight distribution can be awry, not only from front to rear, but from one side to the other, and from one corner to the diagonally opposite corner.

You might opt to carry a larger fuel load than is actually necessary to go the race distance, in the interests of improving the overall balance of the car. Cornerweight measurements should be made with the driver aboard.

This Chevrolet Camaro – driven by John Heinricy/Don Knowles in the 1989 Firestone Firehawk Endurance Championship – is understeering slightly.

6

The major championships

UNITED STATES
There are four major championships in this category of motorsport in the USA. Two are sanctioned by the International Motor Sports Association (IMSA), headquartered in Tampa, Florida, and two are administered by the Sports Car Club of America (SCCA), headquartered in Englewood, Colorado. The SCCA comprizes two distinct elements: SCCA Club Racing and SCCA Pro Racing.

Neither organization pays particular attention to the European-based 'global' regulatory structure.

SCCA Club Racing Showroom Stock category
SCCA Club Racing runs the Showroom Stock category for cars presumed to have been purchased primarily for roadgoing use, and the rulemakers leave very little scope for modifications. Not only must the original wheels and tires be retained, but also the standard brake pads and clutch disc!

The brake lining limitation has been criticised in some quarters, on the grounds that it leaves an insufficient safety margin.

With such tight restrictions, the overall standard of preparation becomes more important than ever. Showroom Stock competitors can make adjustments to the suspension within the manufacturer's tolerances, alter the tire pressures, and buff their treads. Roll cages are mandatory, but they must be readily removable, and mustn't extend beyond the cockpit area.

Although the regulations state that overhaul procedures which would increase performance in the slightest way are not to be utilized, and blueprinting and balancing are considered inconsistent with the 'Showroom Stock philosophy', these practices are widespread – for reasons explained in Chapter 1.

There are four classes in Showroom Stock: SSGT, SSA, SSB and SSC. The classes race separately. In contrast to the 'European system', where classes are defined by engine capacity, the SCCA categorizes models according to a combination of parameters. Factors taken into consideration include braking performance, acceleration potential, power-to-weight ratio, delivered tire size, and gearing. The relevant data are then run through a dedicated computer program to indicate which class the model should be assigned to.

Nuances aside, engine capacity and power output provide fairly reliable pointers to the makeup of each class. The most powerful cars tend to find their way into SSGT – the least powerful, into SSC.

There is now a 'gentlemen's agreement' in effect in Showroom Stock, limiting the showroom price for a new car to a maximum of $30,000. This has effectively outlawed models such as the Porsche 944 Turbo and the Honda Acura NSX.

In a country as large as the USA, geographical factors could limit grid sizes in a championship geared to reducing competitors' financial outlay. For this reason, Showroom Stock events are organized on a regional basis. Instead of one all-embracing national series, there are eight divisional Showroom Stock championships. At the end of every season, the top four divisional championship contenders in each of the four classes battle it out for the ultimate honors at the Valvoline Runoffs, held every October at Road Atlanta, Georgia.

The SCCA's eight regional divisions are: Central, Midwest, Northeast, Northern Pacific, Rocky Mountain, Southern Pacific, Southeast and Southwest.

To be eligible for Showroom Stock, models must have had a minimum production output of at least 3,000 units within a 12-month period, and must not be more than four years old. The following models were eligible for the 1992 Showroom Stock season.

SS GT Class
Chevrolet Camaro IROC-Z
Chevrolet Z-28
Chrysler Conquest
Ford Mustang GT and LX
Ford Thunderbird Turbo
Mazda RX-7 Turbo
Mitsubishi 3000 GT (non-turbo)
Mitsubishi Starion ESI-R
Nissan 300ZX Turbo
Pontiac Firebird Trans-Am and Formula
Pontiac Trans-Am
Porsche 924S
Porsche 944
Porsche 944S
Toyota MR2 Turbo
Toyota Supra 3.0 Turbo
Toyota Supra Turbo

(Above) John Wall Jr., driving a Chevrolet Camaro, leads the field en route to a new Showroom Stock GT Class lap record at the SCCA Spring National meeting at Summit Point, West Virginia, in June 1992. His father, placed third here in an identical car, won the race.

(Below) More GT Class action, as Mark Mitchell pilots his Mazda RX-7 Turbo to victory at Texas World Speedway, College Station, in February 1992. Mitchell is being hotly pursued by the Chevrolet Camaro of Tony Matthews.

SS Class A
Alfa Romeo Milano (75)
BMW 325 iS
Chevrolet Beretta GTZ
Dodge Daytona Shelby Turbo
Dodge Shadow Turbo 2.2
Eagle Talon Turbo
Ford Probe GT
Ford Probe 2.2 Turbo
Ford Thunderbird Turbo 2.3
Mazda 323 16-valve Turbo
Mazda MX-6 Turbo
Mazda RX-7
Mazda RX-7 (non-turbo)
Merkur XR4Ti
Mitsubishi Eclipse Turbo
Nissan 200SX-V6
Nissan 300ZX
Nissan 300ZX (non-turbo)
Oldsmobile Calais 442
Peugeot 505 Turbo
Plymouth Laser Turbo
Pontiac Sunbird Turbo
Saab 900 Turbo/SPG
Saab 9000 Turbo
Shelby CSX
Toyota MR2 Supercharged
Toyota Supra 4-valve
Toyota Supra 24-valve
Volkswagen Corrado

SS Class B
Chevrolet Beretta
Chevrolet Cavalier Z-24
Dodge/Plymouth Colt Turbo
Ford Escort GT
Honda Accura Integra
Honda Accura Integra (three-door)
Honda CRX Si
Honda Prelude Si
Mazda MX-6 (non-turbo)
Mitsubishi Mirage Turbo
Nissan 240SX
Nissan NX 2000
Nissan Sentra SE-R (2.0)
Oldsmobile Calais
Peugeot 405
Pontiac Fiero GT
Pontiac Grand-A
Saturn SL Sedan
Toyota Celica GT-S
Toyota MR2 (non-turbo)
Volkswagen GTi 16-valve
Volkswagen Scirocco

Showroom Stock Class B contenders attack an S-bend at Texas World Speedway. David Daughtery's Mitsubishi Mirage Turbo (note window nets) leads T.C. Kline's Nissan Sentra SE-R.

SS Class C
Ford Escort GT Geo Prism GSI
Geo Storm GSI
Honda Civic DX
Honda Civic Si
Honda CRX
Isuzu Impulse XS
Mazda 323
Mazda MX-5/Miata
Mazda Protege LX
Mercury Tracer
Nissan NX 1600
Nissan Pulsar NX
Nissan Pulsar SE 16-valve
Nissan Sentra (1.6)
Saab 900 16-valve
Suzuki Swift GT
Suzuki Swift GTi
Toyota Corolla GT-S
Toyota Corolla GT-S 16-valve
Toyota FX 16 GT-S
Toyota MR2
Volkswagen Golf GT

■ For further information, contact: Dick Martin, SCCA Club Racing Department, 9033 East Easter Place, Englewood, Colorado 80112. Tel (303) 694-7229. Fax: (303) 694- 7391.

Wiley Timbrook, driving Coyote Racing's Nissan NX 2000, contests Showroom Stock Class B at Second Creek Raceway, Denver, Colorado, in August 1992.

Bryan Cohen, a leading light in Showroom Stock Class A, corners hard in the Bryan Cohen Racing Mitsubishi Eclipse.

SCCA Pro Racing World Challenge

SCCA Pro Racing's World Challenge features races of varying durations, up to a maximum of 24 hours. In fact, there's only one 24-hour race each season: at Mosport Park, Canada. Because the World Challenge encompasses the entire North American continent, with no regional/divisional structure of the kind operated by SCCA Club Racing, some competitors only contest rounds which take place within their general geographical area. Of course, they have no chance of winning the championship this way, but the organizers are happy to accommodate the arrangement.

The World Challenge is divided into four classes, delineated by means of a complex performance formula, as opposed to simply engine capacity. Factors taken into consideration include engine capacity, induction system type, power-to-weight ratio and on-track performance potential. Class A features high-performance models from around the world: it's seen as a showcase for production technology, with cars featuring turbochargers, four-wheel-drive, ABS – even traction control.

Class B features cars with engines ranging from normally- aspirated V8s to turbocharged, multivalve L4s – up to a maximum displacement of 5 liters. Four-wheel-drive vehicles are permitted. Class C features cars with normally-aspirated engines displacing 3.5 liters or less, while Class D features cars with normally-aspirated engines displacing 2 liters or less.

Fitment of a fuel cell is optional in all classes, except in Class A, where this is a mandatory requirement. In Class A, the cage must be welded-in. Bolt-in roll cages are acceptable in the other classes. In all four classes, it is permissable to fit front triangulation struts and a turret brace, and seam welding of the bodyshell is permitted.

Airjacks are prohibited, but an ingenious method has been devised for raising three wheels off the ground simultaneously, within the regulatory restrictions (see Chapter 2).

Almost all of the competitors in this category are professional racing drivers, augmented by some wealthy motorsport enthusiasts – doctors and dentists with a passion for racing. Actor Paul Newman has participated in the series, driving a Lotus Esprit Turbo: indeed, he was fortunate to walk away from a major accident at Lime Rock, Connecticut, in the summer of 1992.

World Challenge Class A pretenders locked in battle in Turn 3 of the Road America circuit at Elkhart Lake, Wisconsin, August 1992. Kim Baker's Corvette ZR-1 leads R.K. Smith's similar car and Boris Said's Mustang, its hood threatening to fly open at any moment! Smith's team-mate – and eventual winner – Bill Cooper, breathes down Said's neck.

Bill Saunders and Neil Hanneman drove their Archer Brothers Eagle Talons to a one-two finish in Class D, during the World Challenge meeting at Road America in August '92.

SCCA Pro Racing permits models with a minimum production output of just 1,000 units per year. The following models were eligible for the 1992 World Challenge, subject to their year of manufacture.

Class A
BMW M5
Corvette
Dodge Stealth AWD Turbo
Honda Acura NSX
Lotus Esprit Turbo
Mazda RX-7 Twin Turbo
Mustang 351
Mustang Saleen SC
Nissan 300ZX Turbo
Pontiac Firehawk
Porsche 911 Turbo
Porsche 911 RS America

Class B
BMW M3
Chevrolet Camaro
Dodge Daytona IROC
Eagle Talon Turbo
Ford Mustang
Ford Probe GT
Lotus Elan Turbo
Mazda RX-7 Turbo
Mitsubishi Eclipse Turbo
Pontiac Firebird
Porsche 968
Subaru SVX
Toyota MR2 Turbo
Toyota Supra Turbo

Class C
BMW 325
Chevrolet Beretta GTZ
Chevrolet Lumina Z34
Ford Taurus SHO
Ford Probe V6
Honda Prelude
Mazda RX-7
Nissan 240SX
Oldsmobile Achieva
Mercedes-Benz 190

Class D
BMW 318
Eagle Talon
Ford Escort GT
Geo Storm
Honda Civic CRX
Hyundai Scoupe
Isuzu Stylus
Mazda MX-3GS
Mazda Miata
Nissan NX 2000
Nissan Sentra SE-R
Saturn
Toyota Corolla TC
Toyota Paseo
Volkswagen GTi

■ For further information, contact: Rob Elson, Technical Administrator, SCCA Pro Racing Department, 9033 East Easter Place, Englewood, Colorado 80112. Tel (303) 694-7229. Fax: (303) 694-7391.

IMSA Firestone Firehawk Endurance Championship

In 1992, America's premier street stock endurance racing series entered its eighth season – during the course of which drivers notched up the two millionth mile!

Cars competing in Firestone Firehawk lie somewhere between the SCCA Club and SCCA Pro Racing levels in terms of the scope for modifications. In deference to the series sponsors, all cars run on roadgoing Firestone Firehawk SZ or Firehawk SV tires with treads shaved to racing depth, or all-season Firehawk GTX covers. Associate sponsorship comes from Bosch and Kendall Oil.

Despite the intensity of the competition, the majority of drivers treat their involvement in the Firestone Firehawk Endurance Championship as a hobby: only 40 of the 131 race winners from 1985-1991 earned a living from their racing. However, success in the series can be a career-builder for professional drivers: Dorsey Schroeder won ten Firehawk races for Paul Rossi's Dodge team, then went on to win Trans Am and GTO championships, and has competed in NASCAR and the IROC series. John Andretti also has participated in Firestone Firehawk, winning his first three races.

Drivers compete for race purses, year-end points funds and manufacturer contingency awards approaching $1 million. The championship's winningest driver is Paul Hacker of Valatie, New York, with over 20 victories to his credit.

Firehawk race meetings are two-day affairs, with Sports Class and Touring Class cars competing together on the first day, and Grand Sports Class cars – predominantly Camaros, Firebirds and BMWs – doing battle on the second. Typically, meetings attract over 90 entries and are televised. The ten-round 1992 season comprized a 2.5-hour race at Lime Rock, Connecticut, and a string of 3-hour races at Road Atlanta, Georgia, Mid-Ohio, Laguna Seca, California, Portland, Oregon, and Road America, Wisconsin, interspersed by two races at Sebring, Florida (4 hours and 12 hours) and two at Watkins Glen, New York (3 hours and 24 hours).

The most successful manufacturer in the history of the Firehawk series is Honda America, which began 1992 with 34 individual race wins and four Touring Class Manufacturer Championships to its credit, and added considerably to that tally during the course of the year.

Models eligible for the 1992 Firestone Firehawk Endurance Championship were as follows.

Grand Sports Class
Audi V8 Quattro BMW M3
Chevrolet Camaro
Dodge Spirit R/T Turbo
Ford Mustang GT and LX
Ford Thunderbird SC
Nissan 300ZX
Pontiac Firebird
Porsche 944
Porsche 944 S2
Toyota Supra Turbo

Sports Class
Acura Vigor
Alfa Romeo Milano (75)
Alfa Romeo Milano Verde
Alfa Romeo 164 S
Audi 200T Quattro
Audi Quattro Coupe 4-valve
Audi 100S
BMW 325e
BMW 325is
BMW 325i 4-valve
Chevrolet Beretta
Chevrolet Beretta GTU
Chevrolet Cavalier Z-24 2.8 and 3.1
Chevrolet Celebrity
Chevrolet Lumina Z34
Chrysler Conquest Turbo Tsi
Chrysler LeBaron GTS Turbo

A Porsche 944 S2 soaking up the punishment of endurance racing. Kelly Moss Racing, based in Madison, Wisconsin, won six out of ten rounds of the Firehawk series, to annex the 1992 championship title in the Grand Sports Class.

Dodge Daytona
Dodge Daytona IROC
Dodge Daytona Shelby Turbo
Dodge Lancer ES Turbo
Dodge Lancer Shelby Turbo
Dodge Shadow Turbo ES
Dodge Stealth ES and RT
Eagle Talon TSi and 4WD
Ford Probe GT
Ford Taurus SHO
Honda Acura Legend Coupe
Isuzu Turbo Impulse
Lexus ES 250
Lexus ES 300
Mazda MX-6 GT Turbo
Mazda RX-7
Mazda RX-7 GTU and GTU-S
Mazda RX-7 Turbo
Merkur XR4Ti Turbo

Mitsubishi Eclipse Turbo and 4WD
Mitsubishi Galant Sigma
Mitsubishi Starion ESIR Turbo
Nissan 240SX
Nissan 300ZX
Nissan Maxima
Oldsmobile Calais Quad 442
Oldsmobile Achiva SC
Oldsmobile Achiva SCX
Plymouth Sundance Turbo
Plymouth Laser Turbo and 4WD
Pontiac Grand Am
Pontiac Grand Am Turbo
Pontiac Grand Prix GTP

Oldsmobile unveiled its Achieva SCX for the 1992 Firestone Firehawk series. In the hands of the ultra-successful Hacker Express outfit, they performed with distinction in the Sports Class – as here, at a soaking Sebring.

Pontiac Sunbird Turbo
Saab 900 Turbo
Saab 9000T
Toyota Camry
Toyota Celica All Trac Turbo
Toyota MR2 Turbo
Toyota Supra
Volkswagen Corrado
Volkswagen Passat 2.8
Volvo 940 Turbo
Touring Class
Alfa Romeo 164L
Audi 100 Quattro
Audi 80/90 Quattro 2-valve
Buick Skylark 16-valve
BMW 318is
Chevrolet Beretta
Chevrolet Beretta GTZ
Chevrolet Lumina
Chevrolet Spectrum Turbo
Chrysler LeBaron GTS
Chrysler LeBaron GTC Coupe
Dodge Colt Turbo
Dodge Daytona
Dodge Shadow ES
Dodge Spirit
Ford Escort GT
Ford Probe and LX
Geo Storm GSi
Geo Prizm
Honda Acura Integra 1.6 and 1.8
Honda CRX and CRX Si
Honda Civic Si
Honda Civic EX
Honda Prelude Si
Hyundai Sonata
Hyundai Scoupe
Infiniti G-20

Isuzu I-Mark Turbo
Isuzu I-Mark RS
Isuzu Impulse
Isuzu Impulse RS
Isuzu Stylus XS
Mazda 323 1.6 and 1.8
Mazda 323 Turbo
Mazda MX-3
Mazda MX-6
Mazda Protoge LX
Mercury Tracer
Mitsubishi Eclipse GS
Mitsubishi Mirage Turbo
Nissan 240SX
Nissan NX 2000
Nissan Sentra and SE-R
Nissan Stanza
Oldsmobile Calais
Oldsmobile Calais IS HO
Peugeot 405 Mi16
Peugeot 505 STX
Peugeot 505 Turbo
Plymouth Acclaim
Plymouth Colt GTS Turbo
Plymouth Laser RS
Plymouth Sundance
Pontiac Grand Am
Pontiac Grand Am 16-valve
Pontiac Le Mans
Pontiac Sunbird
Saab 900S
Saab 9000S
Saturn Sport Coupe and Sedan
Suzuki Legacy

An impressive performer in the Touring Class of the 1992 Firehawk series was this T.C. Kline-entered Honda Prelude Si, driven by John Ruhlin/Dick Ruhl.

Suzuki Justy
Suzuki Turbo
Suzuki Swift GTi
Toyota Camry 2.0 and 2.2
Toyota Celica GT
Toyota Celica GTS 2.0 and 2.2
Toyota Corolla GT-S
Toyota MR2
Toyota MR2 SC
Toyota Paseo
Volkswagen GTi 16-valve
Volkswagen Jetta GLi 16-valve
Volkswagen Passat 2.0

Volvo 740 and 760 Turbo
Volvo 780
Yugo GVX

■ For further information, contact: Bob Manry, Technical Director, IMSA Inc., PO Box 10709, Tampa, Florida 33679-0709 . Tel: (813) 877-4672. Fax: (813) 876- 4604.

Grand Sports Class cars in combat. The Porsche 944 S2 of Jeff Purner/Bill Cooped heads Joe Varde's Chevrolet Camaro and a string of assorted Camaros, Firebirds and BWMs, during the 1990 Watkins Glen 500.

IMSA Bridgestone Supercar Championship

IMSA sanctions this championship for minimally modified versions of the world's most exotic sportscars. Porsche 911 Turbos, Corvette ZR-1s, Lotus Esprit Turbos and the like compete without barriers, this being a single-class series.

Inaugurated in 1991, the Bridgestone Supercar Championship typically is contested over the course of seven or eight 30-minute, televised sprint races at the following circuits: Del Mar, California; Laguna Seca, California; Lime Rock, Connecticut; Miami, Florida; Phoenix, Arizona; Portland, Oregon; Road Atlanta, Georgia; and Watkins Glen, New York.

Healthy entries have been graced by such luminaries as Hans Stuck, Hurley Haywood, Doc Bundy and actor/racer Paul Newman.

With a prize fund of $555,000 up for grabs in the 1992 season, the Bridgestone Supercar Championship was well supported by its sponsors. All of the cars run on Bridgestone Potenza RE71 high-performance roadgoing radial tires, which feature a steel sidewall insert for a rapid, predictable steering response, but have a standard street compound. For the Supercar series, the tire's unidirectional tread pattern has been shaved to a depth of 2/32in. This reduces tread wear under severe racing conditions, as heat-generation and 'tread squirm' are markedly reduced.

For wet weather races, full-tread tires are fitted to maximize water channelling and traction.

The legendary red, white and blue Brumos Porsches are regular front runners, but they have had stiff competition – not least from the exciting but controversial, all-composite, Shelby-powered Consulier GTP. This car teeters on the very borderline of the 'showroom stock' ethos. Although it's a technological marvel, in many respects, it has very little in common with cars one sees in daily use on the highway.

In terms of annual production volumes, several models seen in the Bridgestone Supercar Championship are rare birds indeed. This reflects the liberal approach of IMSA's rulemakers, in sharp contrast to their European counterparts. The following models were eligible for the series in 1992.

BMW M5
BMW M6
BMW 850i
BMW 750iL
Callaway Corvette

Under pressure. Hurley Haywood, piloting a Brumos-entered Porsche 911 Turbo, fends off Doc Bundy's predatory Lotus Esprit Turbo. Bundy went on to clinch the 1992 Bridgestone Supercar Drivers' Championship.

(Above) Cass Whitehead's Nissan 300ZX, pursued by a Consulier GTP.

(Below) Willy Lewis keeps his Mazda RX-7 ahead of team-mate Peter Farrell.

Consulier GTP
Corvette L-98
Corvette LT-1
Corvette ZR-1
Dodge Stealth
Dodge Viper
Ferrari 348
Ferrari Testarossa
Honda Acura NSX
Infiniti Q-45
Jaguar XJ-S
Lexus LS 400
Lexus SC 400
Lotus Esprit Turbo SE
Lotus Esprit X180R
Maserati 430i
Maserati Shamal
Mazda RX-7
Mercedes-Benz 300 CE
Mercedes-Benz 300 SL
Mercedes-Benz 500 E
Mercedes-Benz 500 SL
Mitsubishi 3000 GT

Nissan 300ZX Turbo
Pontiac Trans Am Turbo
Pontiac Firebird Firehawk
Porsche Carrera 2
Porsche Carrera 4
Porsche 911 Turbo
Porsche 928 GT
Porsche 928 S4
Porsche 968
Porsche 944 Turbo
Saleen Mustang

■ For further information, contact: Bob Manry, Technical Director, IMSA Inc., PO Box 10709, Tampa, Florida 33679-0709. Tel: (813) 877-4672. Fax: (813) 876-4604.

Controversial Consulier. The fabulous all-composite, Shelby-powered Consulier GTP teeters on the very borderline of the 'showroom stock' ethos. Although it's a technological marvel, in many respects, it has very little in common with cars one sees in daily use on the highway.

GREAT BRITAIN

In Europe, national championship regulations in this category of motorsport are usually derived from the Group N regulations of the Federation Internationale du Sport Automobile (FISA), the organization which governs motorsport on a global basis. The regulations are published annually in FISA's distinctive *"Yellow Book"*. To be eligible for Group N, models must have had a minimum production output of 5,000 units in a 12-month period, thereby affirming their roadgoing pedigree.

Headquartered in Paris, France, FISA delegates responsibility for implementing its policies to national motorsporting authorities across the world. Motorsport in the United Kingdom takes place under the auspices of the Motor Sports Association of the Royal Automobile Club (RAC MSA), which disseminates its regulations annually in a publication competitors call *"The Blue Book"*.

There are four major British championships catering for the type of cars which interest us.

BRDC/BRSCC Saloon Car Championship

This prestigious Group N-derived championship comprizes not only sprint races, but also 24-hour, 2-hour and 1-hour endurance events. Races are held at the following circuits: Brands Hatch (Indy Circuit), Kent; Castle Combe, Wiltshire; Donington Park, Derbyshire; Mallory Park, Leicestershire; Oulton Park, Cheshire; Silverstone, Northamptonshire (both the Grand Prix Circuit and the shorter National Circuit); and Snetterton, Norfolk.

There are five classes in the BRDC/BRSCC Saloon Car Championship, each defined by engine capacity: Class A (over 3000cc), Class B (2001-3000cc), Class C (1601-2000cc), Class D (1401-1600cc), and Class E (up to 1400cc). An equivilancy factor of 1.7 is applied to models featuring turbocharged engines. Thus, a 2.3-liter car is grouped with cars over 3 liters if it has a turbocharged engine.

Cars competing in the BRDC/BRSCC Saloon Car Championship are fairly heavily modified, at least by comparison with cars contesting the other championships featured in this book. They can have race-specification wheels and tires, a fuel cell, either welded-in or bolt-in roll cages – even airjacks. Nevertheless, they retain strong links with their roadgoing cousins. For example, all of the standard seats, with the exception of the driver's seat, must be reinstalled, together with virtually all of the interior trim. The original clutch unit must be retained – although the lining may be upgraded – and the brake units must be as standard, except for the pads.

In 1992, the harsh economic climate resulted in the BRDC/BRSCC Saloon Car Championship being run without a series sponsor. However, the 24-hour event at Snetterton, which holds FISA International status, was co-sponsored by HEAT and long-standing supporter Willhire.

The following models were homologated for the BRDC/BRSCC Saloon Car Championship, as at 31 December 1991.

Class A of the BRDC/BRSCC Saloon Car Championship is awash with Ford Sierra Sapphire Cosworths! Here, Graham Hathaway powers his immaculate example out of a corner at Donington Park in 1992.

149

Class A
Alfa 75 Turbo
Audi 200 Quattro
Audi 200 Quattro M86
Chrysler Le Baron Coupe
Citroen BX Diesel Turbo
Dodge Daytona Shelby Z
Ford Sierra Cosworth 4x4
Ford Sierra RS Cosworth
Ford Sierra Sapphire Cosworth
Lancia Delta HF 4WD
Lancia Delta HF Integrale
Lancia Delta HF Integrale 16-valve
Mazda Familia 3.1 4WD
Mitsubishi Galant VR-4
Nissan Pulsar GTI-R
Nissan Skyline GTR Turbo
Plymouth Sundance
Renault 21 2-liter Turbo
Saab 900 Turbo 16
Saab 9000 T-16 2.3
Saab 9000 Turbo 16
Subaru 4WD Turbo Sedan
Subaru Coupe 4WD Turbo
Subaru Legacy 2.0BF 4WD
Subaru Legacy 4WD Turbo
Toyota Celica 2000GT 3.4
Volkswagen Golf GTi G60
Class B
Alfa 75 16-valve 3.0
Alfa 164 3.0 QV
Audi 90 Quattro
Audi 90 Quattro B3
Audi Coupe Quattro
BMW 325i
BMW 325iX
BMW M3
Fiat Uno Turbo ie
Ford RS Cosworth
Ford Sierra XR4x4
Mazda Familia 2.7 4WD
Mercedes-Benz 190E 16-valve
Renault 5GT Turbo
Renault 11 Turbo
Subaru Legacy Sedan 2.2BC 4WD
Vauxhall/General Motors Carlton 24-valve
Volkswagen Polo Coupe G40
Volkswagen Rallye-Golf G60
Volvo 440 Turbo
Volvo 480 Turbo
Class C
Alfa 33 16-valve
Alfa 75 2.0 Super
Austin Rover MG Maestro Efi
BMW 318iS
BMW 320i
Citroen BX GTI 16 Soupapes
Daihatsu Charade GT
Fiat Ritmo Abarth 130TC
Fiat Tipo 2.0 16-valve
Fiat Tipo ie 16-valve

Nigel Corner and his Ness Furniture-sponsored BMW M3: front runners in Class B of the 1992 BRDC/BRSCC Saloon Car Championship.

Peter Morss, at the wheel of his Vauxhall/General Motors Astra (Class C), fends off the Suzuki Swift of Sean Andrews (Class E) and the Astra of Rob Squires (Class C) in a round of the 1992 BRDC/BRSCC Saloon Car Championship at Silverstone.

Honda Prelude
Lancia Y10 Turbo
Opel/General Motors Kadett GSi
Oyak-Renault 11 TXE
Peugeot 205 GTI 1900
Peugeot 309 16-valve
Peugeot 309 GTI
Renault 19 16S
Renault 19 GTX
Renault 21 RX
Renault 21 RS
Renault Clio 16S
Subaru Legacy Sedan 2.0BC 4WD
Toyota Celica 2000GT 2.0
Vauxhall/General Motors Astra GSi/GTE 16-valve
Vauxhall/General Motors Calibra 16-valve
Vauxhall/General Motors Cavalier 16-valve
Volkswagen Golf GTi
Volkswagen Golf GTi 16-valve
Volkswagen Golf Syncro
Volkswagen Scirocco 16-valve

Class D
Alfa 33 4x4
Alfa 33 Quadrifoglio Verde
Alfasud Sprint 1.5 Veloce
Ford Escort 1.6 EFi
Ford Escort XR3i
Ford Fiesta XR2
Ford Fiesta XR2i
FSO 1500-125 P
FSO Polonez 1500-125 PN
Hyundai Elantra 16-valve
Honda Civic VTEC
Isuzu Gemini 1600 Sedan
Mitsubishi Mirage 1600
Nissan March Super Turbo
Peugeot 205 GTI (115CV)
SEAT Ibiza 1.5 SXI
Toyota Corolla 1600 GT

Class E
Citroen AX GT
Citroen AX Sport
Daihatsu Charade 1.3i
Fiat Uno 70S
Fiat Uno 70XS ie
Ford Fiesta 1.4S
FSO 1300-125 P
Oyak-Renault 12 Toros R
Peugeot 205 Rallye
Premier Padmini
Renault 4 GTL
Renault 5 TSE
Renault 19 GTS
Skoda Favorit 136L
Subaru 4WD 1.2 KA
Subaru 4WD 1.2 KA Sedan
Suzuki Cultus 1300
Suzuki Swift 1300
Toyota Starlet 1300
Vauxhall/General Motors Nova GTE
Volkswagen Polo Coupe GT
Wartburg 1.3
Yugo 1.3
Yugo 55

■ For further information, contact: Chris Norman, Joint Championship Coordinator, BRDC, Silverstone Circuit, Silverstone, Nr. Towcester, Northamptonshire NN12 8TN. Tel: (0327) 857271. Fax: (0327) 857296.

BARC Production Car Championship

This championship is administered by the British Automobile Racing Club (BARC), based at Thruxton circuit, near Andover in Hampshire. The series typically comprizes twelve rounds, held at Brands Hatch, Donington Park, Mallory Park, Pembrey in South Wales, Silverstone (Club Circuit), Snetterton – and, of course, Thruxton.

In previous years, the BARC Production Car Championship was sponsored by the Firestone tire company, but recession-hit 1992 saw the series unsponsored. Nevertheless, the rule prohibiting competitors from running anything but Firestone tires was kept in force in the interests of continuity, and one of the company's support trucks attended every round of the 1992 championship.

That year, the previous Grand Sports and Grand Touring classes were amalgamated to compensate for reduced grid sizes. This resulted in direct competition between Ford Sierra Cosworths, turbocharged Saabs, and BMW M3s. All three classes in this championship race side by side.

Competitors fielding turbocharged cars are each supplied with a sealed boost control box at tech inspection on race morning. These must be fitted under the hood, and all of the associated pipework must be visible when the hood is open.

Only roadgoing tires are permitted. Race-specification shock absorbers and springs may be fitted, fuel cells are recommended, but airjacks are prohibited.

Although the organizers are pleased to receive submissions for new models, the list of eligible models for the 1992 BARC Production Car Championship was as follows.

Pictured at Snetterton during a round of the 1992 BARC Production Car Championship, Mark Dann pilots Benfield Motorsport's Ford Sierra Sapphire Cosworth to a victory in Class A - headlights ablaze.

Grand Sports Class
Alfa Romeo 75 3.0 V6
Alfa Romeo 164 3.0 V6
Audi V8
Audi Coupe Quattro Turbo
Audi 90 20-valve
BMW M3
BMW 535i
Chevrolet Camaro IROC
Fiat Croma Turbo
Ford Escort Cosworth
Ford Sierra RS Cosworth
Ford Sapphire RS Cosworth
Honda Civic CRX VTEC
Jaguar XJS 3.6
Lancia Delta Integrale 16-valve
Lancia Thema Turbo
Mazda RX-7 Turbo
Mercedes-Benz 190 2.5 16-valve
Mercedes-Benz 300E 24-valve
Mercedes-Benz 500 SL hardtop
Nissan 200SX
Porsche 944 S2
Renault 21 Turbo
Rover 827 Vitesse
Saab 900 Turbo 16-valve
Saab 9000 Turbo

(Above) Grand Sports Class contenders stream through Thruxton's famous chicane during a 1-hour race in June 1992. The Porsche 911 Carrera 2 of Paul Edwards/David Saunders is closely followed by the BMW of Frank Cundell/John Wilson.

(Below) Class War! Terry Flatt's Touring Class Volkswagen Golf GTi and Gareth Downing's Saloon Sports Class Ford Fiesta XR2i negotiate a corner side by side.

Saab 9000 2.3 CS and CD
Toyota Lexus
Toyota MR2 GT
Toyota Supra Turbo
Vauxhall/General Motors Carlton GSi 24-valve
Volvo 760 Turbo
Touring Class
Daihatsu Charade GTti
Citroen BX Gti 16-valve
Fiat Tipo 16-valve
Fiat Uno Turbo
Ford Escort RS Turbo
Ford RS 2000
Honda Civic CRX
Honda Civic VTEC
Mazda 626GT
Mitsubishi Lancer 1.8 GTi 16-valve
Nissan Primera 2.0 EZX
Peugeot 309 GTi 16-valve
Peugeot 405 Mi16
Porsche 911 Carerra 2
Porsche 924

Renault 5 GT Turbo
Renault 19 16-valve
Renault Clio 16-valve
Rover Maestro MG Efi
Rover Montego MG Efi
SEAT Toledo GTi 16-valve
Toyota Celica GT
Toyota MR2 Mk.1
Vauxhall/General Motors Astra GSi 16-valve
Vauxhall/General Motors Astra GTE 16-valve
Volkswagen Corrado G60
Volkswagen Golf GTi 16-valve
Volvo 480 Turbo
Saloon Sports Class
Alfa Romeo 33 1.5
Citroen AX GT
Citroen AX GTi
Ford Fiesta 1.6S
Ford Fiesta XR2i
Rover Metro GTi 16-valve
SEAT Ibiza 1.5 SXi
Suzuki Swift GTi Mk.1 and Mk.2
Vauxhall/General Motors Nova GTE 1.6

This 16-valve, 2-liter Fiat Tipo – operated by Belle Vue Motorsport of Ipswich, Suffolk throughout the 1992 season – typifies cars in the Touring Class of the BARC Production Car Championship. Team co-owner Bill Stilwell is at the wheel.

■ For further information, contact: Dale Wells, Championship Coordinator, BARC, Thruxton Circuit, Andover, Hampshire SP11 8PN. Tel: (0264) 772607 and 772696/7. Fax: (0264) 773794.

Dunlop Rover GTi Championship

This hotly contested one-make championship is built around the Rover 216 GTi. In 1992, the series comprized twelve rounds: two each at Brands Hatch, Castle Combe, Donington Park, Knockhill in Scotland, Oulton Park, and Silverstone (Grand Prix Circuit); and a single race overseas – at Spa-Francorchamps, Belgium. Race distances varied from 24 to 35 miles.

The series runs in accordance with RAC MSA regulations, supplemented by regulations issued by the organizers. Rover Cars supply race-prepared, non-roadgoing Rover 216 GTi 16- valve, twin cam vehicles direct to registered competitors at a special price, which includes the driver's racewear and a mandatory livery design service. Each car is supplied with a kit of parts, consisting of a roll cage, a race-tuned exhaust system, a race-specification seat and safety harness, a circuit breaker, assorted hood/trunk catches, a fire extinguisher, special suspension and brake system components, and spare wheels.

Rover Sport makes a limited number of spare bodyshells available to competitors who severely damage their cars.

The Dunlop Rover GTi Championship is Britain's leading one-make series. The cars are very evenly matched, making for close competition – and good television.

Competitors are permitted to seam weld the bodyshell and undertake certain other modifications, but in most respects the Rover 216 GTis remain closely allied to their roadgoing counterparts. The cars are not fitted with ABS, but brake bias adjusters are permitted. Aviation-specification flexible fuel lines are prohibited.

In addition to the primary sponsors – Rover Cars and Dunlop – the series is supported by Castrol, Delco, Mintex and Philips Car Stereo. The sponsors ran a 'celebrity car' for various guest drivers in 1991, one of whom was Grand Prix team owner Eddie Jordan. This scheme was subsequently discontinued. Most of the rounds are televised, and the status of the championship is such that some rounds support major international races, such as the Formula 1 British Grand Prix at Silverstone.

■ For further information, contact: Chris Belton, Manager, Rover Sport, PO Box 400, Wallington, Surrey SM6 9SQ. Tel: (081) 647-5757. Fax: (081) 669-6553.

Elf Oils Renault Clio UK Cup

This healthy one-make series caters for the nimble little front wheel drive Renault Clio, and invariably provides excellent racing. Rounds are held at Brands Hatch, Donington Park, Knockhill, Oulton Park, Pembrey, Silverstone, Snetterton and Thruxton.

Renault UK supplies competitors with coupe versions of the Clio. When prepared for the championship, they differ from standard roadgoing Clios in several respects. They are fitted with a roll cage and other items of safety equipment, and feature an uprated suspension, a race-specification clutch unit and stiffer engine mounting bushes. The standard fuel tank configuration is altered, though fuel cells are prohibited.

Power steering, which is standard on the roadgoing Clio, is not installed on the competition version, and the cockpit is left virtually bare. The exhaust system is replaced aft of the catalytic converter, and a competition rear axle is optional.

The series is sponsored by various divisions of Renault, together with Elf Oils, CAT GB, Champion, de Carbon, Facom, Michelin and Philips Car Stereo. Renault Sport occasionally fields a 'celebrity car' for guest drivers, one of whom was comedian/motorsport enthusiast Rowan Atkinson.

■ For further information, contact: Tim Jackson, Manager, Renault UK Motorsport, Renault UK Ltd., Western Avenue, London W3 0RZ. Tel: (081) 992-3481. Fax: (081) 993-5945.

Rabid Renaults! A frantic tussle for the 1992 Elf Oil Renault Clio UK Cup, at Thruxton in Hampshire.

Supplier/services directory

UNITED STATES

Aviation-specification pipework
Torino Motor Racing Inc., 1350 M.W. Collins, Orange, California 92668. Tel: (714) 771-1348. Fax: (714) 771-1737.

Camber/caster gauges
Frank Boyce Company, 20 Grove Street, PO Box 72, Windsor, New York 13865. Tel: (607) 655-1218.

Watkins Industries, 780 Second Avenue, Redwood City, California 94063. Tel: (415) 369-3535. Fax: (415) 367-0866.

Canopies
Comprent Motor Sports, 1120 Newton Bridge Road, Athens, Georgia 30607. Tel: (404) 543-1797.

KD Canopy, 5758 Lamar Street, Arvada, Colorado 80002. Tel: (800) 432-4435. Fax: (303) 431-6899.

Landmark Motorsports, 1035 North Main, Orange, California 92667. Tel: (714) 288-9400.

Communications systems
PCI Race Radios, 2888 Grundy Avenue, Signal Hill, California 90806. Tel: (213) 427-8177. Fax: (213) 426-3589.

Racetech Racing Communications, 2162 South Jupiter, Garland, Texas 75041. Tel: (800) 421-3769.

Racing Electronics, 65 Fire Road, Absecon, New Jersey 08201. Tel: (800) 272-7111.

Cornerweight scales
Great Expectations Motorsports, 305 108th NE Avenue, Bellevue, Washington. Tel: (206) 453-6496. Fax: (206) 453-6719.

Innovon Motorsports, 9030 Kenamar Drive, Suite 315, San Diego, California 92121. Tel: (619) 586-1881.

Longacre Racing Products, 14959 NE 95th. Street, Redmond, Washington 98052. Tel: (800) 423-3110.

Dampers
Penske Racing Shocks, PO Box 301, Reading, Pennsylvania 19603. Tel: (215) 375-6180. Fax: (215) 375-6190.

Fuel cells
Aero Tec Laboratories Inc., Spear Road Industrial Park, Ramsey, New Jersey 07446. Tel: (800) 526-5330. Fax: (201) 825-1962.

Aircraft Rubber Manufacturing, Inc., 5271 Business Drive, Huntingdon Beach, California 92649. Tel: (714) 897-2858 FAX: (714) 892-5338 Outside California: (800) 433-6524.

Miscellaneous racing supplies
Baker Precision Products, 2865 Grundy Avenue, Long Beach, California 90806. Tel: (213) 427-2375. Fax: (213) 426-5294.

Essex Racing Services Inc., 2350 Industrial Park Boulevard, Pendley Industrial Park, Cumming, Georgia 30130. Tel: (404) 889-4096. Fax: (404) 889-5256.

Irmo Racing, 1212 Osheal Road, Irmo, South Carolina 29063. Tel: (803) 732-0937.

J&J Racing Ltd., 103 South Church Street, Bally, Pennsylvania 19503. Tel: (215) 845-2848. Fax (215) 845-8820.

Motorsports Spares International Inc., 50 Unit I Gasoline Alley, Indianapolis, Indiana 46222. Tel: (317) 241-7500. Fax: (317) 241-0823.

Pegasus Auto Racing Supplies, 2475 South 179th. Street, New Berlin, Wisconsin 53146. Tel: (414) 782-0880.

Performance World, 7450 Ronson Road, San Diego, California 92111. Tel: (800) 854-6640.

Racer Wholesale, 10390 Alpharetta Street, No. 602, Roswell, Georgia 30075. Tel: (404) 998-7777.

Ron Minor's Auto Racing Specialities, 6511 North 27th. Avenue, Phoenix, Arizona 85017. Tel: (602) 242-3398. Fax: (602) 242-3390.

Silver King Power Sports, 4771 Naniloa Drive, Salt Lake City, Utah 84117. Tel: (800) 866-4631.

Transatlantic Racing Services Ltd., 5730 Chattahoochee Industrial Park, Cumming, Georgia 30130. Tel: (800) 533-6057. Fax: (404) 889-0499.

Race Car Preparation
Autotechnica, 5302 West Woolworth Avenue, Milwaukee, Wisconsin 53218. Tel: (414) 353-8864. Fax: (414) 353-8644.

KZM Racing, 4167 Lyman Road, Hilliard, Ohio 43026. Tel: (614) 771-8311. Fax: (614) 759-7266.

Racewear
Bell Auto Racing, PO Box 927, Rantoul, Illinois 61866. Tel: (800) 237-2700.

Lutz Racewear, PO Box 69, Lyndon, Kansas 66451. Tel: (913) 828-4807.

Simpson, 2415 Amsler Street, Torrance, California 90505. Tel: (310) 320-7231. Fax: (310) 320-7179.

Racing Driver Schools
Bob Bondurant School of High Performance Driving, Phoenix, Arizona. Tel: (800) 842-7223.

Road Atlanta Driver Training Center, Road Atlanta, Highway 53, Braselton, Georgia 30517. Tel: (404) 967-6143.

Regulatory authorities
International Motor Sports Association Inc., PO Box 10709, Tampa, Florida 33679-0709. Tel: (813) 877-4672. Fax:

(813) 876-4604.

Sports Car Club of America Inc., 9033 East Easter Place, Englewood, Colorado 80112. Tel: (303) 694-7229. Fax: (303) 694-7391.

Roll cages
Autopower Indistries, 3424 Pickett Street, San Diego, California 92110. Tel: (619) 297-3300. Fax (619) 297-9765.

I/O Port Racing Supplies, 2718 Telegraph Avenue, Berkeley, California 94705. Tel: (510) 841-5712.

Kirk Racing Products, 1433 Mongomery Highway, Vestavia Hills, Alabama 35216. Tel: (205) 823-6025.

Shoestring Racing, 2600 Morgan Hill Road, Easton, Pennsylvania 18042. Tel: (215) 252-6258.

Safety harnesses
Pyrotect Inc., 301 North Harrison Street, Alexandria, Indiana 46001. Tel: (800) 242-9940.

Seats
Corbeau USA, 4284 Valley Fair Street, Simi Valley, California 93063. Tel: (805) 582-0517.

Timing/scoring equipment
Reliable Racing Supply Inc., 630 Glen Street, Queensbury, New York 12804. Tel: (800) 223-4448.

Vulcan Enterprises, PO Box 50284, Phoenix, Arizona 85076. Tel: (602) 759-7926.

Tires
Leitzinger Motorsports, 3015 Research Drive, State College, Pennsylvania 16801. Tel: (800) 344-3933. Fax (814) 234-3386.

Trailers
Pace American. Tel: (800) 247-5767.

Wells Cargo Inc., PO Box 728-1050, Elkhart, Indiana 46515-0728. Tel: (800) 348-7553.

Vehicle dynamics monitors
Competition Data Systems Inc. Tel: - East (716) 542-4642(415) - West (415) 283-6373.

Computer Aided Racing, 609 Prospect Avenue, No. 18, South Pasadena, California 91030. Tel: (818) 799-1786.

Valentine Research Inc., 10280 Alliance Road, Cincinnati, Ohio 45242.

Wheels
Averill Racing, Hazel Park, Michigan. Tel: (313) 542-9366. Fax: (313) 542-3736.

BBS Motorsport, 1121 Solana Avenue, Winter Park, Florida 32789. Tel: (407) 647-6265.

Taylor Corporation, 8601 Urbandale Avenue, Des Moines, Iowa 50322. Tel: (515) 276-0992. Fax: (515) 276-2587.

GREAT BRITAIN

Airjacks
AP Racing, Wheler Road, Seven Stars Industrial Estate, Coventry, Warwickshire CV3 4LB. Tel: (0203) 639595. Fax: (0203) 639559.

Aviation-specification pipework
Braided Steel. Tel: (0386) 700495.

Auxiliary lighting
Hella Ltd., Marketing Services, Wildmere Industrial Estate, Banbury, Oxfordshire OX16 7JU. Tel: (0295) 272233. Fax: (0295) 270843.

Brake pads
Ferodo Ltd., Chapel-en-le-Frith, Stockport, Cheshire. Tel: (0298) 812520. Fax: (0298) 812600.

Mintex Don Ltd., Marketing Department, PO Box 18, Cleckheaton, West Yorkshire BD19 3UJ. Tel: (0274) 875711. Fax: (0274) 873515.

Canopies
Alfred Bull & Company, Woodbridge Meadows, Guildford, Surrey. Tel: (0483) 61897. Fax: (0483) 573448.

Grand Prix Awnings, Derwent, Hazelmere, Rhayader, Powys LD6 5LS. Tel/Fax: (0597) 810430.

Chemical paint-stripping
Viewpride Ltd., Pickle Works, Bell Street, West Bromwich, W. Midlands B70 7BT. Tel: 021-580-5222/FAX: 021-580-0522.

Communications systems
Aircell Coomunications, 60 Sprowston Mews, Norwich Road, Forest Gate, London E7 9AE. Tel: 081-534-9486. Fax: 081-534-8451.

ARE Communications, 6 Royal Parade, Hanger Lane, London W5A 1ET. Tel: 081-997-4476.

Dampers
J.W.E. Banks Ltd., Crowland, Peterborough, Cambridgeshire PE6 0JP. Tel: (0733) 210316. Fax: (0733) 210920.

Spax Ltd., Telford Industrial Estate, Bicester, Oxfordshire OX6 0UU. Tel: (0869) 244771. Fax: (0869) 240536.

Engine-tuning
Janspeed Engineering Ltd., Castle Road, Salisbury, Wiltshire SP2 7HB. Tel: (0722) 321833. Fax: (0722) 412308.

Mountune Race Engines, The Causeway Industrial Units, The Causeway, Maldon, Essex CM9 7LJ. Tel: (0621) 854029/859441. Fax: (0621) 858317. Nelson Engine Services, Calne, Wiltshire. Tel: (0249) 815929.

Oselli Engineering, Ferry Hinksay Road, Oxford, Oxfordshire OX2 0BY. Tel: (0865) 248100. Fax: (0865) 791656.

Warrior Automotive Research, Unit 7, Bellbrook Industrial Estate, Uckfield, East Sussex TN22 1QL. Tel: (0825) 764833. Fax (0825) 769132.

Exhaust systems
BTB Exhausts Ltd., Unit 3, Great Central Way, Woodford Halse, Daventry, Northamptonshire NN11 6PZ. Tel: (0327)

61797. Fax: (0395) 750233.

Fire extinguishers
Lifeline Fire & Safety Ltd., Lifeline House, New Barn Business Park, Merstone, Newport, Isle of Wight PO30 3BT. Tel: (0983) 521921. Fax: (0983) 522951.

Freight services
Rapid Movements Ltd., 14 Saxon Way, Harmondsworth, West Drayton, MIddlesex UB7 0LW. Tel: 081-897-3603. Fax: 081-759- 1550.

Fuel cells
Aero Tec Laboratories, Inc., 37 Clarke Road, Mount Farm, Bletchley, Milton Keynes, MK1 1LG. Tel: (0908) 270590/Fax: (0908) 270591.

Premier Fuel Systems Ltd., Willow Road, Castle Donington, Derby DE7 2NP. Tel: (0332) 850515. Fax: (0332) 850749.

Insurance services
Adrian S. Flux & Company, 124 London Road, King's Lynn, Norfolk PE30 5ES. Tel: (0553) 692202.

David Keen Insurance Services, 4 Bramber Close, Banbury, Oxfordshire OX16 0XF. Tel: (0295) 254116.

T.L. Clowes and Company Ltd. Tel: 071-480-5371. Fax: 071-481- 4696.

Miscellaneous racing supplies
Demon Tweeks, High Street, Tattenhall, Nr. Chester CH3 9PX. Tel: (0829) 70625. Fax: (0829) 71002.

Raceparts (UK) Ltd., Unit 3, Rockfort Industrial Estate, Wallingford, Oxfordshire OX10 9DA. Tel: (0491) 37142/37740. Fax: (0491) 36689).

Ripspeed Racing International, 54 Upper Fore Street, Edmonton, London N18 2SS. Tel: 081-803-4355. Fax 081-807-7495.

Road and Racing Accessories Ltd., 75 Moore Park Road, London SW6 2HH. Tel: 071-736-2881. Fax: 071-736-6116.

Race car preparation
RaceSpec, Owen Street, Winwick Road, Warrington, Cheshire WA2 7PA. Tel: (0925) 36959. Fax: (0925) 415255.

Racewear
David Sears Motorsport, Units 3/4, Snetterton Circuit, Snetterton, Norwich, Norfolk NR16 2JU. Tel: (0953) 87667/87298. Fax: (0953) 87454.

Grand Prix Racewear Ltd., 10 The Broadway, Gunnersbury Lane, London W3 8HR. Tel: 081--993-7555. Fax: 081-993-5502.

Jaybrand Racewear, Highbury Street, Peterborough PE1 3BH. Tel: (0733) 68247. Fax: (0733) 68249.

Racing Driver Schools
Jim Russell Racing Drivers' School (UK) Ltd., Donington Park, Derby DE7 2RP. Tel: (0332) 811430. Fax (0332) 811422.

John Watson Performance Driving Centre, Silverstone Circuit, Silverstone, Nr. Towcester, Northamptonshire NN12 8TN. Tel: (0327) 857177. Fax: (0327) 858268.

Regulatory authorities
British Automobile Racing Club, Thruxton Circuit, Andover, Hampshire SP11 8PN. Tel: (0264) 772607/772696/772697. Fax: (0264) 773794.

British Racing Drivers' Club, Silverstone Circuit, Silverstone, Nr. Towcester, Northamptonshire NN12 8TN. Tel: (0327) 857271. Fax: (0327) 857296.

British Racing and Sports Car Club, Brand Hatch Circuit, Fawkham, Dartford, Kent DA3 8NH. Tel: (0474) 874445. Fax: (0474) 874735.

Royal Automobile Club Motor Sports Association Ltd., Motor Sports House, Riverside Park, Colnbrook, Slough, Surrey SL3 0HG. Tel: (0753) 681736. Fax: (0753) 682938.

Roll cages
Safety Devices Ltd., 176 Exning Road, Newmarket, Suffolk CB8 0AF. Tel: (0638) 661421. Fax: (0638) 662340.

Safety harnesses
Stockbridge Racing Ltd., High Street, Stockbridge, Hampshire SO20 6HE. Tel: (0264) 810712. Fax: (0264) 810247.

Spark plugs
NGK Spark Plugs (UK) Ltd., 7-9 Garrick Industrial Centre, Hendon, London NW9 6AQ. Tel: 081-202-2151. Fax: 081-202-3283.

Tires
Avon Tires Ltd., Racing Division, Bath Road, Melksham, Wiltshire SN12 8AA. Tel: (0225) 703101. Fax: (0225) 707443.

Firestone UK Ltd., Sunblest House, Fairfield Avenue, Staines, Middlesex TW18 4BA. Tel: (0784) 465651. Fax: (0784) 464992.

SP Tyres (UK) Ltd., Fort Dunlop, Birmingham B24 9QT. Tel: 021- 384-4444. Fax: 021-306-3815.

Transmission blueprinting
R&D Motorsport, Newton Close, Drayton Fields, Daventry, Northamptonshire NN11 5RR. Tel: (0327) 72855. Fax: (0327) 300758.

Vehicle dynamics monitors
Delostar Electronics Ltd. Tel: (0606) 871895. Fax: (0606) 871837.

Wheels
Magard Motorsport, 372 East Park Road, Leicester LE5 5AY. Tel: (0533) 730831. Fax: (0533) 490061.

Revolution Wheels (AWI), Temple Manor Works, Priory Road, Strood, Rochester, Kent ME2 2BE. Tel: (0634) 720227. Fax: (0634) 720201.

Index

ABS, 124
Air bottles, 130
Air lines, 84-86
Accommodation, 10, 130
Airjack tubes, fitting, 48-50, 102,103
BARC Production Car Championship, 152-154
Blueprinting, 27, 68-83
Bodyshell alignment, checking the, 30
Bodyshell modifications, other, 55
Brakes, 10, 84, 85, 124-127, 130
BRDC/BRSCC Saloon Car Championship, 149-151
Bridgestone Supercar Championship, 146-148
Budgeting, 8-11
Bumpers, 93, 96
Camber/caster gauge, 18, 134
Camshaft, 71, 72
Car, selecting a, 6
Championships, selection of, 6
Checklists, 130
Clutch disc, 10, 130
Cockpit, outfitting the, 106-109
Combustion, 72, 73
Conrods, 73
Consumables, 131
Contingency funds, 10
Cornerweight scales, 114, 135
Crankshaft, 73
Crew clothing, 130, 131
Cylinder head 74
Damper-rates, 134
Disassembling the car, 30-32
Doors, 115
Drivetrain, 120-122
Dunlop Rover GTi Championship, 155
Elf Oils Renault Clio UK Cup, 156
Eligibility, 24, 25
Emissions from engine, 74
Engine, 10, 11, 68-83, 116-119, 131
Entry fees, 11
Exhaust system, 75, 119
Exterior fittings, 93
Filters, 11
Front triangulation struts, fitting, 42, 43
Fire extinguisher, 104, 105
Firestone Firehawk Endurance Championship, 142-145
Fuel/fuel system, 11, 51-54. 75, 84-86, 98-101
Gearbox, 11, 120
Geometry adjustments, 134
Identity lights, 92
Ignition system, 75
Induction system, 76
Insurance, 11
Light units, 91, 92
Lubrication system, 76, 78, 79
Mirrors, 115

Nomenclature, guide to, 5
Nutrition, 131
Paint-stripping, 32
Pedal box, 127
Personnel, 11
Pistons, 79
Pitlane procedure, 131
Power band, 79
Presentation of car, 131
Quick-release fasteners, 94, 95
Race numbers, 129
Racewear, 131
Refueling, 131, 132
Regulatory authorities, 24-29
Repainting the car, 56-67
Rev band, 79, 80
Rev limiter, 80
Roll cages 34-41
Running costs, 10, 11
Safety harness anchors, 47, 110-113
Sealing (engines), 77
Seam welding, 44-46
Seats, 110-113
Setting up, 134, 135
Showroom Stock category, 136-139
Spit-type body jigs, fabricating, 14, 15
Sponsorship, 8-11
Spring-rates, 134
Steering system, 116-199
Sunroof, dealing with, 33
Suppliers, 157-159
Suspension, 122, 123
Tech inspection, 132
Testing, 11
Tires, 11, 128, 132, 133, 135
Tools, care of, 132
Towing eyes, 47, 129
Track alignment gauge, 134
Transmission, 120-122
Tuition, drivers, 132
Turret brace, 42, 43, 119
Valves, engine, 81, 83
Valve springs, 81-83
Weight distribution, 114
Weight saving, 114
Wheels, 128
Wheel bearings, 11, 132
Wheelwell flanges, flattening, 55
Windows, 115
Windshield, 132
Windshield wiper mechanisms, 96
Wiring harness, 87-90
Workshop, establishing, 12-23
Workshop practice, 18, 19
World Challenge, 140, 141